JEWISH MEMORIES
OF THE
TWENTIETH CENTURY

by Members of the
North-Western Reform Synagogue
London

Recorded and collated by
David Stebbing

Compiled by
Evelyn Julia Kent

Published in 2003
by
Evelyn Kent Associates
7 Savernake Court Stanmore HA7 2RA England

Copyright © David Stebbing

Printed and bound in Great Britain by
Antony Rowe Ltd Chippenham Wiltshire

ISBN 0 952 3716 0X

Please note: Although these are true stories, they have
been told from memory, recorded and transcribed.
Some of the names and incidental details may not be
accurate

British Library Cataloguing-in-Publication Data
A catalogue record for this book is available from the
British Library

*Dedicated to
the congregants of Alyth
who kindly gave their time
to recount their memories.*

*Let us remember those
who are no longer with us.*

'Jewish Memories of the Twentieth Century' is a treasure trove of eyewitness accounts of a century when it was not easy to be Jewish. They are told by members of 'Alyth' synagogue and give us an insight into the past. Stories from childhood reveal that some members were born here to immigrants to Britain at the turn of the last century. Some members were born in countries that suffered under the Nazi regime; some arrived in Britain on the Kindertransport and lost their families in the Holocaust. Those who were old enough served in World War II. Some, as children, were evacuees. Many lived through difficult days but were able to enjoy happier times.

These stories are a tribute to the contribution they made to the life and prosperity of Britain and are a living testament to the Jewish spirit.

Evelyn Julia Kent

CONTENTS

Photographs on Cover - Front Cover, clockwise:
Family group at seaside - Liesl Silverstone
Airman with wings - John Davies
Musical group - Eva Graham is at the piano
Smiling lady - Kathe Trenter
Soldiers on board - Jules Bennett on the right
Centre - Wendy Greengross with younger brother

Back Cover, clockwise:
Entertainer - Benjamin Barrie
Lady in hat - Maria Alice Phillips
Members of Liesl Silverstone's family
Boy on the beach - Tony Graham
Soldier - Peter Gilbey
Young boy - Roman Halter

PREFACE

The North-Western Reform Synagogue in London, known as Alyth, celebrated its seventieth anniversary in 2003. To commemorate the success of this thriving synagogue, members who were born in the first half of the twentieth century kindly agreed to be interviewed by me to record their reminiscences and their involvement with Alyth. These stories are told in their own words.

When I began this project I did not realise how many amazing stories I would hear. I did not realise that the 'little old lady' who sat opposite me on a Friday night had endured such hardship. I never imagined that the 'elderly gentleman' I spoke to at Kiddush had suffered with his family under the Nazis. 'Ordinary' people with extraordinary stories – some told for the first time, in their own words. I feel privileged to have met so many marvellous congregants. Through them we can all gain an insight into so many different life experiences.

I wish to acknowledge and thank all those who have so generously given their time in helping to compile this book, especially Nicola Baker, John Davies, Jean Davis, Eveleen Habib, Alec Hasenson, Vanessa Lampert, Liesbeth Rubinstein, Cristina Vieira and Sally Woolf for editing and typing the transcriptions. Thanks to Erica and Philip Osmond for proof reading, to Paul Baron for his computer expertise, and to Maurice Kanareck for the glossary and cover.

I am indebted to the North-Western Reform Synagogue for their financial contribution; to Evelyn Kent for turning the manuscripts into a book, and to my wife Julia for her unstinting support.

Finally, my sincerest thanks to all those congregants who were kind enough to share their memories with me.

David Stebbing

JEWISH MEMORIES

OF THE

TWENTIETH CENTURY

1   MARGARET BALLHEIMER

M y father was a lawyer in Frankfurt-am-Main, the eldest son of
Rabbi Caesar Seligman and I was his second daughter, born in
Germany's fourth largest city on 30th November 1923.

Like so many other Jewish families we lived a normal life
until 1933 when Hitler came to power, a time that also coincided with
my change from primary to secondary school. The city had an
excellent Jewish school in those days, 'Philantropin', which I duly
attended until the morning of 9th November 1938, just before the
horrors of Kristallnacht. A tense atmosphere was building up and we
were sent home again as soon as we had arrived. On my return I learnt
that my parents had just been warned that an attack on our flat by the
Nazis was imminent. My mother and I left at once and together went
for shelter to the home of my grandparents who lived well away from
the centre of town. However, my father was not quite ready to leave
home so soon and stayed for a while longer, only just managing to
escape by the back door before the hordes arrived at the front - a
raging mob that stormed up to our apartment, literally then smashing
up everything inside.

In the meantime, whilst all this was going on at home, we
waited anxiously at my grandparents' place for news of my little sister
who had not yet arrived to join us. It was a very tense time but to our
great relief she returned safely at last, much later than expected and
not before witnessing both a blazing fire (our synagogue!) and
admiring a lovely doll which a friend of hers had received. The poor
innocent child was blissfully unaware of all the worry she had caused
us.

After that terrible night my parents decided that it was no
longer safe to just sit there and wait for our permits to emigrate to
America in view of the two year waiting list. Fortunately for us, two of
my father's sisters had already settled in England some years before
and with their help and the support of the Montague family, mainly

1

Lily, my grandparents were able to leave Germany in December 1938. My mother left for England three months later in January 1939 to take up a domestic situation, whilst my two sisters and I arrived in London on a Kindertransport in March. My father came over shortly after in June that year having first wound up his affairs in Frankfurt.

My eldest sister was sponsored by the 'Oxford Group' and sent to Winchester, where she was apprenticed to a dressmaker. My other sister was taken in by a lovely Jewish family (friends of my Aunt), who already had four boys of their own but had also always wanted a daughter. As for myself, I was sent to London to live with my aunt and uncle and their five-year-old son, just off Ladbroke Grove. There I looked after my little cousin and generally acted as the family's 'housekeeper'.

By now my parents had moved to Gloucestershire as guests of Robert Henriques at his farm in Winson, near Cirencester. Robert was a friend of my mother's family in Paris and had opened up a part of his property to house four or five refugee families. The local Rotarians befriended them and did their best to show these people how English people lived by inviting them to their homes and showing them the beautiful English countryside. In particular, one family in Cirencester invited me to stay with them on holiday in the July shortly before the war. They were very special people to me; a Mr and Mrs Jones, the husband a local jeweller and optician, his wife a lady who ran a glass and china shop. Both treated me as a much-loved daughter. Their concern for my disrupted education led them to suggest that I now went back to school and study for my School Certificate, thus enabling me to obtain a better type of job in later life. The money for my schooling was raised by the local community, amongst them several Church of England clergymen. It was arranged with the headmaster of a neighbouring grammar and boarding school that I should start there at the beginning of the 1939 autumn term.

All this was in fact arranged while I was still in London with my aunt and uncle and when it became clear that war would soon break out I was sent back to Cirencester to start my schooling. My good friends Mr and Mrs Jones were unable to put me up this time as they already had several other evacuees with them. They arranged for me to stay with the vicar and his wife in the village of Bilbury until the start of the school year, put back by two weeks due to the fact that war had now broken out.

Although the vicarage was a very large and comfortable house, it was only heated by candles and paraffin lamps. There was an electric generator, but this could only be worked by their son and he was away on active service in India! I found it altogether strange for someone like myself who had always lived with the conveniences of a town. My parents were still living in Winson on the Henriques' farm, only five miles away from my school in Northleach and as I had a bicycle I was able to visit them quite easily. All this was to change however when my parents left Winson in 1940, my father to join the army, my mother to take up work in London. I stayed behind to finish my schooling the following year, thereafter remaining in the headmaster's house and helping out with all sorts of jobs, including cooking and cleaning and looking after the rest of the boarders. I even learnt how to milk a cow as well as caring for the lambs, pigs and chickens which the headmaster's niece had acquired in order to help the war effort.

I finally left Northleach early in 1942 and moved back to London to be with my mother, now in catering. Mother had successfully completed a course in canteen management and was now manageress of a kosher canteen in Stamford Hill, supplying school meals and luncheons to the Jewish community of that area.

One day, during the course of a 'flu epidemic, she was asked if she could spare one of her cooks to help out at another kosher school meals centre where most of the staff were off sick. Unable to spare any other experienced help, she sent me instead. The centre was in Shacklewell Lane synagogue, and I arrived there early one morning to commence my duties. The manager took one look at me and promptly told me to go back to school and not to bother him. When I assured him that I really could cook he relented, if somewhat reluctantly, and allowed me in. To my great embarrassment I was then told that the day's menu was gefilte fish, something I had never ever heard of, let alone prepared and quite unknown as a dish in our family. To cover my profound ignorance I asked each of the other helpers, mostly very old women, how they made theirs and then to produce all the ingredients for me that they usually used. In this way I managed to muddle my way through the entire week.

Then one morning I was told that I would again be moved, to yet another centre, this time at Stoke Newington Town Hall, where the cook was unwell and unable to come in to work. To help me use what there was of my vast inexperience, the manager suggested that I say that I only cooked kosher food. After only one week at the Town Hall, working for the 'School Meals Service', I was next transferred to the 'Londoners' Meals Service', which were heavily subsidised canteens providing healthy and nourishing meals for the local workers. As assistant cook it was my job to prepare all the desserts: steamed and baked puddings, custard and rice puddings for up to 300 people. Being of rather small stature I had great difficulty trying to mix anything up to 36 lbs of flour in the huge zinc bowls provided. I tried standing on a chair, but this was too high and so a special stool was made for me so that I could then reach over the table and bowls to do my mixing.

I stayed with this meal service for several months until offered the position of head cook elsewhere. Instead of being pleased with the offer though, I was rather downhearted. I felt that I was still far too young for such responsibility and also greatly concerned that I might be put in charge of a lot of women, all of whom might be old enough to be my mother or perhaps even my grandmother. The powers that be however insisted that everything would be all right, so rather reluctantly I agreed. I arrived at my new centre in Crondall Street early in 1943. On being asked my name I replied 'Margaret', only to be told 'Oh no, what is your surname?' 'Seligman' I replied and was then informed that in future I would be known as Mrs Seligman, it being the custom in those days to give every cook such a courtesy title. I objected to that and in the end we compromised by my agreeing to be addressed simply as 'Cook'.

Right from the outset of my employment with the Londoners' Meal Service I had made it quite clear that it was my intention to train as a nurse just as soon as a vacancy occurred. This was not a simple matter for me as there were quotas for aliens entering the profession at that time. Once more however the Montague family came to my assistance, this time in helping me to obtain a place at the combined training school of University College Hospital and Hornsey Central Hospital in Crouch End, north London. It was a four-year rather than a three-year course but at least I could start at once, so I gave in my notice and was allowed to leave without having to work out the full period of the contract as normally required.

Not long after, on 15th March 1943, I made my way to the Hornsey Central, eager to start my new career. The sister in charge of housekeeping showed me how to put on my uniform and at 3 pm, a mere one hour from the time of my actual arrival at the gates, I was already on the wards as the most junior of probationers. There was no accommodation for us in the hospital itself and all the staff, junior and senior, lived in the nurses' home. Discipline in those days was strictly observed. At lunchtime Matron served at the head of the table, starting with the most junior at the bottom who then had to wait until everyone else had received their portion before she could begin to eat her own meal. Needless to say the higher you climbed up the ladder the hotter your meals became. At the end of our second year we sat our preliminary exams, the successful candidates then transferring either to University College Hospital or the King Edward VII in Windsor for the next part of our training. In my own case I was sent to UCH, where the atmosphere was very much more relaxed with no petty restrictions between junior and senior nurses.

In June 1947 I passed my final exams and became a State Registered Nurse. Even so, although I had already worked on both ante and postnatal wards, I still had no idea what actually happened in between in the labour wards, so I decided that in order to round off my training I would take a six-month course in midwifery. I was fortunate enough to obtain a place at Queen Mary's Maternity Home in

Hampstead, situated diagonally opposite Whitestone Pond, founded by Queen Mary for the wives of members of the armed forces. The Queen herself paid an annual visit and many of the cot covers and woollies in the wards had been knitted by herself and her friends. At the end of six months I passed my Part One Midwifery exams, though as yet I would still not be allowed to practice as a midwife until I had completed a further six months 'On The District'. Since I disliked the idea of only half a qualification and wanted the practical experience as well as the theory of obstetrics, I therefore applied for a place at the Maternity Nursing Association in Myddleton Square, Islington, where I finished the second part of my training.

In those early post-war days the area we covered had not yet been 'gentrified' and the living conditions of the mothers we attended were generally pretty awful. For the most part there was only one water tap somewhere on the landing of a four or five storey house, with a lavatory in the basement if one was lucky, or outside in the backyard if one was not. There were however also some purpose-built 'Buildings for the Poor' where each flat had at least a kitchen sink, though the lavatories were still shared by three or four families. It certainly gave me an insight into the way the impoverished people of London lived.

At the end of the six months 'On The District' I passed my final examinations and became a State Certified Midwife. Fully qualified, I now returned to University College Hospital as a Staff Nurse, working for a few months in the private wards and then for a year in the labour wards when a vacancy came up. After that I was transferred to the postnatal wards, first as senior Staff Nurse, then as a Sister.

It was during that time that mutual friends introduced me to my future husband, Rudolph, and we married in March 1956. The following year we bought our present house in Hoop Lane where we raised our family, at the same time as taking in up to four elderly people at any one time, mostly ladies who we looked after, all of whom enjoyed being in a home setting as part of a growing family. It was all quite different from today's residential care homes. Throughout the time I studied and worked I still kept in close contact with my good friends the Joneses in Cirencester. They attended our wedding and then the barmitzvah celebrations of both our boys. Sadly they died some years ago, but I am well aware that without their help and support and that of so many other good people I would not have been privileged to have enjoyed such an interesting and fulfilling life.

　　Bless them all.

2   BENJAMIN BARRIE

I was born on Christmas Day 1920 in a small nursing home virtually opposite Euston station. The 'stage' was in my blood. Jack, my father, had originally acted in Fred Locomo's famous company – it was there he met Charlie Chaplin. After serving in the First World War he married my mother, the beautiful Bessie, and settled down to life as a market trader. I have met a lot of funny men in my time but my father was the funniest man I ever knew. He really was a brilliant comedian orator.

In the early 1920s he came under the spell of Sir Basil Henriques at the Oxford and St. George's Settlement Synagogue where he was Sir Basil's right hand man. A great patriot, Sir Basil, known as 'The Gaffer', was the first man to go 'over the top' in a tank, leading an assault in France in World War One. On Yom Kippur, Sir Basil always used to stand in the synagogue and pat me on the head (he was 6ft 5ins) and say 'Ah, Benjamin! I remember when your beautiful mother used to bring you to synagogue!'

My mother was well known for her beauty. I can clearly remember – I must have been about six – being stopped in the street and told, 'Your mother's Bessie the hairdresser. She used to work in Bell Lane. She was the most beautiful woman in East London. You look like your father!'

I had a very happy childhood. My earliest recollection was going to the Jewish infant school in Commercial Street, where I sat next to a little boy who was to be a friend for life. His name? Alfred Marks, the actor. At junior school I was the youngest boy ever to win the prize for elocution. I was a natural on the stage. The school was heavily endowed by the Rothschilds and all the princes of the Jewish religion. So there were lots of prizes and I got quite a large share of them, as I regularly came top every year!

At the age of ten Alfred Marks and I decided to join the Jewish Lads Brigade, then a terribly right wing organisation. There was a particular secondary school I had set my heart on, but there were no free places. It was the depression, the labour government was in crisis, and it was my luck that they cut back on educational expenditure. As a result I lost interest in school.

The time came to leave school and my mother apprenticed me to a hairdresser. I didn't like it, despite being taught by the top man himself, Raymond Bassoni – better known as Mr. Teasy-Weasy on TV in the Fifties.

I was about fourteen when the Blackshirts began regular meetings in the East End. Alfred Marks joined the Young Communist League. I can't say Alfred knew much about politics but he knew the League fought the Fascists. During the terrible times of 1936 when the Blackshirts were marching through East London we used to try to go to their meetings to disrupt them. We didn't see all that many Blackshirts, but we certainly saw a lot of policemen. Once Alfred was actually hit on the shoulder by a mounted policeman's baton – not hard – more pushed out of the way.

In August 1940, Alfred Marks and I volunteered for the RAF. I did pretty well and was offered a chance to go to Edinburgh University to take an aeronautical engineering degree, but as I was keen to fly I became a flight engineer instead.

Whilst stationed in Blackpool I performed in Ralph Reader's 'Crazy Gang' show. He was keen for me to join the RAF concert party, entertaining the troops on a permanent basis, but I didn't really want to do that because I was very keen to actively fight against Hitler.

Soon we were sent to Canada for flight training – in theory a nice, safe place, but when we got to Vancouver Island it was promptly shelled by the Japanese. We were put on flight patrols looking for Japanese submarines. On one such flight our undercarriage refused to lower and although I had a cartridge to force it down, that would not work either. But the pilot was brilliant. He flew around for an hour to use up the petrol, did several shallow dives (which didn't work out) and finally made a perfect belly landing, saving all our lives. However, it was a shock to my system which left me with a souvenir – a bad back. It was Stanley Leaf, the osteopath who founded Champneys, who told me my bad back was due to that belly landing.

I was forever being 'discovered' in the RAF, winning talent contests and doing shows. At heart I really wanted to be a serious actor, but comedy, jokes and impressions were the way I got into the spotlight. So when I arrived in Canada I found my reputation had preceded me and I was dropped straight into the concert party. This time it was called 'The Small Show'. We had Hughie Greene (Canadian by birth) and quite a number of stars. Hughie was a great character, a wonderful bloke, and we used to have a lot of fun. Believe it or not, that English Vaudeville show is still running every summer in Vancouver Island.

It was a Friday night in Vancouver Island and if I wasn't flying I always made sure I went to synagogue. Now one night I noticed that the fellow sitting next to me was a merchant navy chap. I was struck by the fact that he was reading the siddur upside-down, but I didn't pay too much attention. We got chatting and he turned out to be a Jewish refugee from Vienna. He had a little moustache and wore a sailor's uniform, but the odd thing was he had a strange square cap with a little flag, not the usual round hat with a crown. A few weeks later, there he was again still reading the siddur upside-down. The synagogue people were very hospitable. So one night he was invited back to dinner and it turned out he made what I can only describe as a bit of an assault on this girl. Now really, a nice Jewish boy if he is invited back to dinner there is no way he would assault the hostess. I could have got him 'fixed up' for this because being a big star in the show I had plenty of supporters and they would do anything for me. However, the guy just disappeared.

Now by sheer coincidence, one afternoon not so long after, I was hitchhiking into town and got a lift from a man in his forties. I mentioned I was Jewish and he invited me back for dinner. I gathered he had been a captain in the First World War. When he asked me whether anybody had ever tried to wheedle information from me on RAF activities I said 'No'. But it prompted me to tell him about my suspicions over this so-called naval refugee officer. Next thing I knew

I was sent to the guardroom and the security officer waiting for me says 'You had dinner with Colonel Strong last week.'

'Not me.'

'Oh yes you did! You told him his wife is the best cook in Canada!'

So then I put two and two together. The guy who gave me the lift just happened to be head of security in Vancouver.

'But he was in civilian clothes,' I protested.

'He's no civilian. He just wears civilian clothes.'

So I ran through the whole story about the naval officer who read Hebrew upside-down. Next thing I knew my Entertainment Officer congratulates me.

'Mazeltov Ben! You've got yourself a spy! They arrested that fellow – he's an escaped U-boat commander.'

'So, what happened to him?'

'What usually happens to spies?'

And that was the last I heard of that.

One time I hitchhiked my way to Hollywood – what a time! It was there I danced with Lucille Ball. I met Deanna Durbin. Hoagy Carmichael played the piano. I met Frank Lesser. I had lunch with Abbot and Costello – I've still got their autographs. It was all great stars – Gary Cooper, Universal Studios, Anna May Wong, Academy Award dinners, comedians, actors, scriptwriters and songwriters. You know the song 'The Good Ship Lollipop' that Shirley Temple sang? That was written by Harry Ravel, who also wrote 'Stay As Sweet As You Are'. Some time ago I helped the late Benny Green, the broadcaster, with material for his programme on Harry. And where did Harry come from? Chapel Lane in the East End, where my family lived when I was born. Some journey!

After they dropped the atom bomb I was sent to Germany where my school German came in handy as I was in charge of 150 prisoners-of-war. I never let on that I spoke German but I certainly understood when they saw me coming and announced 'Das schwein kommt...'.

On leaving the RAF I was recommended for the Alexander Korda Scholarship at RADA. I went to Gower Street and did my audition pieces in front of Dame Edith Evans, Ralph Richardson, John Gielgud and the principal, Kenneth Barnes. But the scholarship paid only £2 per week (it was 1946), so my uncle got me a job. Suddenly I was in handbags and earning £30 in an afternoon. After that I never bothered about becoming a serious actor and took over as sales manager instead.

Having made quite a bit of money I decided to retire at about thirty. I bought a farm in the country with the idea of raising chickens, but they were wiped out by a poultry disease. So in 1964 I started a sales promotion company, Premium Agencies, which grew into one of Europe's leading promotion companies, now called Worldwide Ideas.

In 1979 I met my wife, Alana, – it was purely by accident, over the phone. Imagine meeting the most gorgeous twenty-four year old and me already in my late forties! But somehow, fate made sure we got together. Alana embraced the Jewish religion. She was a professional librarian, and I am proud to say that she became the founder of the regenerated library we have at Alyth Synagogue today, in which she is involved closely with Alyth's Lynette Chazen-Hart.

3   JULES BENNETT
DESERT ADVENTURE

I was born in 1920 in London, and my family moved to Dollis Hill in north-west London in 1929. I attended Kilburn Grammar School, leaving in 1937 with honours in Matriculation. I joined the London County Council as a town planning technical assistant. In early 1939 I enlisted in the Territorial Army and was called up at the outbreak of war in September that year.

It was April 1941 and my army unit had just left Cairo, heading for Benghazi in Libya, 750 miles west along the northern coast of Africa. We planned to meet up there with the King's Rifles for the onward sweep to the west, playing our part in driving the Italian Army out of North Africa – or so we thought!

My unit comprised 71 men and 30 new three-ton trucks loaded with transport spare parts, which could service a brigade. After an uneventful 500 miles' progress we were approaching the town of Tobruk when a dispatch rider came to meet us. We soon learnt the news – the Germans had landed further west and were heading for Tobruk from the other side, complete with an air force, a large fast tank force and mobile guns.

While our Commanding Officer headed for Tobruk, we set up camp about six miles west of Tobruk with our vehicles spread out a hundred yards apart so as not to present an easy target for air attack. We posted guards and slept until dawn when we learned that the enemy was very close. Two of us occupied a machine gun nest, built of sand-filled four-gallon petrol drums, on the summit of a small hill. The machine gun was a Hotchkiss made in 1918, which we knew from practice tended to jam in those sandy conditions after one bullet had been fired. The transport officer took up position forty yards ahead of us with the unit's one anti-tank rifle.

One man, after an earlier adventure, had been nicknamed 'the Colonel'. He was, we thought, the bravest man in the unit. He would dismantle enemy shells, enter captured dugouts without testing for booby traps, and set fire to any piece of enemy equipment we found. The Colonel slumped down and said 'Ben, I'm afraid.' With all my twenty years of life's experience I reassured him and said we were all nervous but we were determined not to show it. Another companion lay prone near us, his rifle loaded and ready, his finger on the trigger, while he read silently from the Bible.

Meanwhile, immediately to our rear, we found an Australian infantry unit had arrived and was trying to dig in positions in the rock-hard sand. Our second-in-command remonstrated with their Commanding Officer, as we would be caught in their line of fire. The Australian in plain language told him he did not care and we could do what we liked – or words to that effect. He had been instructed to form the second line of defence there and that was that. Waves of German planes were now flying overhead fairly low, and with no anti-aircraft fire to impede them shells began to fall in the area. I decided that as soon as action began I would remove my identity discs, which bore the legend 'Jew', and bury them.

Then the CO returned from Tobruk and signalled that we should follow him at two-minute intervals. I shouted the message to the transport officer who swore and said 'What's the good of that?' I could have told him that his life had just been saved, but thought better of it.

Over the next hour we left our position and drove into Tobruk. There we were dispatched to a piece of waste ground on the shore. We found the remains of Italian army dugouts, comfortable but flea-infested, and I resolved never to use them. Shortly afterwards, bombs started raining down on us, so I abandoned my resolution and took cover with the fleas.

We learned that Tobruk was now surrounded by the enemy. Water was scarce and we were forbidden to wash or shave. Each day our water bottles were filled and we received tea and bully beef. But other than keep a lookout for air attacks we could do nothing.

On the eighth day, in the evening, we made our way on foot to the docks. There we boarded a small freighter. The ship had been bombed on its journey to Tobruk, with many of its Mauritian troops on board killed. The remaining soldiers were still on board, very nervous and inexperienced. I was immediately placed at the top of a short gangway leading to the bridge. Wearing my steel helmet, with fixed bayonet and loaded rifle, I was instructed that if there was any panic and anyone tried to get to the bridge I was to kill him.

As darkness fell we began to steam – very slowly – out of the harbour. At the front of the ship, one ship's officer on the port side and one on the starboard held hand torches focussed on the two small pylons marking the exit from the harbour and, with shouted commands to the bridge, they guided us carefully out to the open sea.

We turned east and, following the coastline, slowly made our way towards Egypt. Enemy planes inspected us from time to time but, probably due to the ship's small size, did not attack us. We had to keep calming the Mauritians though until the danger had passed. After about a week we came into Alexandria, unkempt, unwashed and bearded. Just before we landed I had one inch of water in my drinking mug, which I used to become the only soldier aboard who landed clean-shaven!

This short episode was just one of many adventures that befell me in the Middle East. For those of you whose age does not permit a memory of the up and down nature of war in the Western Desert, I will conclude by saying that after many battles, some lost and some won, the Allies eventually drove the enemy out of North Africa.

After many travels and adventures I left the Army in March 1949, married Anita and worked in our family soft furnishing company. In 1960 my brother and I set up a table glassware-decorating firm, which I left ten years later to become a Life Assurance consultant.

I was president of a Friendly Society Lodge and subsequently in the 1960s became Chairman of the North Western Reform Synagogue and Treasurer of the RSGB.

After my wife died in 1998 I moved to Cheshire, where my son is a cardiac consultant. My daughter, who lives in Israel, is

Secretary General of the English Speaking Residents Association based in Herzlia. Between them they have four children, all of whom are a source of pride to their aged grandfather!

4   RITA BRODIE

I am the younger of two children. We were both born in London, my brother Jack in 1919, and I followed in 1924. Our mother was also born in this country but father came over here as a toddler. He was originally from Kishinev, then part of Russia, his name Sidney (born Isaac) Fleminger.

My paternal grandfather, Samuel, came from Czernowitz, capital of Bukovina, which was then within the Austro-Hungarian Empire and since 1940 has been part of western Ukraine. As a young man he was encouraged, for whatever reason, to travel to Kishinev, then in north-eastern Rumania, possibly in order to pursue his religious studies. In due course, he met and married a girl by the name of Yetta Goldberg. Their first-born was my father Isaac. Soon after his birth, the Goldberg family, Samuel their son-in-law, Yetta his wife and their infant son, all packed up and made their way to Constantinople, where the Goldbergs had relatives, and where my father's brother Harry was born. Thereafter, the whole family made their way to settle in England.

On my mother's side her family too were immigrants to this country, though mother herself was born here. Her parents originated from Eastern Europe, coming to England in the early 1880s from a place called Jeludok, which I believe is in the northern part of Poland. Unusually for those days my grandmother had been extremely well-educated in many respects. She was brought up by her grandfather, a Rabbi or Rov, who treated her the same as any of the boys in his class. In this way she gained a considerable knowledge of Judaism and the Torah.

My father's family first lived in the East End of London and my father was sent to the Jews' Free School, founded by the Anglo-Jewish Establishment, one of whose main aims was to turn immigrant children into English gentlemen. That really suited my father, who had always looked up to the English and tried to dress and behave as he felt an Englishman should. This turned out to be a no-win situation

17

when he was a youngster. Living just off Brick Lane he found that as he walked down the street on his way to work the gentiles at one end would revile him for being a Jew, whilst his own people at the other end would taunt him for trying to be different. He appeared not to take any notice however, and despite the humiliations never ever did change his attitudes or dress to appease his critics.

Both my parents were the eldest children of immigrant families and as such a good deal of responsibility fell upon them during their childhood. Their busy parents, both working to make ends meet, unfamiliar with the English language and with English ways, often depended on their English-speaking eldest children to help bring up and guide their family in this new environment. My father always wanted to be a doctor, but this was financially impossible. After leaving school he took a job as a laboratory assistant at St George's Hospital, later studying at night and eventually qualifying as a MICE (Member of the Institute of Chemical Engineers).

My father was spared the horrors of the trenches in the First World War as he was in a reserved occupation. In 1919, shortly after the fighting stopped, he married my mother, Bessie Prince, whom he had met through mutual friends. They set up home in the Upper Clapton Road, where I, Marguerita Estelle Fleminger, was born and where I lived for most of my youth. My parents were always keen to move further out to north-west London, but this was beyond their means and so we stayed in Clapton until war broke out. In later years they managed to send my brother to Clifton College, whilst I attended North London Collegiate School.

Although my father was not particularly religious, he would make Kiddush every Friday night and celebrate all the Jewish Festivals. However, my mother was more observant, probably for her mother's sake. She kept a kosher house and would not allow me to write on Shabbos when I was small.

After my brother's barmitzvah he was sent away to the Jewish house at Clifton. I was sent to a cheder in Seven Sisters Road one afternoon a week, but after an unhappy few weeks there I left and was taught Hebrew and Jewish studies by a private teacher at home instead. Despite my Jewish upbringing, most of my school friends at the North London Collegiate School were non-Jewish, and I remember going away on holidays with them and their families, while at the same time keeping to a strictly kosher diet.

It was not until about 1937 or so that I first began to be aware of what was happening in Germany, due to the fact that my parents were now getting pleas for help from people (possibly relatives) trying to get out of Europe. My mother spent a great deal of time trying to obtain permits for them to come to England. Even then I did not realise the enormity of the problem. It was only in 1939 while we were on holiday in Eastbourne that I first met a man who had been in a concentration camp. I remember him showing me the numbers tattooed on his arm. He also taught me to play patience, a card game that he said had been the only way he had managed to keep sane while imprisoned. At Eastbourne that last summer before the war I had just finished the lower fifth form at North London Collegiate School. I expected to sit School Certificate at the end of the following June, then do two years in the sixth form and go on to Cambridge. However, things did not go according to plan.

On 3rd September, when Neville Chamberlain announced that Britain was at war with Germany, no one knew what to expect. Were we about to be bombed, invaded or what? As many schools in London were being evacuated, it was decided that my mother and I would remain in Eastbourne where I was enrolled in St Winifred's, first as a day scholar, later as a boarder when my mother became ill and had to be admitted to hospital. Sadly she died in May 1940 – still a relatively young woman.

For the first few months of the war life on the home front was pretty uneventful, but in May 1940 everything changed. The western front suddenly erupted, British troops were taken off the beaches at Dunkirk and France capitulated. Britain was now in the frontline, the south coast vulnerable. In Eastbourne the seafront was covered with rolls of barbed wire. Invasion was expected at any time. Schools in the area were now being evacuated in their turn. St Winifred's moved to the Surrey countryside, where it doubled up with an existing boarding school. We were all pretty squashed together, as you can imagine, and hated the other girls who kept the best dormitories for themselves.

My memories of that part of my life are rather disjointed, but I do recall that we had to do all our studying and revision for biology on our own as our science teacher had gone off to do war work. When the time came to sit our School Certificate we had a pre-fabricated wooden hut in the school grounds to serve the purpose. German bombers were attacking airfields and factories at this time, but no one was really immune: bombs could easily miss their intended targets, or bombing planes fail to reach them, their deadly cargo then randomly jettisoned on the way back to the Continent. Not surprisingly therefore we had the occasional air raid alert even in the depths of the countryside.

I well remember the night before we sat our history exam, when there was an air raid alert at about two in the morning. We all rushed down to the cellars and stayed there until the 'all clear' sounded. Another time we watched a dog fight over the skies above, finding it far more exciting than the lesson we were supposed to be having.

July came, school finished for the summer and I returned to London in good time for the Blitz. I was staying in Golders Green in my aunt's house, where my father also stayed for the duration of the war. They had no air raid shelter, and when the sirens went off and we heard enemy planes we all squashed into a cupboard under the stairs or crept under the dining room table as the safest places to be. Of course some people had Anderson shelters at the bottom of their garden, and there were also public shelters as well as the safety of the depths of the London underground stations. At night one had to pick one's way past all the people sleeping on the platforms.

My most vivid memory was the night of the Great Fire of London in December 1940. I do not know how many incendiaries the Germans dropped on the city that night, but in Golders Green, which was on the other side of London, the whole sky was lit up, bright enough to read a newspaper in the garden.

Not long after, I was sent out of the country. After my mother had died it was decided that I should join my father's family in South Africa. This was easier said than done. Ships taking civilians there were few and far between and one simply had to wait until told when and where to report. The travel warrant finally came in April 1941, when I was given five days notice to report to the docks in Glasgow with my luggage, identity card, gas mask and ration book, assured too that my passport and ticket would be handed to me on board ship. My father came with me on the train to Glasgow and we stayed overnight with an aunt and uncle of mine. The following day we said goodbye to one another and I boarded the City of Nagpur of Ellerman Lines Ltd., in the company of soldiers being sent to South and East Africa, as well as some wives and children going to join their families. I was only sixteen at the time.

We left the Scottish port in the company of a tanker, first going north then turning south on about the fourth day, at which point our ship and the tanker parted company, the latter heading for the USA. Our City liner ploughed on towards the African continent. That evening we went to bed as usual. It was nearly the end of April. We were in the middle of the Atlantic, far from land, midway between Newfoundland and Ireland. Suddenly we were woken by the sound of running feet in the passage outside. Hurriedly my cabin mate and I put on our shoes and coats, grabbed our life jackets and made our way to the lounge as directed. We did not know what was happening, but could hear gunfire. The next thing we knew, a door opened into the lounge from outside. An officer came in and told us not to worry, because those were our guns we could hear. Perhaps so, but we could also hear more distant firing. Another few minutes went by, then the officer suddenly announced that we had been torpedoed by a submarine and that we should make our way to the lifeboats. Quickly we all pushed our way on to the deck outside. I tried to get on one lifeboat only to find that it was already full, and was directed to another on the other side of the ship. It was with some difficulty that I made my way over, for shelling and firing was still going on and the deck was burning fiercely. Fortunately my lifeboat was still there and I waited my turn to get in, accidentally treading on a wounded seaman lying at the bottom of the boat as I did so. Somebody handed me a baby to hold, but luckily the mother then joined us and took it back. We were really overfull by now, having had one of our lifeboats destroyed by enemy fire, but despite the chaos all around we were lowered slowly and gently until we came to rest safely in the waters of the Atlantic, at once pulling away from our stricken ship, on fire and slowly sinking. The captain and some of the crew were on a life raft nearby. The submarine, which had previously surfaced and fired at us, was now approaching our lifeboat. As it came nearer, a man speaking good English called asking whether we had any officers amongst us. Of course we said no. But the most frightening thing for me was the fact that I knew very well by now the way that Jews were being treated by the Germans, and I was terrified that they would bring me on board and take me to Nazi-occupied Europe with them. Thank goodness the submarine then went away and my worst fears were not realised. Sixteen men had been killed in the attack, but everyone else had managed to get away, though of course I did not know this at the time. Fortunately we were also unaware that no SOS had been sent, and that the chances were it was most unlikely we would ever be found.

The night passed – we were in the middle of the Atlantic eating dog biscuits, or so it seemed to me from the taste. Actually it was hard tack and I had to make do, since the chances of another ship being anywhere near us were about one in a million. Anxiously we waited and waited. Then at last we heard the sound of an aircraft. As it came closer, we recognised it as a Catalina flying boat. It circled around us, flew off again and we settled down to wait once more. At last at about midnight, to our great delight, a British destroyer approached, took us all on board and brought us home to Glasgow. I was back where I had started, though without luggage, papers and only very little money. We were actually provided with temporary papers and enough money or travel vouchers to get home. By this means I was able to take a taxi back to my aunt and also tell my father when I phoned him in London that I was safe, very much to his relief.

Eventually I left for South Africa once more, this time in a convoy that took thirty days to reach Cape Town. There I went to live with my father's cousin, Annie Brodie, and her husband, Emanuel, who was in the glass business. At the time they had only the two younger sons living at home. Their eldest son, Bernard, was away in the army. He was the man I was later to marry, though I did not know this at the time.

I found South Africa somewhat of a shock. There were many people who were pro-German, their attitudes often leading to fights in the streets of Johannesburg. There were other people however, like my future husband, who gave up everything to join the armed forces and then willingly 'went north', a euphemism for those who volunteered to serve outside the borders of their own country, in his case the Italian Front. As for social life, the Jewish community in Cape Town kept very much to itself, and I remember the degree of disapproval I encountered whenever I wanted to go out with a non-Jew.

In South Africa I continued with my studies. I enrolled at Cape Town University, took my Masters in psychology and was awarded a scholarship to do further research. At that stage I wanted to go back to England as the war was now over, but was advised to stay where I was as British academia was having great problems trying to accommodate the many ex-servicemen applying for courses. So instead I remained in South Africa, working for the Council for Scientific and Industrial Research and doing research in industrial psychology for which I received a doctorate. In the meantime my father had come out to South Africa, where sadly he died. When I finished my Doctorate in 1949 I returned to England where I went to work for the Industrial Health Research Board, doing research into human behaviour in industry.

Towards the end of 1950 Bernard Brodie came over to England. We had got to know each other well over the years in South Africa and now we renewed our acquaintance, and eventually decided to get married. We had a small family wedding at the Bayswater Synagogue and the Dorchester Hotel, and afterwards we went back to live in Cape Town. Being unable to follow a career in industrial psychology in Cape Town, I did a variety of voluntary and research projects, perhaps the most notable being the setting up of a public information and advisory service for children with special needs, a day centre for such children in Guguletu township, and various play groups and a toy library to assist 'non-white' children for whom no other such services were then available.

By this time my husband held a top position in a very large glass and timber firm that had been started by his grandfather in Cape Town at the turn of the century. He was a fine businessman and a concerned employer, supporting a variety of causes. He was highly regarded in both the Jewish and general community in the Cape.

We had always had strong reservations about the way South Africa was going, and in the 1950s we considered leaving the country and perhaps moving to New Zealand. However for a variety of reasons it was not until 1976, after the youngest of our three children had finished school, that we finally made a move and came back to England.

To bring this abbreviated biography up to date – our three children all live in London, and happily my husband was able to enjoy watching the early years of our five grandchildren before he sadly died in 1998. Our children Valerie, David and Philip live full and varied lives, all three making their individual contributions to society. Valerie is a highly experienced counsellor working in a voluntary capacity, David was awarded an OBE for his work on behalf of low-income taxpayers, whilst Philip has done a considerable amount of charitable work and is presently a Warden at Alyth.

5   GEORGE COOPER

M y name is George Cooper. I was born in Newcastle in 1912. My father's name was also George and my mother's name was Marion. I think my father was born in Birmingham, and my mother in Port Glasgow. Her maiden name was Stearment. I believe my grandparents were born in England. I have a brother Leon who lives in Australia and is an engineer. I have never been to Australia. I had four sisters whose names were Betty, Sylvia, Marion, and one whose name I cannot remember. Sadly all of them have died. I have a niece who lives in Durham, but I have not kept in touch with my family in Newcastle.

During the First World War my father was a manager at Swan & Hunter shipyard and worked as an engineer. I don't know if he went to college. We did not talk very much in my family – the depression caused an awful lot of trouble. I went to school in Eaton Road, Newcastle. I left at fourteen on a Thursday night and started work the following morning as an errand boy in a shop. It was very hard to get work in the depression – life was tough.

I had my barmitzvah in Elzik Road, Newcastle – a very orthodox synagogue. Unfortunately my father could not go to synagogue on a Saturday because of work. Money was so tight that you were not even allowed to have influenza or you lost your job. We always had enough to eat, but there were many around us who were really starving.

At the age of sixteen I left home and worked for a firm of tea merchants, Rangston Tea. I taught myself to drive, there was no test then. I travelled by car to Northumberland, Durham, Yorkshire, part of Lancashire, Leeds, Sheffield, Sunderland and Berwick selling tea to restaurants and cafes. Eventually when I was working in Leeds, living in digs, I got fed up with this. I had some money from my father and went down to London where I lived in Walworth Road, Elephant &

Castle for a number of years. Here I made a friend who was a first-class painter and decorator, and worked with him for a while.

Again I got fed up and decided to go to go to Eastbourne, where I was introduced to a doctor who was the medical officer for Sussex. (Prior to all this, in about 1933, I had attended medical school at Newcastle University, but I cannot remember how I got in or what examinations I took.) The doctor advised me to train as a nurse. I trained at St. Mary's, Eastbourne and then in another hospital. Eventually I passed my exams and became a nurse. In fact, I did psychiatric nursing. I worked in Hurst Park and Haywards Heath for a number of years. Then I did private male nursing in Eastbourne. One of my patients was an ex-army major. I also worked with two or three doctors.

When war came I was in reserved occupation. I volunteered to join the royal naval base, but failed my medical. I decided to join the army in the Royal Reservist Corp. I was in the army for three weeks, and then transferred to Doncaster, which is where I met my wife. Her family had moved and bought a house there, having been bombed out of London. Her father had a job managing a big furniture store in Doncaster. I had had no contact with the Jewish community in Eastbourne although I had many Jewish friends. In fact, I only went to synagogue twice – once in London and once in Wales – I seemed to have lost touch completely, and it was only when I met my wife that my involvement returned.

When I was in the army in Doncaster I had the job of driving the company van that carried the band around. We went to various dance halls. One day I was at one of these dances with a friend of mine, Ronnie Allcock. The band was already set up – I had delivered it earlier. Ronnie was with a girl I knew called Mary. Then I saw a girl in a green dress with very black hair – a beautiful girl. I asked her to dance, and we never stopped dancing. From that moment my life really began to lift – she was the most wonderful thing that ever happened to me. Her name was Cecily Lange. She came from the East End and was born in Redlands Road, just off Sydney Street. Her grandmother had a big delicatessen store just on the other side of

Better Street. We married very quickly in Barnet in March 1940 as I was forever on embarkation leave, waiting for my posting to North Africa.

I was in the North African campaign and the whole of the Italian campaign. Once I remember we were in San Marino for about a month. We lived in water up to our knees every day – wet blankets, wet clothes – but we got through it. I met many Germans and was in Trieste for about three years. However, I never knew about the atrocities happening in Germany. If I had known I would never have been so friendly with the Germans.

I had many experiences, both good and bad, whilst in the army. I saw a lot of action whilst abroad. I was doing deliveries – petrol, bombs, etc. – and finished up on tank transporters, which took me to Yugoslavia where I met Tito who was a really nice man. I ended up in a place called Spitz.

I made many good friends. When I was in Trieste there were four families and we used to see each other every Sunday evening and go to pubs, singing and dancing. Two of the four men had been in the police force and I was always welcome as I had money and cigarettes – one good thing about being away from home. I was away for four and a half years, although I got twenty-eight days leave a year. I remember one night after returning from leave at the end of the war I told the families in Trieste I was going back to England the next day. There was silence and it was very sad. At the end of the evening everybody was crying. This will always live in my memory.

When I came back to England I was transferred to all different places on the south coast. I did another year in the army before I was demobbed. I finished up as a Sergeant. I got my Civil Defence Medal, Africa Star and Italy Star. I was demobbed in 1946.

My wife and I had lodgings in Barnet and it was a long time before we got established. We lived in a flat above a shop in Finchley Road until eventually we bought a house. I worked for Blue Star Miners for some time. At that time we had been married about six years and my first son was born and had his brit at the hospital.

Unfortunately he developed encephalitis, which was never diagnosed, and after that he could not walk. Then his epilepsy became really bad and he had fits day and night. I nursed him all the time – and he was doubly incontinent. In fact, until I retired I had a job where I could come home as much as I wanted (despatch work for the patisserie firm, Sheraton), as I had to force-feed my son. Then my second son was born. It took a little while for my first son to accept his baby brother.

My first son died when he was forty-six and we looked after him at home all that time. For the first few years my wife had it very hard in our flat in Finchley Road as we had to carry my son down a few flights of stairs. Councillor Young arranged for us to have a ground floor flat in Childs Hill, Cricklewood Lane. There were 184 flats and we were the only Jewish people. We had a lovely flat and did a lot of entertaining. My son used to go to Harperberry Hospital for ten days about two or three times a year to give us a break.

My wife was in touch with Doris Down, the founder of MENCAP, and we were two of the founder members. From then on my wife worked really hard for MENCAP, which held two or three balls a year. My wife used to organise the tombola, which raised £2-3000 at each ball. Yes, my wife devoted so much time to MENCAP – she was on the main committee. Harry Secombe and David Jacobs were also on the committee. I was vice-chairman of MENCAP for many years. I am still a member but no longer involved.

My younger son went to school at Christ's College and was head boy. He went to Exeter University and became a solicitor, but decided he did not want to practice. He now has a wonderful job which takes him all over the world. He lives in Shepherds Bush and is forty-seven and not married – a wonderful chap. I see him every weekend.

I have belonged to Alyth for many years, and my younger son went to religion school and had his barmitzvah there. My wife died thirteen months ago – life isn't the same without her. She was always beautifully dressed until the day she died – everybody talked about her. The synagogue was really wonderful to me.

JOHN DAVIS
6
THE FLYING TOOTH

The oldest of three brothers, I was born in 1922 into a comfortably off family. My father, a captain, had been awarded the Military Cross in the First World War. Periodically, even after twenty years, pieces of shrapnel would work their way out of his body. Later he became a prime mover in organising what was to become the annual Jewish Ex-Servicemen's Remembrance Parade. I can still remember the boyhood nightmares inspired by the march past of wheelchairs, the blind, the lame and the limbless.

Our synagogue was Upper Berkeley Street. We were there most Sabbaths for the children's services, then on to Selfridges for the delicious Sabbath treat of an ice-cream soda. I was educated at Highgate School, where I started the Jewish Circle in 1939. I also distinguished myself by captaining inter-school boxing matches. Never rising to more than 5ft 4ins in height, one day the inevitable happened and I was matched against a six-footer. I lost – but survived to tell the tale.

Just three days after my eighteenth birthday I applied to join the RAF. My ambition was to be a pilot, though I had never set foot in an aircraft. But my eyesight and maths were inadequate, so I was accepted as an Air Gunner. There followed three months of maths studies and eye exercises until I found myself accepted for the desired pilot training. Off to Canada for the flying course – a very exciting experience! I was trained to fly single-engine aircraft – Tiger Moths, Hurricanes, Spitfires, Kittyhawks, etc. As time in the RAF progressed, losing colleagues became part of the experience – some because they failed their training, but more because they were killed in operations. So I ceased making friends; it was too painful losing them.

As for me, my first flying accident resulted in a lost tooth. This was to prove singularly appropriate in the light of my involvement with the dental profession in subsequent civilian life. My second solo flight in a Hurricane was even more dramatic. I had a dreadful crash and landed suspended upside-down by my seatbelt. On this occasion my short stature saved my life, as my head avoided direct contact with the ground.

Somewhat to my surprise I was allowed to continue on to operational training near Chester. This was a fun period. Saturday night was always special. Since camp washing facilities were so rotten – a bare hut, icy winds and snow gusting through unglazed windows, boiling water but no means of temperature control – I regularly repaired to the bliss of a soak in the Chester Bath House, then went off to the dance.

With training complete, various spells were spent in strafing attacks over France, in northern Ireland and West Africa. In spring 1942 I arrived in the Middle East. There, one evening on my way back to the tent, a truck loaded with drunken South African troops knocked me down. I suffered acute cerebral oedema and I was bedridden for three long months with my leg in traction. When the weights, etc, finally came off, a large colony of bedbugs was exposed. They had been my constant companions for two months – at last the mystery of my rash was explained.

One night my fellow convalescents and I, all on callipers and crutches, decided that a celebration was in order, so we took a taxi to a nightclub where we seated ourselves at a table. The girls of the club duly arrived. Their routine was to order expensive 'champagne' and then attempt to arouse their man. During these proceedings a look of horror swept across one girl's face, until she realised that what she was stroking was, in fact, a plaster cast.

Having recovered from the accident, I was passed fit for non-operational flying and sent to work ferrying fighters from West Africa to Cairo. I later spent some time in a desert village called Azizia – the hottest place on earth. This was preparation for our landing in Sicily. Since then I am only happy when I have a glass of water by me.

September 1947. My first night flight since the accident was to prove a terrifying ordeal. My mission was to deliver a Kittyhawk to Bari, Italy. Refuelling in Catania, I calculated I had just enough time –

and fuel – to scrape a landing in Bari before night fell. But events did not go according to plan. My first handicap was that I had no map of Italy – none was available. Then a tremendous thunderstorm broke out, forcing me to fly across the Gulf of Taranto at sea level, only to find Bari airfield was totally under water with rockets signalling it was too dangerous to attempt a landing. To complete the picture, there was a total absence of radio communication with Bari. What to do? Inspiration! I remembered Lecce, an airfield with night-landing facilities, forty miles east from a lighthouse in the Gulf of Taranto. Would I make it? It was pitch dark and I was dangerously short of fuel. Panic struck me. Should I climb and bale out? I chose Lecce. Locating the lighthouse I turned east, and there before me lay winking the most welcoming landing lights in the world. I executed a hurried turn. A beautiful landing! At that very moment my engine died. The fuel had finally run out. Shock and terror left me physically unable to extricate myself from the plane.

The whole of my RAF service saw no anti-Semitism. Indeed I was always particularly popular at breakfast since if bacon was served there would be one or two rashers for my neighbour. I had one roommate, an ex-policeman, who had been a member of Sir Oswald Mosley's fascist Blackshirts. We talked in great depth, and became bridge partners. Sadly he was killed while flying and I organised his funeral. Strange. For the record, I was never hit by the Germans, but American friendly fire got me twice.

Summer 1945. A unit 'unofficial' trip. The war in Europe had finished; chaos was everywhere. My task was to fly a Palestinian Jew into Italy. There he would organise the escape to Palestine of Jews as illegal immigrants. A tricky trip.

The war was over, but the RAF was not yet ready to send me home. I became an Operations Officer, first in Cairo, then Tobruk, and finally in Tripoli. In Tobruk I was responsible for receiving the monarchs of Morocco, Algeria and Tunisia on their way to Mecca to give thanks for victory. Here I fouled up. Unable to distinguish between kings and servants I took them all to the Officers' Mess. The food (a regal dinner of corned beef) was 'incorrect', and the intricacies of our toilets defeated them. If relationships with these countries are somewhat strained, it could be my fault.

Tripoli, at the time I went, was one third Italian, Arab and Jewish. The Jews and Arabs had lived together in harmony for two thousand years. But political events were moving fast. Whilst Tripoli was left temporarily in charge of a British officer (the second-in-command) who had a history of supporting the Arab cause, the 4th November 1945 pogrom took place. One hundred and twenty Tripoli Jews lost their lives. Immediately on his return to Tripoli I managed with difficulty to get in to see the Area Commander to discuss the situation. He took the firm action necessary, called out the British troops and the pogrom stopped immediately. I arranged for the British Board of Deputies to be informed, but by then the concentration camps and refugees from Europe were more pressing than the deaths of a hundred and twenty Jews in Tripoli.

So home for demob in early 1946. My Flight Lieutenant's uniform came off for the last time. The excitement of being together with my parents after five years of separation was an enormous thrill. But to be alive was the biggest thrill of all. Into the family dental supply business I went, at the princely annual salary of £300.

In 1948 Israel was created and was immediately attacked by Arab neighbours. I telephoned the Jewish Agency to offer my experience. Later a mystery call led to a meeting on a bench in Hyde Park. A long walk, talk and investigation of my credentials brought the request that I be ready to pick up an ME109 in France and fly it to Israel. The waiting was long. Then came the first armistice so I withdrew my offer of help.

I was introduced to my future wife, Hilde Meyer, by a mutual friend. Eighteen months after our Upper Berkeley Street marriage we were blessed with the arrival of our daughter, Susan, and six years later by Daniel.

In 1954 I started my own dental production business, which gradually grew to 40-strong employees. By 1979 we had grown to be one of the largest suppliers in the UK. Eventually I was able to fulfil a long held ideal of mine, a 'co-ownership' business, with employees as shareholders. Legal advisors took ten years to bring this to fruition, as it was unusual. Unfortunately it did not last when the company moved into loss making. My son, Daniel, now runs the enterprise, which is owned by a Finnish dental manufacturer.

I served two stints as President of my Trade Association and was largely instrumental in the formation of the British Dental Health Foundation, a charity building public awareness of the need for mouth care. This was followed by the creation of a special dental charity, the Cordent Trust, financed by my company, with me as Hon Secretary for the first twenty-eight years. Cordent initiated many original dental projects, especially bringing dental care to underdeveloped countries.

Aged sixty-nine, retirement arrived. It was surprising and rewarding to receive three different 'Life Achievement Awards' and to be the only non-dentist in Europe to be elected to the International College of Dentists.

The word 'retirement' has never appealed – I do not regard myself in this category. I am student, teacher and writer. I represent local bodies, serve on the Local Council of Christians and Jews, care for the housebound, help with the homeless, am uncrowned King of Litter for the Garden Suburb, act as librarian, help slow readers in school, garden, ramble, play bridge, sing with a choral society, and have four wonderful grandchildren. I still have time for bowls and summertime pre-breakfast swims in Highgate Pond. Long may it continue, in health, and with Hilde alongside.

7   KATINKA EASTON (SEINER)

I was born in Budapest on 7th November 1933, many moons ago, and was an only child. My mother was called Anna and came from the north-east corner of Hungary and my father's name was Imre (a very Hungarian name). My grandfather, whose photo is hanging on the wall, was a gentleman farmer and had a big estate in a north-east part of Hungary. He had vineyards, and I have good memories of when I was a little girl being allowed to drive a horse and cart. My grandparents died of old age, but part of my family died in Auschwitz. My favourite uncle – he was a wonderful man and a Zionist – taught me how to write Hebrew.

My grandfather had a big family business – similar to Fortnum & Mason in London – and when he died my father took over. My father's father was very clever, and was even an MP at one time in the Czech Parliament. He was very orthodox, although my father was progressive. We always had a Friday night dinner and a poor person at the table. I remember my mother lighting candles and my father blessing me with a handkerchief. We were very privileged Jews and when I was young I did not know what it was like to be poor.

Back in Budapest at that time, Jews were not allowed to go to university. We lived in quite an elegant street and I used to go for a walk with my nanny, near the Danube, past a smart restaurant – and there was a notice that said 'Dogs and Jews not allowed.'

The Germans came in 1944. Now I hate sewing because I can remember trying to sew a yellow star on to my coat. There was no help in the flat at that time as non-Jews had to be sent away from Jewish homes. My piano teacher stayed in our flat as she was thrown out of the house where she was living. Generally, we felt that the Hungarian people did not support us.

We received a postcard from my cousin in Auschwitz (who survived and now lives in Australia) saying 'Arrived Auschwitz, having a good time'. Her mother and daughter died in the gas chamber. I didn't know what Auschwitz was. I didn't really know what was going on. We had a very large flat and people kept coming and going – in every room or two rooms there was a family living. My mother would sit in her bedroom, receiving people one after the other and promising to save their lives. We also had to move to 'safe houses', and went from place to place. My father was in a forced labour camp and the family business was confiscated. At that time we lived in Pest and were destitute. We then went into hiding in Buda.

I had a brother who died two years before I was born and I believed that he was looking after us. At one time we went to a convent, and we thought that this was it – the Russians were coming and we would be okay. However, suddenly one day the doors burst open and a Hungarian soldier marched my mother, myself and two more people down to the square. Suddenly we were standing in the street. The soldier looked at me and said I reminded him of his brother Joseph. He offered us the chance to escape whilst he turned away to light a cigarette, having threatened to shoot us if he turned to find us still in his sight. We ran for our lives. After this, we went back to our so-called Jewish house. This was a horrendous place as everybody was waiting to be killed. I was about nine at this time.

Eventually we saw my father again at the home of one of his employees, where he was waiting for us. This was one of our hiding places, and this was where I learnt to play chess and bridge. I also had to do some darning. Whilst we were staying with my father's employee, his wife was very nervous about hiding us. During the day she sent us down to the coal cellar in case somebody came, but in the evening we were allowed to come out. However, one day in November, she said she could not take it any longer and we had to go. My mother had some Swedish papers, so we went to a Swedish house at about nine or ten o'clock that night because there was a curfew and Jews were not allowed out during the day. While we were at the Swedish house we were liberated by the Russians. The Hungarians never admitted they supported Hitler.

Life in Budapest was dreadful at that time. There was no running water, no electricity, no gas, no food – we were starving. We eventually got back to our flat, and bit-by-bit my father managed to retrieve some of his fortune, but a lot of it was stolen. My cousin and aunt came back from Auschwitz. They just rang the bell – it was really wonderful to see them. We started to live a little. I went back to school. We had very good teachers, and we had a few good years – dancing, hiking and swimming. I went back to studying. We only mixed with Jewish people.

Then the Russians started causing problems. The Hungarian police came with machine guns and made my father hand over the keys of his business. The family then felt that the only thing to save us was to become working class, and for me to work. Somebody we knew arranged an audition for me at the operatic theatre and I started working. However, there was a problem since one of the directors realised who I was, my background, etc. He used to be an errand boy in our business in 1944. My father had given him money and help, and then he went into a forced labour camp. He had almost been thrown out of the theatre. He told the artistic director about me. There was a big meeting, and a woman who was a Nazi started saying nasty things about me. However, they still did not throw me out.

One day I felt I had had enough, and in 1956 I applied to the Royal Academy of Music, where I stayed for three years. However, in Hungary life was not very good to me and I was just hanging on, studying music. Generally people were as poor as we were. My cousin and aunt sent us parcels. I gained a higher scholarship and did some teaching and worked at the opera house as a soloist.

In 1956 there was a revolution. I went marching for four days until the Russians intervened. Our house was riddled with bullets. My mother was very distraught at the time. Life was not safe in Hungary, so arrangements were made with my aunt, who was crossing from Austria to England, for us to be smuggled out of Hungary into Austria. At that time the borders of Hungary were closed (except to communist officials) and surrounded by barbed wire, making it impossible to leave. One evening there was an unexpected ring at the doorbell. (Everyone in those days was petrified that it might be something bad. It had happened a few times to quite a few of my friends and they didn't survive the treatment.) A man stood there and said he was sent by my aunt. My parents were quite old, but I managed to persuade them to come. Only my father had a passport.

We met the man again, who told us to meet at a certain place in the dark where we would see a big lorry, which was supposedly collecting some wheat. When the time came, my mother and I got into the lorry. When we got off we were given some soup, but from there we had to go on foot in the snow. Conditions were terrible, but we knew we had to keep going – it was like a death march. However, eventually we made it into Austria. We went to Vienna where we had friends and stayed for a few days. Then we came to England. My father followed on later with his own passport.

In England I continued my career in opera, and sang at The Festival Hall. I met my husband when the Royal Philharmonic Orchestra went to Glyndebourne. Our wedding day was on the anniversary of my departure from Hungary. I have been back to Hungary since to sing, but I really hated it there.

8   LASZLO EASTON

My name is Laszlo Easton, formerly Laszlo Ekstein. I was born in Hamburg, Germany, on 14th July 1920. My parents Eda and Maurice managed and owned an auction room in Hamburg and later opened an antique shop. I had one brother called Andor, four years younger than me (our names are Hungarian). My brother and I were educated in a Jewish school in Hamburg which also covered secondary education. During the First World War my father was an officer in Hungary in a very anti-Semitic regiment. Before my father joined the army he was trained as a Rabbi. When he left the army he went to Germany. My mother also came from Budapest, Hungary.

Up to 1933 my life was okay. My grandparents lived in a block of flats in Hamburg which was only for Jewish people and had its own synagogue. It was a donation from one of the wealthy Jewish people in Hamburg and we used to go there with my parents every Friday night and Shabbat morning. But I always found my grandparents too religious.

I became interested in music when my parents and I went to a restaurant in Hamburg where there was always an orchestra. At that time the orchestra had a Hungarian leader who played the violin and I copied him with an umbrella. My parents then arranged for me to have violin lessons, and one of my teachers was the leader of the Hamburg Philharmonic Orchestra. Eventually I had a Jewish Hungarian gypsy teacher who was absolutely marvellous. After the lesson he used to discuss the bible with my grandmother. He taught me to love music and enjoy playing the violin.

In 1935/36 forms were sent out and anybody who had anything to do with art and antiques had to join the Chamber of Culture. However by 1937 my parents were very worried about my brother and me, and decided to send us to England. My father had a client who was a ship's chief-engineer on the Ellerman Line, which travelled from Hamburg to Hull. In exchange the client took some gold coins from my father's antique shop.

I was seventeen at the time and the client took my brother and me to the ship and went through customs with the gold coins - I was scared stiff at the time. Those gold coins paid for most of our school fees in England. We went to a boarding school in Kent organised by Lady Reading and Victor Gollantz. The school was called Bunscourt and the headmistress was Anna Ettinger who brought children over from Germany. My brother and I stayed at this school for about a year and a half. I had been taught to speak English at school in Hamburg by an Australian elocution teacher. This enabled me to work for a year and a half on the stage through the Maccabi Club. It was very risky as I had not been naturalised, but they changed my name - so luckily the authorities never found out.

In 1938 I left school and came to London. I stayed in digs in Stamford Hill until my parents came over in August 1939. I went to a polytechnic to study electrical engineering and then worked for EMI in Oxford Street as a radio engineer for most of the war. Before this I worked for a man called Levy who employed Jewish refugees. He ran the Aberdale Cycle Company, a cycle factory in Edmonton. I then volunteered for the air force but was turned down because of my Hungarian origin. By this time my father was dealing in antiques in England and we lived in Hampstead.

Whilst working at EMI I met H.G. Wells. I went to his house in Hanover Terrace to repair his radiogram. I needed a record with a singer to test his radiogram, but H.G. Wells said he did not have one, as he did not like to hear the human voice in an unnatural way.

My brother joined the army. He started being trained in Inverness and then was drafted into the 51st Highland Division. He had to change his name when he served in Normandy. He was wounded, went back and was killed during a night patrol, just before the end of the war when the Germans retreated. My mother never got over this. Therefore it was lucky that they didn't accept me.

After the war my father opened an antiques shop in Jermyn Street and I joined him. He specialised in small antique paintings, porcelain, etc. We bought our stock from auctions, from abroad and from other dealers. Some stock we bought over from Germany as household goods.

In the antique shop we had some very prestigious clients: the Queen's lady-in-waiting, famous actors, Mrs. Kennedy, Peter Wolstenholme, Vivien Leigh, and Prince Philip just after he was married to Princess Elizabeth. In fact when Prince Philip came in the shop my father did not know who he was, and thought he was a dealer interested in some pottery soup terrines which were made in Holland and Germany in the 17th century. Prince Philip asked my father why he had quoted him a lower price than on the ticket and my father replied, 'You're in the trade aren't you?' Prince Philip said, 'I could be.' At that moment the chauffeur put his head round the door and said, 'Your Royal Highness, I cannot stop outside the shop. Do you mind if I wait for you outside Fortnum & Mason?'

When we realised who it was my mother wanted to apologise. She said, 'Excuse me sir, we didn't recognise you, you were so simple.'(In Germany that is a compliment).

Next day the secretary came in and said that His Royal Highness had enjoyed himself immensely.

My father died in 1955 when he was sixty-six years old and I carried on the business with my mother who died at the age of ninety-two. When my mother died I carried on the business with a partner.

My father had one surviving brother in Hungary and he once came to visit us. In Germany my grandparents were quite old and fortunately died before they were taken to the concentration camp. Some of the family went to Israel. One of my father's brothers was a cripple with one leg. He went to Israel to Mea Shearim and had fourteen sons.

We still had friends in Hamburg who owned a jewellery shop. They had kept a Kiddush cup for me that I had been given for a barmitzvah present. We visited them after the war. One of my father's customers was a dentist and was involved in a group against Hitler. He managed to escape execution.

During and after the war I had a social life. I was a member of the Maccabi Sports Club and we went to the theatre, concerts, etc.

My first marriage was to a girl I met at a music society in 1947. We were married for seven years. She unfortunately died when our second daughter was born. I looked after the children with several nannies who I threw out one by one, partly because half of them wanted to marry me and the others weren't any good. Then I had an English lady who used to look after Mrs Churchill. She made a stipulation that she would only stay for six months, and she was marvellous.

After two years I met Katinka - my mother and my friends had tried to matchmake but I was not very keen. My mother and I saw a picture in one of the music magazines of a girl from Hungary who was a singer at a concert at the Albert Hall. My mother found out where she was living and managed to get the girl, Katinka, into the shop. We went out and after two months we decided to get married. We were married at Upper Berkeley Street Synagogue. My wife brought up my two girls. We had one son together in 1960 who is a doctor in Leeds.

Although my grandparents were orthodox, I joined Alyth Gardens as I had always been reform like my parents. During my first marriage we lived off the North Circular Road. I moved to Finchley with my second wife. When my son Andrew was little he went to Kerem House, and my daughters went to King Alfred School. When they were older one daughter went to a boarding school in the country and the other daughter went to university to study medicine and became a psychiatrist, as did my son Andrew. He was at University College School, Hampstead and then went to medical school at the Middlesex Hospital.

We were invited to Hamburg by the senate (about fifty groups a year from all over the world are invited). They took us to concerts, theatres, Jewish clubs, but most of the Jewish people from Hamburg came from the east - there are hardly any Germans or ex-Germans there now. We were treated extremely well and stayed in good hotels. In fact, Katinka actually sang in one place there. Before we left Hamburg we went on a steamer on a lake in the middle of Hamburg.

We were followed by a police barge to protect us. Katinka was asked to sing on the ship and she sang 'Yerushalyim'.

On another occasion in Hamburg, before lunch, I was asked to make a speech in the Town Hall. This was quite strange, as during the war it had been taken over by Hitler. I still speak fluent German.

9   CHARLES EMANUEL

I was born on 15th December 1944 at the Jewish Memorial Hospital in New York City, the son of Morris and Viola Emanuel, and brother of Harold Marc Emanuel. Whilst I do not remember anything about my first few years of life, I realise now that the closeness of my family, both emotionally and physically, was an important factor in my life. Until we moved to Long Island we lived in the same apartment building as my paternal grandmother (my grandfather died before I was born) and a number of aunts and uncles as well. My maternal grandparents also lived nearby.

At the age of three I moved with my parents (I don't remember being asked my opinion) to the town of Elmont, New York, which was a small suburban town just outside New York City. In 1948 there was almost nothing there but a few small local shops, a farm where you could buy fresh milk, a few schools, and a number of young families like ours where the man worked in the city but was willing to commute so that the family could have a nice home and some fresh air. When we moved in I do not think the road was paved yet.

Most important for our family was that there was no synagogue, so my parents along with a number of other Jewish families started one. I am told by my father that the reason it became Reform rather than Conservative was that the Reform movement offered more money to help us get started. Being founder members meant that the synagogue became an important part of our life for the next eleven years when we lived in Elmont. My father taught in the religion school as well as serving on the board. He was both chairman of the board and president of the synagogue among his other duties. Every Friday night and Saturday morning we went to services. When I started Hebrew at the age of six at the synagogue's weekday classes I could not read any Hebrew but knew many prayers by heart. As I got older I sang in the children's choir and lead children's services with my brother for the High Holy Days.

When I was thirteen the Reform movement opened its first summer camp called the Camp for Living Judaism. My brother, who is three years older than me, went as a counsellor. I went as a camper. The experience was wonderful as I was able to live and study Judaism in a much more relaxed and informal way while still swimming and playing baseball, which were my two real passions. For three years I attended the summer camp and I probably would have continued. However, my father who worked for the government was promoted and we moved to Washington DC.

Whereas the experience at the summer camp had opened my eyes to living a Jewish life outside a family setting, my two years in Washington opened my eyes to the political side of life in general, and Judaism in particular. While both of my parents worked for the government, they had gone to university in the Thirties and were liberal in their approach to the political scene. In Washington I met senators and congressmen as part of my everyday school life. I heard J.F. Kennedy speak at my school during his campaign for the presidency in 1960. I also became involved in two Jewish youth movements. The first was my synagogue youth club. The rabbi, Eugene Lipman, was heavily involved in social action, civil rights and ecumenical activities. The one activity I particularly remember was a musical programme called 'We sing for Judaism' where a group of us within the youth club formed a choir and performed in churches and schools. We also discussed our Jewish beliefs and practices with the group, which included black churches and youth clubs.

At the same time I became involved in the B'nai B'rith Youth movement. Although much more social in character, this allowed me to express my political side as well. As vice-president I also chaired the social action group, whose activities included organising parties at orphanages and old-age homes as well as discussions on social issues of the day. For instance, we went to a segregated restaurant in Maryland to have an honest and frank discussion as to why blacks were not allowed to eat in this restaurant. Considering the restaurant was quite expensive and the only blacks that would be able to eat there would probably be professionals, businessmen and even ambassadors from the African embassies in Washington, one would have thought they would be welcome.

I was asked by both the synagogue youth club and the B'nai Brith club to be the chairman in my senior year in High School, but before I could make a decision my father informed me that he had received another promotion and we would be moving to Chicago.

Moving to a new city is never easy, but moving at the beginning of my senior year in High School was particularly difficult. Everyone had made friends during that last year and thought more about where to go to university for the next year rather than developing new relationships. However, the one place that I found welcoming was the synagogue. My parents and I continued to go to services. I was involved in the youth group and even came second in a citywide sermon contest run by the Reform youth movement in the area. I was very pleased the next year to enter my freshman year at the University of Wisconsin. Officially I studied mainly the history of Hebrew, but the University of Wisconsin was a relatively left wing campus, and the Hillel Foundation (the centre of Jewish student activities) and its rabbi encouraged both civil rights and pro-Israel activities. While civil rights were nothing new, Israel now played a major role in my Jewish life as I became more and more involved in Hillel activities. During my university years I also used my swimming ability to return to the Reform Jewish summer camp programme where I taught both swimming and Judaism to the campers.

My Jewish activities were so much part of life that by the time I graduated university (1967) it was no surprise to anyone that I applied and was accepted to study to be a Reform rabbi at the Hebrew Union College - Jewish Institute of Religion, in New York. After my first two years I decided to take a year 'off' to study in Israel. In June 1969 I left for Israel, first to study at Ulpan Akiva in Netanya, then to work at a Kibbutz in the Galil, then to study at an Ulpan in Arad and then for the last four months to study at the Hebrew Union College in Jerusalem. I met Peduth Amar in Arad. Peduth had been born in

Morocco and studied Law in France. We were married on 27th December 1970.

In the summer of 1971 I returned to my parents' home in Worcester, Massachusetts where I interned at our congregation that summer and the next summer. I was ordained in June1973, and one month later our first son, Ilan, was born. The three of us moved to Huntsville, Alabama, where I started my first job at Temple B'nai Shalom. Huntsville was an interesting town. It had been a small, southern town with very few Jews, but in the early 1950s the United States government set up an army base there dealing specifically with the space industry. Huntsville became a boom town, with the help of people such as Werner Von Braun, a German scientist who had come to the United States after World War Two. When I arrived the town had approximately one hundred and fifty thousand inhabitants with around one hundred and forty Jewish families. Although there were two congregations, a Reform and a Conservative, for the six years I was there I was the only rabbi, the Huntsville rebbe so to speak. In 1977 our second son, Yaniv, was born.

In 1979 I accepted a position in Leeds, England. My reason for going to England was two-fold. Peduth was not very happy being so far from her family who all now lived in Paris, and England seemed like a good family move. Also, being on the more traditional side of the American Reform movement, I found the British Reform more to my liking.

I stayed in Leeds for four and a half years and then accepted the position of Rabbi at the North Western Reform Synagogue in London. I became much more involved with the Reform Movement and the World Union for Progressive Judaism. From 1987-89 I served as Chairman of the Assembly of Rabbis of the Reform Synagogues of Great Britain.

At the time of writing I am still serving as the Rabbi of the North-Western Reform Synagogue.

10   BEATRICE FOSTER

I thought I would let you know about my early days in the film industry. I left school at fourteen having learnt shorthand and typewriting. In January 1931 I went with an uncle who owned a cinema to Wardour Street, where all the film companies were situated. There I obtained a position with United Artists. They were just about to distribute the first Mickey Mouse films made by Walt Disney. We had a charming American Managing Director who one day brought round four of the film stars who had formed United Artists, and introduced us by name. So I met Charlie Chaplin, Douglas Fairbanks Snr, Gloria Swanson and Sam Goldwyn. Another day someone asked me if I would type a letter for Douglas Fairbanks Jr. I was petrified, but he was charming. I saw quite of a lot of him as he was producing a film in London. I was so sorry to read from the newspaper that he had passed away aged ninety. Then I was asked to go into our cinema to take some notes for Howard Hughes – thought I might be discovered but no such luck! I also saw Walt Disney in person.

In 1943 I worked for Odeon Cinemas. A concert was held at the Odeon, Leicester Square, for the American Forces and some of the staff were allowed to attend. I remember seeing Bob Hope, Adolphe Menjou, Frances Langford and quite a few others.

In 1951 I went to New York for the first time and stayed with my sister who was there on holiday. In 1958 she met an American in London, who she subsequently married. One day walking down Fifth Avenue I saw Rosalind Russell and Robert Cummings and I also saw ex-King Peter of Yugoslavia and his wife. Another day I was in one of the stores and in walked Joan Crawford – great excitement – everyone stopped dead to watch her. I also saw Greta Garbo several times as she was living quite near the hotel where we were staying. Earl St John is a name I often see on television in connection with the older films. I worked for him for a few weeks when his own secretary was ill.

11   PETER FREAN

M y parents were Hannah and Kurt Freedman. I was born in
Hiezing, Vienna, on 23rd January 1914. My father had a shop
selling paint and brushes, which had been started by my grandfather. I
have a younger sister Lilly and there was another child who died in
childhood. During the First World War my father was in the Austrian
army. My mother and I followed my father around wherever he was
stationed. After the war my father went back to his business.

My mother was the eldest of five children. Before my
grandfather was in the paint business they were distillers somewhere
in Eastern Europe and they came to Vienna in 1848. My other
grandfather came from a long line of rabbis, but his son didn't follow
them and had a furniture factory.

I went to school in Hiezing and had a barmitzvah at Temple
Gunzit. At secondary school I studied for matriculation. I came to
England in 1933 while my family remained in Vienna. My first job
was decorating at the Mount Royal Hotel in the West End. At first I
lived in the Bayswater area, bed and breakfast, hotels, etc. During that
time I went back to Vienna to visit my parents. When the situation
deteriorated in Austria I got my parents and sister over to England.
They had a flat in Battersea.

In 1940, during the Second World War, I was interned in the
Isle of Man and then Canada. I came out of internment when I
volunteered for the Pioneer Corps and enlisted on the 22 July 1941. I
finished up as a gunner in the Education Corps. I was also sent to
Belgium for a short time.

I left the army in 1945 and went back to my business of fancy
goods. I went round the stores selling. I had an office in Newman
Street, then in Reading, and then came back to another address in
Newman Street. My business was always a one-man business,
although I had a helper in the office. In 1947 I became a naturalised
British citizen.

I was introduced to my wife in 1956 and we were married in Hampstead Registry Office. We then lived in Highgate for five years and later bought a house in Windermere Avenue. Our three children were born in 1960, 1962 and 1964. We joined Alyth in 1972. All the children went to Brooklands School.

Our eldest son went to City of London, our middle son to Christ's College and our daughter to Henrietta Barnett. Paul, the eldest son, then went to Cambridge and now lives in New York. Michael spent a year in Israel, and then trained for youth and community work and he now lives in Morden. Ruth went to Sussex and took a physics degree. She now lives in Italy.

At Alyth we became involved with Soviet Jewry through Harry Lightman's sister. We both went to Russia at different times. We visited the Refusnik people. I brought back a book of photographs including a Russian synagogue that was destroyed. These are now exhibited in a museum.

12   EVA FREAN

I was born in the fur district of Vienna on 18th June 1925. My family were second generation Austrian. My father was a doctor and the youngest of eight children. His father died when he was about fourteen. My father was the only one in his family who had studied at medical school in Vienna. My mother was one of the few women admitted to law school in Vienna. It was a four-year course but she left after two years to get married. I have a brother Hans who is two years older that me and lives in Canada.

Until I was thirteen I went to school in Schüttel Street in Vienna. In March 1938, when Hitler came to power, the Jewish children had to leave the school. I then had to go to a Jewish school further away from the city. My brother went to a secondary school and was sixteen when he left. The year before Hitler I remember going on a skiing holiday where there were six Jewish girls and some non-Jewish girls who were not very nice to us. On the whole you kept your head down.

My brother and I came to England in 1938. We both came independently. My brother got a place through the Quakers at a French school in Yorkshire where they had a number of other refugee boys. I went to the same school as a day girl for one year. My parents arrived during that time, in March 1939. My father had been in prison for a short time in Vienna and was released on the condition that he left. He did not have any work when he first came to England but my mother had a domestic job in Edinburgh. There were a number of doctors from Germany and Austria who were allowed to re-qualify within twelve months and he did this in Edinburgh. My father was also interned but eventually got work in Birmingham as a doctor.

I joined my parents in Edinburgh and went to a private girls' school called Primary School for Girls where the headmistress took in one refugee child. I felt very isolated. I was there for two years. When war broke out the whole school was evacuated to Bracken Bay. I got my school certificate there. I was the only Jewish child at the school so

I had no Jewish education. However I did have religious instruction in Vienna. I left school in 1941 and joined my parents in Birmingham. My parents had Jewish awareness but did not keep anything, except my father kept Yom Kippur but worked. And we always had a Seder at home.

I had two cousins in Vienna who managed to escape. The parents of one of them didn't and the other one went to Shanghai and is now in Israel.

When I lived in Birmingham it was wartime. I worked in a day nursery. Then I went to Birmingham University to study social sciences and lived with my parents. I had taken the Scottish leaving certificate. I graduated after two years and came to London. When I first arrived I shared a flat in Swiss Cottage. My first job was in Camberwell as a social worker. You saw the parents and the kids who had tonsillitis, minor illnesses - recovering from the war.

Then I decided to take a course in fostering which was government sponsored. I did this in Cardiff for a year. I was offered a job in Nottingham and lived there for three years. I then went to Switzerland for a year. I wanted to work with children, spoke German as a language and worked in a psychiatric observation centre near Zurich. I was there for six months and then did a similar job in Lausanne, which was French speaking.

I came back to my parents in Birmingham. I went for some more training at LSE to become a psychiatric social worker for two years. I took a job with Middlesex County Council. This was in about 1955/56. At that time I shared a flat in Hampstead.

When I met Peter we moved on to Highgate. We had three children and I went back to work part-time after seven or eight years. I worked for the London Borough of Barnet for about twenty years.

We have been back to Vienna with our daughter. I returned again two years ago with my son and daughter-in-law. As far as my feelings are concerned I have been and that is it.

13   GHITA FREUND

I am known as Kitty. I was born in Liverpool on 5th February 1913.
My parents came from Russia and their real name was Turneritch.
My mother's family name was Read (when they came off the boat in
England they were asked if they could "read" and this became their
name). My mother's father came from St Petersburg and my father's
father was a bandmaster to the Tsar. My father, Sam, was a glass
merchant like his family in Russia. They were quite prosperous and
had businesses in Liverpool and Sheffield. My parents didn't have a
good marriage and my mother, Flora, got a legal separation from my
father - they couldn't get a divorce. She came to London with me
when I was eighteen months old.

My mother and I stayed with her sister, whose husband was
the headmaster of Norwood Jewish Orphanage. We stayed with them
until my mother could find a job. I called my uncle 'daddy' and my
Aunt, Esther. My father went to Boston before the war - he never
supported us and we never saw him again.

I went to a school orphanage until I was eleven. The
orphanage had a hundred and fifty children. Then I won a scholarship
and went to Streatham High School. This was quite a shock as I had
been very sheltered in an all-Jewish atmosphere. When I got the higher
education certificate I attended Fursedown Training College for two
years and became a qualified teacher. My first job was in Addington
Gardens, west London, where I taught for four years. At this time I
lived with my mother whose family business was running a small
hotel.

I had cousins who were like brothers to me. One was Marcus
Kaye, a member of Alyth Gardens. One day I went with a rabbi, who
was a friend from Liverpool, to a dance at Bayswater Synagogue and
met Hans. I was always in contact with Hans - we wrote to each other.
I arranged an exchange-teaching job in Pretoria. I travelled by boat to
Cape Town, where I knew some people from Liverpool who looked
after me.

Hans and I were married in December 1939 in the synagogue in Pretoria, (which later became the place where the treason trials were held). When Hans went away to war I became involved in nursery education, which was just starting in South Africa, and we used to speak in English and Afrikaans. I did nursery school teaching for most of my life.

When we first married we had a nice little flat in Cape Town. Then when Hans returned from the war we lived in Kimberley and finally Cape Town. During this time my son David was born. This was quite a difficult time as we worked in an orphanage which the owners did not know how to run - in the end we walked out. Hans took a job teaching and I got a job in a nursery where I could take the children. My daughter was born in Cape Town and her name is Erica. At this time we lived quite comfortably as we both worked.

After the war things got really bad politically, and we were involved in supporting the Africans we taught in night schools. After six years Hans came to England and found a job in Feltham. My daughter and I joined him in 1966 after selling our home in South Africa. David stayed behind and got an art scholarship, went to Germany and came to England a year later. Erica trained as a teacher in England. At first we rented a flat and two years later we bought the house where we now live. I taught at a college of higher education in Twickenham until I retired.

Hans' close family went to either America or England. His father died while he was on the boat going to South Africa and his mother had already died.

Most members of the Leo Baeck Lodge in Fitzjohns Avenue are German refugees, and I am one of the few English-speaking people. We have a day centre. We joined, as Hans was already a member of the B'nai B'rith in South Africa. When new people join our Lodge they have to give a little talk about themselves and I couldn't believe the stories I heard. When I retired the first thing I did was to collect stories and I have collected seventy-five life stories.

We have been married for sixty-one years. When we had our diamond wedding anniversary the Leo Baeck Lodge (where we are very active members and of which I was president at the time) gave us a marvellous party and we had a family party. We also had a letter from the Queen.

I have three grandchildren. My eldest granddaughter Louisa is a harpist and plays at The Festival Hall. Both granddaughters have degrees and the boy is just leaving High School.

14   HANS FREUND

M y father's name was David Freund and he was born in
Mysowitz. His family came from Upper Silesia, Yuvashlazie.
Although my family was very academic - we even had rabbis - my
father was different and ended up in the textile business in Berlin in
1906 in the working-class district. My parents met in Berlin where
they were married. My mother's name was Lotta. I was an only child,
born on 9th November 1910.

I was four when the First World War broke out. My father
became a soldier but he never had his heart in the war. He was
stationed at a place called Kustrin. He had an understanding with the
Sergeant-Major that he wasn't keen to be sent to the front. My mother
ran the business whilst my father was in the army. One of my earliest
memories of the war was my father telling us that he had heard that the
British had promised that they would give the Jewish people their own
homeland.

At the end of the war my father left the army and went back to
work in the textile business. I attended school near where we lived - it
went from elementary to high school. I had my barmitzvah at an
orthodox synagogue and sang in the choir for many years. Then I went
to university to study German and English literature. I went to a few
universities, including London, and eventually took my degree in
1933, the year Hitler came into power

Life in Germany before 1933 was not too bad. However one
day the Germans boycotted the Jewish shops, except my father's as he
had a good relationship with the local people. I did not come across
too much anti-Semitism where we lived or at university, but can
remember a sign opposite our shop, which said 'Jews are our
misfortune'.

In 1933 I came back to England as an exchange student at
London University. The university gave me an unpaid job to allow me
to stay here. I lived at 53 Albany Street. I had relations who lived in

Fitzroy Square with whom I stayed for quite a long time when I first arrived at university in London.

I first worked in a toy firm in the city. I couldn't get a proper job as I didn't have a work permit. However my boss paid me £3 a week out of his own pocket. I met Kitty at a dance at Bayswater Synagogue. The rich Jewish people bought tickets at £1 each.

In 1936 I went to South Africa and Kitty joined me a few years later. We were to remain there for 30 years. A businessman (a friend of my father) offered me a job in Johannesburg. I decided I wanted to become a teacher so I obtained a teacher's diploma which added to my degree - around 1937/38. We were married in 1939 just before the war began. I applied to change my name from Freud to Freund. However when I joined the army they changed my name and I became Harold Freund.

I had just got a permanent job in Victoria and just before the war broke out I managed to obtain British citizenship. I volunteered for the South African Air Force when things got bad. The army found out I was well qualified in teaching and I became an information officer. Then I was sent to North Africa. During this time I was captured and wounded in the leg. I escaped in 1941. One day we were in a truck, I was in front sitting next to the driver, and we were rescued by British troops. They took us back to Alexandria.

After the war we went to Cape Town where Kitty took a job in the Jewish orphanage.

In 1966 we returned to England. We got a flat in Bayswater and I took a job at Hendon High School, where I taught for many years until I retired. Originally we belonged to the West London Synagogue and then joined Alyth Gardens.

We have two children – a boy and a girl. On Sundays I taught Jewish boys at Harrow School until I was eighty. Then it was suggested I teach Jewish girls in Wycombe Abbey - I did this until a year or so ago. I also used to teach in the reform synagogue in Cape Town and Germany.

15   DENISE FRIEDMAN

My parent's names were Julius Zlotover and Margorie Tarshish. My father was born in Wales and grew up in Dublin and my mother was born in Liverpool. Both their parents came from Russia. My grandfather first came to Wales with his wife and four children. Two years later my father was born but his mother died when he was two. My grandfather moved to Dublin with his family and later became the equivalent of a JP. So my father came from a very well known Jewish family, and my grandfather in Dublin was the first president of the main synagogue. He lived next door to Isaac Herzog, who became the Chief Rabbi of Ireland, and who married my parents in Liverpool.

My father met my mother in Liverpool. He qualified as a dentist at the Royal College of Surgeons in Ireland. After he qualified he moved to London, set up practice and changed his name to Salter. I was born on 3rd May 1926 in Platts Lane, London. We later moved to Golders Green. I have a younger sister Rhona married to Tony who has just retired as a judge. I went to several schools in London – Frognal and Henrietta Barnet

I really didn't know very much about the war, but in 1938, at the start of the war, my family evacuated to Dublin to a place called Mount Merrion, which is a very pleasant area on the way out to Bray. We had a lot of family and friends there. My father did not practice in Dublin as he had a skin complaint. He managed the family furniture shop started by my grandfather. He had three widowed sisters who depended on him to keep the shop going.

I went to different schools in Dublin, including The Mount, and then on to Trinity College where I studied sociology. I had a really good time and a good Jewish social life including university balls. During the war there was no shortage of food in Dublin, only petrol rationing. There were loads of cherries in the Irish countryside, which was very unspoilt. We all had bicycles.

My father came back to London in 1945, bought a house in Wimpole Street and then the rest of the family followed. My sister hated it as she missed the countryside in Dublin.

My father's first practice was in Kilburn and then he held a surgery one day a week in Harley Street.

I had various secretarial jobs which I hated. Later on I became an interviewer and ended up in Praed Street, where I was a manageress for two years. Then I married Roy. We were married by Rabbi Reingold at Upper Berkeley Street Synagogue because my parents were members there. I worked for a couple more years until I became pregnant with my first child.

I had very little Jewish education. My parents were not at all religious and I had no feelings towards Israel at that time. It was my son Colin who became interested. After I had Colin I was a housewife for about ten years. Roy encouraged me to study and I chose the Bar and qualified in 1965, by which time I had two children aged ten and seven. After attending Hereward House they went to Highgate School.

I was lucky that we could afford an au pair and I really enjoyed the Bar very much. I used to travel, leaving the house at 7am to get to some court by 10am I first worked in local magistrates courts and then specialised in family and criminal law. I was a prosecutor for Scotland Yard. Then I became a part-time immigration adjudicator. I was chairman of various social security tribunals. I kept working for many years until I eventually retired.

I have always been interested in Alyth and was a member of the Guild. As regards my hobbies: I used to play some golf, and in the early days we played tennis and still play bridge.

I have only been back to Ireland once and I took Roy with me. Trinity College now has a modern glass library, my school has been knocked down and there is a motorway outside my old home. The Jewish community is now very small.

16   RONALD (ROY) SAMUEL FRIEDMAN

This is the biography of Roy Friedman, born in Glasgow on 15th June 1926. My father's name was Sydney and my mother's name was Sarah Minnie, although she insisted everybody called her Minnie. My mother's maiden name was Zimbler. My mother's father came to England in the 1850s. My father was born in Hull in 1879 where his mother was also born in the 1850s. He ended up owning two cinemas. When he was about sixteen his parents shipped him off to South Africa as he was a tearaway and he got an ostrich farm there. Eventually he came back to England and died in 1954 at the age of seventy-five.

I had three brothers and three sisters. My older sister was twenty-two when I was born. My youngest sister died four years ago aged over eighty, and my youngest brother two years ago aged eighty-six.

When we first came to London my father was still in the cinema business. He had the cinema in Greenock, Scotland, and he bought one in Hendon, which he eventually sold to the Classic chain. It is now a shopping precinct.

We came to London when I was four, which is why I lost my accent. We stayed with my mother's mother in Hackney. We then moved to 951 Finchley Road, Golders Green, opposite Golders Hill School, which I attended aged five until eleven. Then I went on to Highgate School until I was eighteen. I had a private Jewish education and I don't quite know why I didn't go to Cheder. Perhaps because Highgate had Saturday school and my parents thought six days a week schooling was enough. A man came round to give me barmitzvah lessons. He was a Palestinian Sabra staying in England as a law student. I saw him about fifteen years ago in Tel Aviv. He gave me barmitzvah lessons as well as a general Jewish education.

My barmitzvah was at Dunstan Road United Synagogue. My school was evacuated to north Devon just after my barmitzvah. I came back to London in 1942 when I was sixteen. I can remember the headmaster authorising a Jewish circle for the evacuated Jewish children to meet for prayers when the others went to Chapel. We had Jewish lessons, as well as being given one box of matzo per person at Pesach. We fasted on Yom Kippur from teatime to teatime. As far as anti-Semitism was concerned it was always there since it was a Christian school. I can remember one particular boy making some rude comments so I punched him and broke his nose.

When the school came back from Devon one of my sisters told me to go and join the local Jewish youth club at Dunstan Road. At school I was aware of what the Germans were doing to the Jews, as we all were. The Jewish circle of about fifty boys included some refugees. After I matriculated I took a higher school certificate. The headmaster said that instead of the normal term end, after exams boys could break for the summer holidays as individuals after each had taken their last exam of the school year. In 1944, near the end of term, a V1 rocket bomb landed on the Second Eleven cricket pitch. At that time I was still living in Finchley Road with my parents.

I volunteered for the army and was called up on 1st November 1944. I joined up because I didn't like the Germans and still don't. I went into the Intelligence Corps, serving in the Field Security Branch. I chose this as I thought it would be exciting and interesting. Each security section consisted of eight or nine men, i.e. a commanding officer who was a captain or major, a sergeant major, possibly a staff sergeant and a couple of sergeants. The others were lance corporals who, when with an active unit, always wore three stripes as a local acting unpaid rank. All army recruits went to basic training before being allotted to regiments or corps. I went to York with the Rifle Brigade. When I went to the Corps Depot we were trained so as to be able to hold our rank with infantry, motorcyclists, truck drivers and administration units in case we were attached to other units. We also went to the school of military intelligence. Our infantry training was first of all three months in Anglesey, then with the Dragoons in Enniskillen and two weeks with Guards Sergeants as instructors back at our own depot.

In October 1945 after my training, I was sent as a lance corporal to the Intelligence Corps depot in Karachi (India and Pakistan were one country) on the ship Winchester Castle. I can remember sitting on deck with my life jacket. Six of us managed to disembark at Bombay, ostensibly as a baggage party, and had a look round the town. The next day we took a train to Lahore and then journeyed on to Karachi where I met up with a Jewish boy, Monty Jonas, who was a school friend. We then flew down to Indonesia to replace a Field Security section that had been shot up and killed or taken hostage by the Indonesians. As a Field Security section we were responsible for everything, from lecturing on morale to running counter espionage at grass roots level in Batavia, now called Djakarta.

The British went into Java and Sumatra to rescue the people from the camps, take the Japanese surrender, and hold the town until the Dutch, who were mainly in Europe, came back to reclaim their colony. The Indonesians, who had been taught by the Japanese that they were part of The Greater South East Asia Prosperity Sphere, did not want to go back under Dutch rule. They assumed that anyone in a green uniform was British and anyone in a khaki uniform was one of the very few Dutch. We arrived in khaki uniforms – but not for long! We were not allowed out unless we were armed. We slept with pistols under our pillows. Our unit was self-contained in a very nice house with no army discipline. The town was divided into areas. We were each allocated a section and we had to report back any activity to the sergeant major and commanding officer who collated it all and reported to Division, in our case the 23rd Indian Division – The Fighting Cock, part of the 12th Indian Army Corps.

There wasn't much of a British army there. The Japanese were guarding the prison camps where the Europeans had been interned, and where those en route from other Japanese camps in Indonesia were sent for medical treatment and processing before going home. The Japanese guards were protecting the internees from the Indonesian terrorist/freedom fighters. I was in Indonesia for six months.

I also had one piece of pleasure. I arrested the German who was the link between the German Gestapo in Java and the Japanese Kempei Tai, which was the same as the Japanese equivalent of the Gestapo. As Field Security we did not arrest people personally, but when we pinpointed somebody the military police went in and arrested them. However, I got permission to arrest this guy myself. Some time later after his arrest they found in his house some official seals. In the course of finding out how they had got there I saw a Japanese Kempei Tai officer, whose name was Nakamura. He told me the British had arrested a Chinese motor mechanic who said he had worked for the Japanese - which he had not. His interest in the welfare of the Chinese motor mechanic seemed surprising, so I commented on it in my report. This tied in with another report of a very beautiful Eurasian woman who boasted she was richer than the Queen of Holland and slept on a bed of gold. This woman turned out to be Nakamura's mistress and they had plundered rings, gold, diamonds and money worth millions from the Dutch. Nakamura was hoping to use this to fund a post-war Japanese espionage ring.

Around this time there was an incident. Quite often some of us went as individuals on patrol with other units, such as the Paras, the Ghurkas and other infantry. In my case I was with the Dutch navy on their only submarine in that area. However to dig up the Nakamura loot, which was in various petrol cans, we went on our own as a complete unit. We drove to an out-of-bounds area which was under Indonesian control. For some reason our CO did not tell the military police. Our jeeps were parked about fifty yards from the place we were searching – a passing military police unit saw them and decided to remove them. I believe they knew we were there and were prepared to leave us stranded.

I heard the engines start, challenged and, being a coward, fired over the vehicles. A very angry and frightened voice called out in unrepeatable language that the people involved were British. Later they complained they had been shot at - and our CO replied that we had been reprimanded for not shooting to kill! We collected the cans full of the looted items and took them back to our mess where they were opened – unwisely.

The CO let us look saying, 'You'll never see anything like this again'. He then resealed the containers, but not before letting us take unlawfully three souvenirs each, so long as they were not of great value. I took a signet ring for a girlfriend. When the boxes were handed over to HQ it was alleged that millions had been stolen by our commanding officer and sergeant major – all the town's intelligence personnel from the brigadier down were shipped out and replaced, in case they were involved.

As a unit we were split up. Some of my section went to Saigon (French in those days) some to Malaya, and others, including me, to Singapore. At first it was very miserable because my girlfriend was in Djakarta and a lot of friends had gone to other places. We eventually settled down in Singapore and were quite happy. We had dance halls and shows, and food was cheap. The local people would not accept the British currency and we didn't recognise the Japanese currency. Therefore we were given free issue of Japanese currency to spend in local shops. We were also given a free issue of cigarettes and Scotch, so we were able to save our army pay. This stopped when we left Java.

In Singapore I dealt with political intelligence. There was a large Jewish community. The Japanese were not anti-Semitic; that is European Jews were treated the same as other Europeans, but Jews from the Middle East, such as Persia and the Yemen, were treated as Malayan and Chinese population and not put into camps.

We had to spend six months with an operational unit before being commissioned, but when my time came the war was over. I was given the choice of my own command and signing on for a year, or home leave. I took leave and was home in the winter of 1947, but was back in Singapore in time for my twenty-first birthday. I had jaundice on the ship travelling back and spent a long time in the ship's hospital.

When I returned to England in 1948 as a Sergeant I couldn't get a job. I tried to get into the film studios but one had to be a union member and the union was not taking new members until the old ones had their jobs back. I then tried to get into advertising but ended up at the Law Society School in Lancaster Place. I did three years articles instead of five because of war service, and then became a qualified solicitor. I used to work with the Golders Green Jewish youth club, where I had been as a boy. I then met my wife Denise and we were married in 1952, (when the King died) at Upper Berkeley Street Synagogue. Our wedding reception was at a restaurant called Gunters, off Curzon Street.

As far as Israel was concerned I wanted to go and live there. I only worked for Jewish firms. My first job was at a firm called Kaufman Seigal. I then worked for Malcolm Slowe for about a year. Denise has a cousin called John Fredman and we joined together to set up Friedman Fredman & Co. The firm was in Manchester Street. John's father was a property man and he gave us what little work he could. I also had my own clients.

When we were first married we lived in St. John's Wood and belonged to the United Synagogue there. Eventually we joined Alyth and it was strange at the beginning. Our son Colin was born in 1954. Brian was born two and half years later and we moved to Kingsley Way in the Suburb. We stayed in this house until Colin was married – more than twenty years ago. Both boys went to Kerem House School, opposite where we lived. From there they went to Golders Hill School, where I had taught between leaving school and joining the army, and then on to Hereward House and then Highgate.

I became a warden at Alyth in 1974. I joined the Council at the time that Joyce Rose was the first woman chairman of the Council. I continued further studies at Leo Baeck College after I retired from my practice in January 1990. I obtained a BA in Hebrew and Jewish studies just before my seventy-first birthday. Denise and I have just celebrated our Golden wedding on 18th February 2002.

17

PETER GALGUT
GROWING UP JEWISH IN SOUTH AFRICA

I was born in Pretoria, South Africa, in 1946 - blissfully unaware of the turmoil that had just swept through the world.

My father, a South African Air Force pilot, had fought in North Africa alongside the RAF and my mother had served in the SA Women's Auxiliary Services. Towards the end of the war they married. On returning home my father found that his legal practice no longer existed and he had to rebuild his career from scratch. So my parents started life in peacetime owning virtually nothing.

Of course I had no idea of their struggles. My earliest memories were of our home, a farm outside Pretoria, where we grew fruit and vegetables to supplement the family income. My childhood years were filled with hot South African sunshine, beautiful blue skies and lots of room to roam around and play – always under the watchful eye of my African nanny. It seemed perfectly normal to have a large African lady always there to look after me and attend to my every need, whim and fancy! We also had a 'house boy', a 'cook boy' and several 'garden boys' - all grown men of course.

Apart from seeing photographs of my parents in uniform and one day finding some ration books, I had no idea what the war had been about. I later learnt more as the implications for Jews came closer to home.

The Afrikaners bore a huge grudge towards the British, whom they saw as being the usurpers of their land and country. Moreover, with their generally Aryan features and Germanic attitudes, the Afrikaners had great empathy with the Nazi cause. On the basis that my enemy's enemy is my friend, the Afrikaners sided well and truly with the Germans and vented their spleen where possible against the Jews. In contrast, most South African Jews spoke English and signed up for military service as part of the war effort on behalf of the colonial power, Britain. While we escaped the excesses of the violence seen in Europe, pitched battles between Jews and Afrikaners in the streets of Johannesburg and other SA towns were not uncommon.

Then after the war, remnants of families in Europe, if they could be found, were brought out to South Africa to be housed and cared for by the local Jewish community. At around the same time, the Afrikaners at last achieved power and took over their country. How would they deal now with the Jews?

In fact, the relationship between the two peoples was undoubtedly complex. On the one hand, with their deep-rooted Calvinist, puritanical religious commitment, the Afrikaners recognised and respected the Jews as 'the holy people' who had originated from the Bible. Indeed, many Afrikaner families read chapters from the Bible every evening, so they were knowledgeable not only of the New Testament but also the Hebrew texts.

On the other hand, there was a strong streak of antipathy towards the Jewish community, vastly complicated by the whole ethos of apartheid. This was not just a division between Blacks and Whites, but a fine-tuned ladder of privilege with the Black Africans at the bottom and the mixed race, Asian, Chinese and White communities going up the rungs of privilege. And, of course, some Whites were 'whiter' than others - non-Christians were considered as second class Whites.

This rather schizophrenic existence improved considerably after the State of Israel came into being. Israel's precarious position, vastly outnumbered by the Arab world – like David and Goliath – struck a very strong chord with the Afrikaners facing an equally hostile world. The connection was cemented when many Israeli advisors came to South Africa to help train the South African military machine.

As I grew up, the 'natural' way of things started to seem increasingly unnatural to me. Petty instances of apartheid were all around me: park benches and shop counters clearly demarcated for Whites or non-White - anyone with a white skin automatically going to the head of a queue - the children's story *Black Beauty* being banned, and on and on.

When I trained as a dentist I was at first fascinated by the absurd situation of having White and non-White clinics, and then profoundly angered that non-White professionals were forbidden to treat the supposedly 'superior' Whites. On one occasion, a Whites-only ambulance called out to treat a road accident victim was sent back to base when it was discovered that the boy was black. He had to lie there waiting for the Black ambulance to turn up.

I found myself increasingly at odds with everything associated with the South African Government and, as compulsory conscription loomed, I worried about possibly having to take up arms to defend the regime.

The crunch came when I realised I was being 'bugged'. As President of the Student Dental Council, a student leader in one of the most liberal universities in South Africa, and most definitely opposed to the regime and everything it stood for, I was clearly of interest to the authorities. One day I received a note under my door asking me to meet a friend and colleague on the football pitch after lectures. I was given specific instructions to burn the letter. Intrigued, I met my friend as arranged. During the rendezvous he told me he was a Government spy with a remit to keep an eye on me. At first I laughed, insisting he must be joking. Did he think he was James Bond? But then he started recounting personal details about myself, my girlfriend and other aspects of my life that he could not possibly have known as a casual friend and fellow student. With the hair slowly rising on the back of my neck and cold sweat appearing on my brow, I decided the time had come to leave South Africa.

18   JOHN GEE

I was born in Bethnal Green on 14th May 1911. My father's name
was John Isaac Gee and my mother was Sarah. Her maiden name
was Isaacs. They were both born in England, my mother from Dutch
parents and my father from Russian or Polish parents. My sister Jessie
was two years younger than me. We lived in Forest Gate. Originally
my father had his own business as a ladies and gents hairdresser. I
went to school in Forest Gate.

In 1916 during the First World War my father went into the
army. I can remember when I was three my mother and my sister saw
father going away to war. He was in the army for just over two years.
He trained soldiers in the Gymnasium Department. Then he was sent
to France. While he was in France they found out he could speak
German, so he was sent back to England as an interpreter for the
prisoners-of-war. He finished up the war on the Isle of Sheppey. I can
remember going there with my mother and sister.

The original school I went to was a council school. I can
remember going there when I was four and there were only one or two
Jewish children. In the first class my teacher was Miss Dickens, a very
kind teacher, and she gave me the job of looking after the goldfish
bowl. I can remember sandbags right up to the tall windows and when
there was an air raid we used to go down to the basement of the
school. There were the Zeppelin bombs. I vividly remember one being
shot down and it landed just outside the London area. Parts of the
Zeppelin were on exhibition at The People's Palace in the East End of
London.

I had my barmitzvah at Earlham Grove Synagogue, Forest
Gate. I had my secondary education at Sir John Cass in the Minories, a
grammar school. I can remember learning Shakespeare and Henry V. I
studied analytical chemistry, as my family wanted me to be a chemist.
I left school and went into a firm that dealt with metals called D W
Metals & Company. I started with a small firm, a man and two
brothers, and they more or less taught me the business. They bought

and sold metals and scrap metals. Eventually I left and started on my own in the early Thirties in Bow, East London.

When the Second World War started I was called up. However, the Ministry of Supply wrote to me and said I would probably be called up but they wanted me to be scheduled for the metal trade. Two days before I got the call up I contacted them and they told me to report to Crawley. They stopped me going into the army because I worked in the metal trade in schedule operations.

In the 1920s and 1930s I had joined the Polytechnic in Regent Street and did exercises in the gymnasium. I used to run round the outer circle of Regents Park three nights a week – getting home at 11 pm and getting up at 7am. I lived at home with my parents until I got married in 1937. I met my wife at a family house in Tottenham. One of my uncles had some friends there and I used to play quite a lot of football. One Sunday my father said we were going to visit Uncle Harry. He had some friends there and one of the girls was Marie - her single name was Cohen. She was seventeen and I was twenty-two. We just passed the time together. She had a lot of friends. Her father had a business in Tottenham.

Marie's father was a difficult man. She had a stepmother because Marie's mother had died in 1916 when she was a baby. Her father went into the army and took the two girls, who were evacuated, to a foster mother in Norfolk. When the war ended Marie's father remarried a lovely woman. Marie's sister was two years older and there was a younger sister from the second marriage.

Marie and I became very friendly. She was at Tottenham High School. Then she worked as secretary to a legal firm in the city. I used to meet her after work and go to the theatre and take her on outings. She was in the Girl Guides in those days and sometimes I used to go down to her camp at weekends. We were married on the 6th June 1937 at the Hackney Synagogue and bought a house in Woodford Avenue, Ilford.

In 1937 war was imminent and I was in the metal trade which was called a reserve occupation. Marie became pregnant but she had complications so we got in touch with a surgeon, Morris Johns, at Queen Charlotte's Hospital. He then transferred her to a hospital run by nuns near St. Albans. She had a caesarean and Richard was born. Our second child, Nicholas, was born at the same place. Then Jeremy was born at Queen Charlotte's.

In 1947 we moved to Oman Avenue off Anson Road, Willesden, and lived there for forty years. The children all went to a local primary school in Moira Road where Leon Brittain was also a pupil. The three boys transferred to Kilburn Grammar. Richard won a scholarship to University College London and became a solicitor, then a recorder and was one of the first solicitors to be nominated to become a judge. He retired two years ago. Nicholas is an accountant. Jeremy became a freelance cameraman. Among Jeremy's films are Charlotte Gray and Sliding Doors. When these films have been shown at the cinema Marie and I have gone along to see Jeremy get all the credits.

I carried on with my metal business throughout the war and right up to the late seventies. Then I just felt like a fish out of water. I looked at adverts in The Times and Telegraph and eventually found a firm called John Brown Construction Company in Praed Street looking for an assistant on accounts, aged between twenty-three and twenty-five. I went for an interview and filled in a form. I was called back ten days later and offered the job of assistant accountant on the project accounts. I was put on one or two month's trial as a paid job. At that time they were developing the first oil rigs in the North Sea and this was part American and part English. There were fifty-two representing America and the same here. There were about eight floors in the building and the English side had one floor.

A chap in his late sixties told me to settle down at my desk to see what they were doing, but he covered up what he was doing. I said to him 'Look, I have been given this job to assist in the Accounts Department' and after a couple of months he was my best friend.

I was sent up to town next door to Westminster Abbey - the Sanctuary – to deliver the secret documents being sent to the American side of the company. I was with the company for about seven and a half years and left when I was nearly seventy-seven.

Marie worked at St Godric's College in Hampstead and saw over twelve thousand students. She is often recognised today. She taught and was also on the administration side and retired in 1984. Pupils came from all over the world. At that time we lived in Littledale Lodge, Finchley.

We were originally members of Neasden Synagogue, Dollis Hill, where our three sons had their barmitzvah. But I did not like the Rabbi. When my father who lived in Ilford died, the Rabbi was very rude to me. Richard and Nicholas used to go to a Reform synagogue in the East End to teach Hebrew and got a certificate. I met Dow Marmur and joined Alyth and went on to the Council for two and a half years. During that time I attended a lot of shivas and funerals. I was treasurer of JACS for eight and a half years and distributed the Alyth Centre magazine for about fifteen years.

The first time we went to Israel was before the Six-Day War and the last time was about four years ago. We have also been to Australia, Canada, Sweden and Las Vegas. I was on the management committee of Hammerson House before it was even built over fifty years ago and never thought I would be here as a resident. I resigned only two weeks ago. For the last two years Marie's forgetting everything. We have been here nearly five months now. The food is very good - you can have what you like.

Sue Hammerson and Marie were girl guides together - we both had three children. When Sue Hammerson's husband died aged forty-two she gave the land of her eight-bedroom house to build a home in his name.

The difficulty now is that I am on the inside looking out and not on the outside looking in. Marie and I have now been married for sixty-five years and we had a letter from the Queen. We have eight grandchildren and three great grandchildren, two of whom are girls.

19   PETER GILBEY

I was born on 11th February 1913. My parents' names were Percy and Anne. My father was born in the East End and my mother was born in Wolton Road, south London. My mother's maiden name was Levy. My father was a publican. He owned the Crooked Billet in London, N1 and the Exeter Arms in London, NW8. I was born in the Crooked Billet, which is no longer there. My parents had the pub for fourteen years. I had an older brother James, three years older than me, who died four years ago.

I went to Hoxton House School and then to Shoreditch Central School. I went to Hoxton & District Hebrew classes four times a week at one of the LCC schools just off Hoxton Street. My parents belonged to Shacklewell Lane Synagogue, where I had my barmitzvah. Other than that we had a little shul in New North Road. Before the war growing up in Hoxton had to be experienced. It was a very rough area - it had a market all the way through. There were a number of Jewish families, most of whom were shopkeepers. And there were a couple of publicans. However people respected you, especially publicans, as they had to be of a certain standard because of the strictness of getting a licence. My parents moved to the Exeter Arms in 1940.

I left school very early because of the war. I went away near Yeovil, Somerset, with two sisters-in-law of my father. It didn't last very long as it didn't work out. When I came back all my school friends had gone. My parents said I should help them out in the pub. Then the bombing started, which was quite horrendous. My father, who was forty-four, wasn't called up as he was a sick man.

I went to synagogue and belonged to a boys club, which was quite unique. Many of the boys who went there reached great heights and we have reunions every year.

I volunteered for the Air Force in 1943. My brother was called up into the Kings Royal Rifle Corps.

Even though I left school early I tried to learn as I went along. The medical examination for the RAF was very strict and they put me on reserve because of my age. The aircrew schools got filled up, so when it came to me they said I could go on the ground staff of the Air Force. I said that I would like to go into the army. I was sent to Northern Ireland where there was quite a problem, even in those days. They wanted to send me back there when I went up for the selection after my initial training, but I was not happy, so they sent me to a gunnery school in Brookwood near Aldershot.

My father became seriously ill. He was quite a young man and my mother wrote to the War Office telling them, so I was sent home for a month, which I wasn't very happy about because it meant leaving my friends and curriculum. This happened two or three times. Eventually I got posted to Exeter and moved around a bit. I enjoyed the army and the discipline did not worry me at all.

Before the war, Mosley and his blackshirts were really bad where we lived. However there were a lot of people who didn't like them and some that did, but when war broke out it dampened down and they put Mosley in prison.

In 1944 I was in the Royal Artillery. I was the observation officer's assistant. I learned a lot there like logarithms, etc, which I had not learned at school. After Brookwood I was posted to Watford and then Exeter. I never actually went abroad, mainly because of the situation at home, of my father being ill, although my brother went abroad.

Soon after the war was over, when I was at Exeter, I was kitted out for the Far East. Then the war ceased very quickly in the Far East so we got our embarkation leave. There was also mention of Palestine. There were a number of Jewish soldiers and they were not allowed to go - Rabbi Brody was senior chaplain to the British forces. I was discharged at the end of 1946 because the travelling from Exeter to Paddington every weekend to see my father took its toll on me. My brother came home in January 1947. My parents had their silver wedding on the Sunday and my father died on the Monday, aged fifty-two.

Hilda and I met during the war at a barmitzvah. Hilda worked in a bank. We were married at St. John's Wood United Synagogue and the reception was at Porchester Hall, Bayswater. We lived in a flat at the top of a house in Allington Road, Hendon Central.

I worked in the pub with my mother for ten years, and during that time we moved to a three-bedroom house in Kenton. Our daughter Pamela was born in 1951, and our son Michael just under two years later. However, again life took its toll on me, travelling backwards and forwards to the pub. We tried to buy an off-licence but they were very expensive. During that time I took up a Trade Association. My area was the second most important in London - Marylebone and Paddington. The first one was Westminster and Chelsea. I worked my way up and when I was twenty-nine I became chairman of the licences division of publicans, which covered an area from Tottenham Court Road to Notting Hill. It meant that I represented all the licensees on certain committees within that area as far as the brewers were concerned. We had an annual dinner where we used to ask certain members of the trade to be President. Gerry Lambert, the secretary of my association, was a retired police superintendent - one of the wisest men I have ever met and I learned so much from him. At the age of twenty-nine I chaired a dinner with Hilda for five hundred and fifty people and the mayor attended. Distillery chairmen and brewery directors were at those dinners and I got to know a lot of people. I never had meat and they always put out fish or an omelette for Hilda and me. I was re-elected chairman for a second year, which was quite something.

The association knew we were looking for a place but couldn't afford it. One day a senior manager from one of the big firms came to see me and said they were discussing closing one of their shops as nobody had ever made a go of it, and he had put my name forward. The shop was in Temple Fortune. I went to have a look at it. The shop didn't have a beer licence – only a wine and spirits licence. Anyway, we said we would take it and managed to get a mortgage. We got a licence but the other off-licences appealed in the Court of Appeal. However we won the appeal and took over the off-licence in 1957 and stayed there for four years. Threshers came along and wanted to buy my shop. After much thought, I gave in and sold it and we moved here, forty years ago this year. The children went to school in Childs Way.

I took a job in a small chain of off-licences owned by Mr Curtis, who was my colleague. In 1977 there was a bad problem and Mr Curtis called me into his office one day after seventeen years. He said he had just sold the business to a north country firm, which made me redundant. Three days before the takeover, the chairman and managing director of the takeover company came to London and asked me to come in with them and I worked for them for four wonderful years of my working life.

Next I got a job with BMW. They put me on three months trial. I worked long hours and wasn't too well as I had been in hospital for surgery. I left BMW and got a job in a stockbroker's office, Schweider Miller, and I was very friendly with a senior partner. However I wasn't very popular there as the staff didn't like the idea of someone coming in from the outside and earning as much as they were earning, so I left of my own accord.

After BMW I went to a property development company. I really learned a lot there. I was working for a very orthodox man and I saw he was overstretching himself so I got out. Then I went to a firm which imported pushchairs, but I didn't stay long.

I then became self-employed and had the job of delivering very up-market cars. Phil Rosen referred people to me and I started a business consultancy, which I gave up two years ago. I had a number of clients and it worked out quite well.

I first became connected with Alyth in 1959 when we had the off-licence in Temple Fortune and had to open on Saturdays. Hilda's parents had always belonged to the United Synagogue and we belonged to Kinloss, where the children went to Hebrew classes. The secretary of Alyth used to come into the shop and buy kosher wine. Although we worked on Saturday, Mr Frohwein used to pass this shop and Mr Coffer, who in those days was the director of Palwin, also used to walk past the shop on Saturdays and raise his hat. I became a warden in 1964 and have been on the council under nine chairmen.

Those four years in Temple Fortune in the shop were some of the happiest of our lives. Pamela won a scholarship to South Hampstead, and Michael went to Christ's College. He is now a senior lecturer and a senior research fellow at The Royal Free Medical School and has a PhD. Pamela went to Goldsmiths and became a teacher and taught at a senior school in Muswell Hill. She eventually became a careers officer. Before this she studied sociology and economics at The London School of Economics.

20   EVA GRAHAM
RESCUED TIME AND TIME AGAIN

I have to dig back deep into my memories to recall many of the events I am about to tell, because I was born in 1938, so I was just a baby, a toddler and a very small child when these things happened to me.

I was born in Czechoslovakia (now called Slovakia). My mother made couturier clothes before she was married, she was a daughter of the Witzman family in Zozboler, where they were major manufacturers of cheese. If you go to the Castle Museum you can now see many of their cheese labels on display. As an infant I remember sitting beneath a cheese-cutting machine on the factory floor, munching the rejected cheeses which had not been properly cut by the equipment!

At first, when the Germans invaded, my father who was an engineer from Zilina (where I was born) was allowed to continue his profession. I clearly remember the yellow star sewn on to my school coat at that time.

When the 1944 Czechoslovakian uprising was put down and many of the Jews in Zilina were herded away, my parents made a sacrifice that was to save my life, but not theirs. They placed me in a convent with a lot of other children. I am probably one of the few Jews around with a certificate to say I was baptised. I'm not sure what the synagogue will make of it, but it's a fact! I don't really know what happened to my mother or my father. I believe my mother was deported and I have heard that she grabbed a child, believing it would save her, but, in fact, it was the opposite. I understand my father survived almost to the end of the war. He was, apparently, a smoker and exchanged his food rations for cigarettes. I believe he starved to death. I have been told this information by others. Whether these stories are true or not, there is no way I can say.

Of the convent, I have very little recollection. I understand there was a large number of children there. I do remember peeling potatoes. One of my worst memories is having measles, because I remember I was in a darkened room (to protect my eyes). The convent looked out over the main square in Zilina and I have terrible, terrible visions of three men hanging from gallows. That memory, and Silent Night sung in German, make my flesh creep.

In 1945, when I was about seven, the war came to an end. I was taken back to my mother's town, Zozbolen, and looked after by a lady – I have no idea who she was. I only remember she lived in a maisonette up some stairs and always wore black. So, really I don't remember what happened to me in that part of my life.

A year later, in 1946, when I was around eight, my Uncle Michael, my mother's only brother who had emigrated to England before the war, arranged for me to be collected by his lodger – I think he was a journalist. My uncle paid an exorbitant price. And so I arrived in Croydon on an aeroplane in 1946 and came to live with my Auntie Ellie and Uncle Michael and their four year old daughter. Three months later my uncle died. Apparently, my cousins in Palestine (as it then was) wanted me flown over to them, but my Auntie Ellie, who was only my aunt by marriage, would not hear of it and that caused a family rupture.

Auntie Ellie was an amazing woman, because although I was not related to her other than by marriage, she was as good to me as any mother could be. Ellie's little girl, then four, was a sickly child. Her doctor also happened to be the doctor from the Jewish children's home, supported by the West London Synagogue, Lindfield House. It was decided that the country air would do us both good. The children, about sixteen all told, ranged in age from four to eighteen. Apart from my cousin and me, they had all gone through concentration camps. I was sent there for the Easter holidays and had the most wonderful time. I stayed there most of my young life. We were sent to the local county school for our education. Considering all that had gone on, it was a very happy time, lots of art, music and fun.

78

Then the decision was taken that to have a group of Jewish children living in the countryside, isolated from the Jewish community in London was not a good idea. So they moved the home to Isleworth, where we were sent to school locally. I finished my education by completing a two-year hotel management course at Acton Technical College and came out with flying colours at the ripe old age of eighteen.

In 1956, I was secretary of a Jewish youth group and, as such, was invited to their international conference in Switzerland. The committee offered to pay for my stay if I could make my own way there. That was fine, except it meant going with two boys I had never met, one called Tony Graham. In those days, it just wasn't on for a girl to travel alone with two boys. I thought my aunt would never let me go, but she responded 'Darling, if you can't look after yourself by now, you never will!' With that I was off to Switzerland! And if you were to speak to Rabbi Lionel Blue he would be very surprised to learn that Tony Graham and I ended up by getting married, because he always said I was really, really horrible to Tony on top of a mountain in Switzerland. Anyhow, forty-three years later, Tony and I are still together. Within six months we were engaged and I was nineteen when we married.

I worked for less than a year, as the hours in the hotel industry were unsociable. My first job was with the Hotel Rubens. I started in June and was due to work on Rosh Hashanah, so arranged to switch my shifts with another girl. I explained the position to the hotel manager, Joe Conrad 'I don't care if you are a bloody Jew,' he said, 'that's the day you are meant to work and that's the day you will work!' I looked at him and said, 'I'm Jewish and proud of it and you can stick your job!' and left.

I soon decided to concentrate on voluntary work. I used to do the books for the Reform Synagogues of Great Britain and I think I was there for about seventeen years.　　I also worked with Marion Steinberger, who was the forerunner of social services at Alyth Synagogue.

When the school opened at the Manor House, I left RSGB and for about ten years helped as a welfare assistant doing all sorts of things, artwork, lunch-time duties, whatever was needed.

I have three children, now in their thirties and forties. We are a very unusual family in that my husband is an accountant and all the family are involved in the business. My daughter even used to bring her children to work until they were old enough to go to school. So Tony had the best of both worlds, with the children and the grandchildren there! As a family we work together and play together.

Despite the disruptions in my childhood, I think basically (and hopefully my friends and family will agree) I'm a fairly normal person. I don't think of the Holocaust as something that happened to me, because at the end of the day, if you wear your heart on your sleeve and tell everybody what a raw deal you had in life, nobody really wants to know. The Holocaust happened to me and all the Jews in Europe. I can't speak for people who were sent to concentration camps, because, luckily, that was not my fate.

I don't remember my parents as people – I can't put a face to them. I was twenty-two before I actually found some photographs of them. My theory is that if you can't personally remember someone, you can't really mourn for them, because you can't recall – 'This is what my mother looked like, what my father looked like', or 'This is what I did with my parents before the war'. I simply don't remember.

The worst thing about being an orphan is that you can't ask anybody, 'What kind of people were my mother and father? Were they nice, were they horrible? Were they fat, were they thin? Were they this, were they that?' You do not know. And that is something that has taken me a very long time to come to terms with. I had this terrible hope that one day I would meet someone from my parents' town and they would say 'Oh, I know your parents!' But it never happened. Time is marching on, and now I don't think it will happen. I have a wonderful family. I have a lot more than many others. And for that, I am extremely grateful.

TONY GRAHAM
21   BOYHOOD MEMORIES OF THE SUBURB
AND COUNTRYSIDE

I was born in Middleway in Hampstead Garden Suburb in 1934. At that time some parts, like Winnington Road, had not yet been built, so the Suburb in those days was very peaceful. The main road through Market Place was not the major A1 that it is today. It was then just a very minor road that did not lead anywhere. There were no cars around; no cars parked in the street at all. Now when I walk you can hardly see the street for parked cars. In streets where there were no garages and no cars, the little cottages had no bathrooms. When it was bath time the tin tub came off the shelf! Today lots of those same houses have BMW's and Range Rovers!

In those days we had road sweepers who came every day and kept the place immaculate. Now I don't think I see a road sweeper in six or seven weeks. I go out and pick up the litter myself. I don't object to that, but I can't clean the whole suburb, unfortunately.

However, not all my life has been spent in the Suburb. During the war, I was evacuated to the countryside, and in the school holidays I found myself a very lucrative job working in a dairy for five hours a day, seven days a week. Mr. Godwin paid me ten shillings and sixpence (55p) and occasionally treated me to a fish and chip lunch – a delicacy in those days. Fifty-five pence was a lot of money in those days. In fact I enjoyed it so much I skipped school and continued in the dairy during most of the autumn. I would get there very early in the morning and the first thing I did was to wash the bottles that had been collected the previous day. The milk arrived in great big churns and I had to ladle it out into the bottles. Fortunately they had quite wide necks and when you put the fresh milk inside nobody could actually see how much residue was left behind from bottles not being properly cleaned. As each churn was three feet high, scooping milk from the bottom could be quite hazardous for a lad like myself. The next step was to put the cardboard tops on the bottles.

Mr. Godwin would then arrive to get the horse out of the field next door to the dairy. The horse was really quite a reluctant worker and had to be persuaded with a bunch of juicy carrots. Even when he was harnessed to the two-wheeled trap he was extremely sprightly. We had to hang on grimly in case he reared up on his hind legs. That was the way I spent the whole morning, seven days a week, delivering milk. I probably went six months that year without any education whatsoever, but what I was being educated in was selling, giving change and keeping the customers happy.

Later we were evacuated to a remote village in Cornwall where I was sent to the village school – just two classrooms. I caught up on my missed schooling quite easily. I eventually won a scholarship to Haberdashers and took my O levels at fourteen and five subjects at A level at sixteen.

In those days you could not go to university at seventeen. So in 1951 I became articled to an accountant for five years. You had to pay a premium of £250 to the firm to get articled and my salary was two pounds and five shillings a week (£2.25p).

The office was the dingiest of places, very bleak and dark. I was given a very old hand-written book and was told to start adding up figures – this was well before the days of electronic calculators. If you can spend the whole day adding up figures and survive you will probably make a good accountant! Once qualified I went into my uncle's electrical business and at a very early stage in my career was involved in the management and financial control of the company.

As far as Alyth is concerned, my association goes back quite a long way. At one stage I was a cub there. As soon as I reached the age of sixteen I joined the youth group and met my wife-to be, Eva, so Alyth has been quite a major influence! Of course then the youth groups were major activities. I think it has tended to fade in recent years, but in those days they really had very ambitious programmes that kept us very occupied socially.

Eva and I were married in 1957. We came to live in the Suburb in 1959 and I still live there now next door to my parents' house where I was born.

22   MARIANNE GRAYEFF

I was born in 1910, before the First World war tore Europe apart; my childhood a normal and happy one. I grew up in a medical family. My father, Dr Louis Zander, was a respected and well-liked general practitioner in the locality where we lived in Berlin. Then early in 1933 the Nazi 'earthquake' shattered our lives.

The first member of our little family to be affected was my older brother Rudolph. He too had qualified as a doctor, at the University of Berlin, and had taken up his first job at a hospital in Neukoln, a suburb of our city. Like father he did well in his chosen profession, until one day he was informed by the management that although they were very pleased with his work he would nevertheless have to leave as the Nazis would not allow them to employ Jews any longer. Forced to resign, he managed instead to make his way to America. My father, after forty years service to the community, had retired by then, whilst my mother was in a Home run by the Berlin Jewish Community, too sick to be cared for any longer in her own surroundings.

A further serious blow came when the Nazis told father that as a Jew he could not be a doctor and that since he was not a doctor he was not entitled to any pension. Perverted logic if ever there was. Fortunately he had managed to save some money and was able to exist on that.

It was always my ambition to become a teacher and in 1928 I was accepted in the Geography Department of our university. I was lucky that this department was perhaps less prejudiced in outlook than some of the other departments of the university, many of which closed their doors to Jews well before mine. I completed my university studies in 1934 by successfully passing before a Public Examination Board, the result of which also qualified me to be a teacher. Quite soon after, admission to universities was closed to all Jews, and I was thus one of the last Jewish students to be allowed to sit an examination.

In such political circumstances my chances of ever getting a position as a teacher within the German state system were absolutely nil. Certainly no school would even consider me by 1934, so just whom could I teach?

Paradoxically, my opportunity arose almost precisely because of this ban. It stemmed from the fact that with so many Jewish children having been thrown out of the state schools, they were now all entirely dependent on Jewish schools for their education. Many of these were now either being enlarged to cope with the extra pupils or even brand new ones set up. Therefore I had no difficulty getting a post.

My first job as a teacher was in a Jewish school for boarders in Caputh, near Potsdam. I stayed only a short while until April 1934, before moving on to another school situated in the western part of Berlin. This had been newly set up by permission of the Nazis and had about a hundred pupils, ranging in age from six to fifteen years, together with five or six teaching staff. I kept the same class throughout and taught every subject as the pupils progressed through the system.

Outside of their homes it was these schools that provided the little security that Jewish children enjoyed in those days. Only in these surroundings were they able to feel relatively safe, knowing that the teachers were their friends. Otherwise danger was everywhere. I soon became aware of just how disturbed some of these children became after the trauma of seeing their fathers being arrested and the impact this had on their mothers. Even in the parks notices began to appear bearing the words 'Jews are not admitted.'

So far as I was personally concerned, this vilification of Jews by the Nazis had the effect of making me value my Judaism more profoundly than ever before and instilled a desire to give it more positive expression, though this was obviously difficult under the circumstances. My father could see clearly enough what was happening in Germany and at various times begged me to leave, saying that this was his dearest wish. At last I agreed, fortunate to have the help of my mother's brother, a timber merchant from Silesia. He knew some people in England and through them managed to find me a family in Surrey who offered me a position as a domestic servant, the only work permitted to me, this being one of the conditions of entry to the country.

I arrived in England in February 1939 and settled down to household chores and helping look after the children in the house. When inevitably war broke out some seven months later I was ordered to attend a tribunal to be interviewed as an enemy alien. I had little, if any, English as yet and would have found it difficult to answer all the many questions on my own. However, my employer was a good man. He came with me and with his help was able to get me classified as a friendly alien, due account having been taken of my previous record of persecution in Germany.

I was now safe in England with no desire ever to meet a Nazi again. I had a terrible fear of falling into their hands and that was something that would haunt me for a long while yet. Surprisingly, perhaps, I would soon swap this ideal of safety for the terrors of U-Boat infested seas. While still in Germany I had become very friendly with a boy called Felix. His sister had already left Germany for Australia in 1937. As soon as he too received his coveted permit for that country, her brother followed in March the following year. However, away from the horrors of Hitler's Germany, life was still not easy for him, and every application he submitted for a post in a school or university was turned down. At last he was offered not one post but two; the first a temporary one for a single term at a good public school in Adelaide, the other in New Zealand, as lecturer in German for the Autumn term at the University of Otago in Dunedin. He accepted both, leaving Australia for New Zealand in February 1939, when his short contract in Adelaide expired. In Dunedin the post was made permanent at the end of the year. He stayed on for thirteen more years, a classical scholar and philosopher, teaching German language and literature and at the same time building up the German sub-department of the university into a full department in its own right.

It was while still in Australia that Felix wrote offering to apply for a permit for me to come over as well. I accepted, but by the time the permit reached Berlin I was already in England. My father sent it on to me, but soon after I received it war broke out and the permit was cancelled. Once more it seemed I was an enemy alien. However, having waited no less than two years for this piece of paper I was determined to have it renewed.

I went to Australia House to plead my cause. I was interviewed by a man who asked me endless questions in endless detail (though I believe he forgot to ask what boot laces I wore). After about an hour of this interrogation, he did at least say he would recommend that my permit be renewed, which was a relief. But he was then unable to say just how long this would take. This was not such a comfort, especially when he added that it could take months, years or perhaps not at all. By this time I hardly knew what to say and it was only at the door, on my way out, that I plucked up the courage to ask whether he would perhaps put in a good word for me. This he promised to do. You can imagine my utter surprise and sheer delight when the renewed permit arrived by return of post. Perhaps he had been testing me in some way when he spoke about the length of time it might have taken.

In anticipation of soon leaving England, I left my family in Beaconsfield and came to London to live with a friend. Here I was offered passage on a ship for Australia, (an offer that was later cancelled when this particular vessel was requisitioned to carry troops to Norway). Later I was offered passage on another ship, the SS Orontes, sailing to Sydney in May 1940. These were dangerous times. Nevertheless, I set sail in her from Southampton for my new home many thousands of miles away, the captain taking a very lengthy and circuitous route via the Cape, dodging possible U-boats by means of constant changes of course.

Despite the odd alarm we reached Cape Town safely, and British Passport holders were allowed off to enjoy some brief time ashore. However, being of German nationality, I was given no such privilege and had to remain on board. I did not really care. It was only the Nazis and their attitudes that I feared. Leaving South Africa we sailed on to Ceylon (now Sri Lanka), arriving at last off the coast of Western Australia. My heart sank when I saw what it was like. This was not the countryside I had expected. All I saw was a dried up land, without trees or bushes, everything yellow or burnt, a part of the Western Australian Desert. It was really depressing and not until we reached Perth did I begin to feel any better. It was such a lovely city.

Next we came to Adelaide, then to Melbourne, where again many went ashore. Even I was allowed off this time, rules being far laxer here than elsewhere, at least at the time. Finally we arrived in Sidney, where I found a letter waiting for me from a woman who was later to become my sister-in-law. Enclosed was my permit to stay in Australia and, despite first impressions, it was not long before I learned to love the dried up, yellow and burnt Bush.

It was an amazing experience being there in June 1940. At first the war seemed totally unreal to me. A barbed wire had been strung across Bondi Beach 'to keep the Japanese out should they have had the crazy idea of coming ashore here', though its main use seemed to be to hang up the towels to dry after we had gone swimming. I felt I had never known so much peace in all my life, the war in Europe soon all but forgotten, except of course by those families who had members serving overseas. Life seemed otherwise to be completely unreal. But then came Pearl Harbour and everything changed once more.

My first job in Australia after I arrived was again as a domestic. However, later I obtained a teaching position in the Sydney Church of England Girls Grammar School. The Headmistress was a true friend and I stayed with her for two years. In the meantime, Felix and I had kept up a correspondence in which, after a while, he asked if I would marry him. I agreed, moved to New Zealand and we were married in Dunedin early in 1943. Both our children were born there, Leonie on the last day but one of that year and Michael in March 1947.

According to reports I received later, both my parents died in Germany in about 1942. Mother died in her nursing home when she and all the other patients and staff committed suicide by poisoning after being informed by the Nazis that they should all be prepared to 'travel' the next day. By that time everyone knew this could only mean deportation and death, so it was better not to spin out the agony. When the Nazis came next day, all they found were dead bodies.

My father died after taking a walk in his small garden. He collapsed on the stairs on his way back and died the next day without ever regaining consciousness. Almost certainly he too had committed suicide. He was a doctor after all and knew just what he needed to do. For many years I seldom spoke about the horrors of the past, preferring for my children's sake to live in the present rather than the past. Only now do I feel that I can be more open about what happened and that there is no danger of traumatising my children, as I have seen other parents do to theirs under similar circumstances.

In October 1952 we returned to England as my husband felt that he could not do much more at Dunedin for various reasons. We settled in London and in 1977 joined Alyth. Felix was my life's companion for many years. Sadly he passed away in 1981 but I have my two children, eight dear grandchildren and one happy little great grandson, all of them a great comfort to me. Thinking back, my life has been a mixture of never to be forgotten sadness and joy. I am thankful for the joy.

23   WENDY GREENGROSS

I was born in St. Mary's Road, Brent, in April 1925, quite near the tube station now known as Brent Cross. My mother's name was Miriam, née Abrahamson. She was one of five children, four girls and a boy. There was also another sister but she died in infancy. Her immediate family had been in England since the middle of the 19th century and were well settled in the East End of London. Other members of the family had gone to live in Canada and Israel.

Morris Greengross was my father's name. Unlike the Abrahamson family, he and his parents came to this country much later. They left Pinchovew, Poland, in the early 1900s and went to Winnipeg, Canada. However, they stayed for only two or three years, as they were defeated by the harshness of the climate.

Moving back eastwards, they came to England in about 1906 when Morris, their only child, was thirteen years old and settled in London. Shortly after their arrival the little family was reduced still further in size when my paternal grandfather announced one day that he would go to America to see what it was like and would send for the family to join him. That was the last we saw or heard from him.

My father went to the Jewish Free School and then left to be apprenticed to a manufacturing jeweller. He received his first tools as a gift from the Jewish Board of Guardians, later the Jewish Welfare Board (before changing its name once more to Jewish Care). He was always grateful for this help. After the Second World War he was invited to become a local councillor for Holborn and spent the next fifteen years deeply involved as Councillor, Alderman and Mayor. During the Thirties and until his death in 1970, he was first Chairman and then President of the Trades Advisory Council. This was a body that had been established to settle disputes between Jewish businessmen, with the aim of preventing such disputes appearing in court and thereby possibly fuelling anti-Semitism.

My mother, Miriam, was educated at the Central Foundation School. When she left she became a secretary at the Fleet Street Office of the Glasgow Herald, where she worked until she met my father and married him in 1924 at the Great Synagogue in the East End. I was born a year later and my only brother Alan four years after that. Alan was educated at University College School (UCS) and went to Trinity College, Cambridge, after doing his National Service in the RAF after the war. He has devoted a great deal of time and energy to local government in Holborn, Camden and on the Greater London Council and has been deeply involved in town planning. He was awarded a Knighthood after the dissolution of the GLC.

My own education began at the West Hampstead Day School, the first Jewish Day School in the country. We received a solid, orthodox Jewish education but were also profoundly influenced to accept Zionist aspirations. Joe Gilbert, one of the founders of Habonim, was Governor of the school and as a result the school had one of the first Gedudim in this country. We were officially too young to be full members, but the experience was extremely positive, and Habonim, - the friends I made there, together with its ideals - was an extremely important part of my teenage years. In 1936 I started at South Hampstead High School and remained there until 1943. During the war years I was evacuated with the school to Berkhampstead in Hertfordshire.

My family spent nearly all the war years in London, although when the air raids became very bad they went to stay in Bournemouth and later went to North Wales. By now my father's business was concerned with making diamond tools for the war effort. At nights and weekends however he was an air raid warden, helping to rescue people trapped in damaged buildings and ensuring that those who were taking cover in the shelters were as safe and comfortable as possible.

During school holidays I would return to London except when the raids made this too dangerous. Oddly enough, we seemed to take these most unusual circumstances in our stride. Food though was in very short supply, but even then, whilst there was not much meat, fish, butter or eggs and only very limited amounts of sugar, fresh fruit or tinned food, most people did not go hungry. There were still lots of root vegetables available, bread most of the time and fruit in season if you were lucky enough to know someone who had a fruit tree!

I seemed to live in a world where extraordinary things were taken for granted. With hindsight I know that many spent the war years sick with worry about brothers, sons, fathers, lovers. I had no very close relatives in the armed forces myself, though I did have cousins in the Royal Air force. I clearly remember travelling home on the underground at night or even early evening and seeing families camped on the platform, preparing an evening meal or getting ready for bed. I remember too the long nights in an air raid shelter, hearing the anti-aircraft guns and the noise of enemy planes overhead.

I had decided early in life that I wanted to be a doctor and was lucky to have had no family opposition. Perhaps this was partly because we already had a dozen or more doctors in our scattered family, including a remarkable woman who was in practice in Canada. However, in England it was very difficult for women to become doctors at that time as there was a strict quota system. In those days in London only three medical schools out of a total of twelve accepted any women. University College Hospital and Kings College Hospital took twelve women each (16%), and The Royal Free. It was not until the end of the 1940s that all hospitals, including The Royal Free, had to take their 16% share of female doctors. I was lucky enough to be offered a place at UCH and spent five very happy years there.

In January 1949 I qualified as a doctor. After doing a range of house jobs I was then offered the opportunity to do some research at the Chicago Lying-in Hospital. At the same time I was awarded a Fulbright Scholarship to enable me to take this up. While waiting to travel to the USA, I decided to fill my time doing locums until the date of my sailing. In 1950 one of these temporary jobs was a two-week stint at Southend Hospital. It was there that I met my husband-to-be, Alexander Kates, also working as a locum and who, as I discovered, actually lived less than a mile away from me in London. He had served in East Africa as a surgeon throughout the last three years of the war. At the time we met he was about to take his finals for the FRCS examination in order to qualify as a practising surgeon. Having met, we became engaged within a week, and not for a moment have I ever regretted my rather precipitate decision. He was a wonderful man, a tower of strength, who supported me wholeheartedly in all that I did. We were married at the Golders Green Synagogue, Dunstan Road, in 1951.

We took over a large general practice in Tottenham. In our new practice I did the morning surgery and also all the calls that came in during the day. At the same time my husband worked as a surgical registrar during the day, then came home at night and did an evening surgery and any late calls that came in, as well as all the night calls, which usually varied between ten and twenty calls a month. We had one free half day a week, on Thursdays when there was no evening surgery, though we were still on call twenty-four hours a day, seven days a week. There was no deputising service then and whenever we went out we would have to leave a telephone number where we could be reached. Any cinema or theatre we visited had to know just where we were sitting, and it was not unusual for a doctor's name to be flashed across the screen during a film. It was accepted as part of the doctor's lot.

As time went on I realised that there were areas in which I needed further training and so attended a family planning course. I asked the doctor responsible for training how best I could cope with the numerous patients who were coming to see me with physical symptoms such as sore throat, indigestion or headaches, but were actually suffering from anxiety, worry or depression. The concept of psychosomatic illness had not been accepted, other than as a way of dismissing symptoms that nobody thought worth treating. Indeed, the very idea of a patient needing a medical symptom in order to get psychological help was unrecognised. My request for help resulted in my being offered training to become a Marriage Guidance counsellor. I was offered a place on the London Spread Course, which involved attending training every Thursday evening for six months. As this was the only time I could spend with my husband, I accepted on condition that he attended as well. We did the training together, but by this time

I was pregnant for the third time and therefore declined any further commitments. However, my husband did start counselling and continued to do so for the next three or four years. I believe as a result of this training he became a much better orthopaedic surgeon. He learnt to listen to what his patients said, answered all their questions and took their anxieties and worries seriously - a most unusual quality for a surgeon at that time. His patients adored him.

We had only been working together for a few years when my husband decided that the future of General Practice lay not in small single-handed practices, which were then the norm, but in larger Group Practices. To this end we spent a great deal of time in the 1950s locating a suitable plot of land for this purpose and getting the requisite permission, until eventually we were able to construct the first purpose-built Group Practice in London and only the second in the whole of England.

In the meantime my family was growing. In just seven years we were fortunate enough to have five children, three boys and two girls, all of whom obviously became a very central part of our lives. At the same time I was still very much concerned with my work, with emphasis on the educational side. I worked for Marriage Guidance and also visited schools, youth clubs, colleges and schools of nursing, talking to young parents, teachers, nurses and youth club workers about sex education and the need for young people to have some understanding of personal relationships and a responsible attitude to birth control.

One day Marriage Guidance (later Relate) contacted me about one of their publications. They wanted to republish 'Sex in Marriage', a pamphlet that had been successfully received a few months previously, and the editor now asked me to also write a new booklet entitled 'Sex in the Middle Years'. It was a runaway success, aided by a huge amount of publicity in the Sunday press but it left me with a somewhat spurious notoriety. It was apparently the first time it had been suggested publicly that anyone, particularly a woman, might be able to enjoy sex after the age of forty. Following the appearance of my booklet, I was then invited as the gynaecological consultant to become part of 'In Practice', a radio medical programme. I was also appointed programme consultant for the BBC's Programmes For Schools on relationships and sex education. At the beginning of the 1970s I became a regular member of the innovative Radio 4 counselling programme 'If You Think You've Got Problems' devised by Thena Heshel. It ran for nearly eight years.

The 1970s were an extremely interesting and productive decade for me. I was acting as Programme advisor to the TV soap opera 'Crossroads', working very closely with the scriptwriter and director. I was also the first Agony Aunt for the recently re-launched Sun Newspaper, writing a weekly column 'Heart to Heart with Doctor Wendy', which entailed having my picture plastered over the backs of buses. All these things gave me an extremely high public profile, but fortunately my family seemed to take it all in good part.

During the 1950s and 1960s I had also been working with AJY (Association of Jewish Youth), chairing the Development and Training Committee As a result of this, at the end of the 1960s I was invited to teach the Rabbinic Students at Leo Baeck College. The work I did with them gradually extended to include marriage and relationships in general for the first and second year students. At the same time, Irene Bloomfield was working with fourth and fifth year students helping them develop skills in their pastoral duties. With the enormous and enthusiastic support of the faculty, she and I developed a Pastoral Care and Counselling programme for Rabbinic students that became an integral part of their studies. It was a role we continued for more than twenty years, Leo Baeck College probably being the first seminary in the world to establish such a course.

At much the same time in the Seventies the Rabbinic Assembly began to feel that there was a need for a Progressive Jewish Counselling service. After many years of deliberation we established the Raphael Counselling Centre with a wide brief that included helping survivors of the Holocaust who, during the Seventies, were just beginning to feel able to talk about their experiences. The group of Rabbis working with Irene and myself also set up a working party to look at the halachich, emotional and psychological situation of Jews who did not seem to fit into the sexual categories to which they had been assigned. In 1985 the RSGB published and supported a booklet I had written entitled 'Jewish and Homosexual'. This was the first public, positive statement on the subject made by any Jewish group and one of the very first in the world made by any religious organisation. By this time too I was writing extensively, in books, booklets and articles in newspapers and magazines, on marriage, parenting, sex, and a wide range of other problems, as well as doing a great deal of broadcasting.

The issues raised were equally important for people with disabilities and in 1972 I was invited to become a founder member and later Chair of SPOD, which stood for Sex Problems of the Disabled. Over the years the name changed to become politically more correct, though the acronym stayed unchanged. I also wrote a book about the sexual and emotional problems of disabled people that was called 'Entitled to Love'. As a result I was invited to become a Trustee of the Leonard Cheshire Foundation, which had been started in the late 1940s. I stayed with the Foundation for nearly twenty-five years and came to know Leonard Cheshire when he was still alive. He was an outstanding man, deeply religious and extraordinarily charismatic. During the 1970s the Leonard Cheshire Foundation was run centrally by just a small professional staff, aided by twenty-five extremely hard working Trustees. As the organisation grew, however, there came the need for increasing expertise. So over a period of some twenty years, the Cheshire Foundation became ever more professional, in time coming to employ more than 7,000 staff, looking after 2,000 people in residential care as well as another 20,000 in their own homes. Rigorous standards of care were demanded by both local and central government. These standards were in the forefront of all the changes that gradually came about in the care of people with physical disabilities, as well as those with learning difficulties. In the 1970s many of these were still infantilised, having always had even minor decisions taken from them. By the turn of the new 21st century however they were already being treated as autonomous adults, making life choices that most other people take for granted.

During this time too, a group of people working in disability organisations set up the 'Residential Care Consortium' with the aim of raising standards of care in residential homes, as well as 'Carematch', a computer based matching service for people with severe disabilities, to help them find appropriate care. I chaired both of these.

My husband and I became members of Alyth in 1979 and over the years I also did an increasing amount of work with the RSGB, chiefly because of my connection with the College. I became a member of the Board of 'Manna', a founding member of Community Outreach and also initiated Care in the Community. All of these were with the enthusiastic support of Rabbi Tony Bayfield, and based on his ideas.

In April 1982 my husband died unexpectedly after a relatively short illness. I found his death very difficult to cope with, although I continued to do a certain amount of work. I think many were surprised that I should find it so difficult to come to terms with my loss. I believe they thought that my ability to be able to give some help to others would also ensure that I would sail through my bereavement with little problem. In fact it took me more than two years to begin to get a new focus, and I only began to recover after going through a life-threatening illness that took nearly six months out of my life. During this time I was a member of Dow Marmur's working party on The Future of the Family. I also gave the keynote address at the RSGB National Conference.

In 1982 I was invited to be a member of the Government Commission examining Human Fertilisation and Embryology, generally known as the Warnock Committee. This took me into a whole new field of medical ethics with which I had been marginally involved for many years. As a result I was asked to become a member and later Chair of the Ethics Committee of one of London's largest private hospitals.

My brother's wife, Sally Greengross, Director General of Age Concern (now Baroness Greengross of Notting Hill), had often spoken about our writing a book together for older people. The result, 'Living, Loving and Ageing' was published in 1991. I had never written a book with a co-author before and we had very different approaches and styles, but we sorted out our difficulties and built on our already close relationship, in this way encouraging more open discussion about older people and their relationships.

I left the Leonard Cheshire Foundation in 2000 and have, during the last four or five years formed an increasingly close association with Alyth, its members and staff. I am grateful for the sense of community and friendship that is on offer. I am also eternally grateful to my husband who supported and encouraged me in everything I did and to my children who are endlessly supporting and loving.

24   ROMAN HALTER

I was born on 7th July 1927 in Tamoleh Chodecz in north-west
Poland. My parents names were Moshe and Sala Halter. My family
was very orthodox. My father's father was the Gerer Rabbi. My mother
was my father's second wife and my sister was six years older than me.
I was the seventh youngest in the family. The family Halter split each
name - originally it was Federhalter. Those who became lawyers in
Poland could not qualify - you worked for a solicitor and did all the
brainwork.

In 1902 my father came from the Russian Army. Things were
bad for the Jews during training. Some of the Russians used to cut off
the fingers of the Jews. My father was physically fit and mentally quite
alert. When certain parts of the forest were cut down, he used to
supervise and live in the forest. He had a horse and a tractor, and his
mother sent him very good provisions. When he was called up for the
army he could ride very well and he was a supply officer. He made
money with his brother and made his way to England as he had two
more brothers living here. He stayed here for three months and then
returned. His half brother from Liverpool went to Canada. (When we
got married we went to Winnipeg and found a home. We also found a
whole clan of Halters living there.)

Where we lived was next to Germany, which was very
unfortunate as the murders started here. It was compulsory that
everybody including Germans, Poles and Jews went to the same
school. I had my Hebrew education at seven in the morning at the
cheder before I went to school. The rabbi was the judge, the teacher,
the adjudicator for the entire community and also the chairman of the
council.

Next door to us was a timber merchant who provided a good
living for my father and grandfather, as this was far more profitable
than being a scribe. On the other side of us lived a family called
Eshner. They were German Poles and I used to go to school with Carl

Eshner who was two years older than me. However in 1939, as soon as the Germans came in, all the Germans in our town became enthusiastic supporters of Hitler. Within weeks the schools became conscripted with the SS. Some weeks later they used Jewish boys and girls as live targets for shooting. Carl, who was my friend and not yet fifteen, was also taught to kill. The community was suddenly divided - those who became killers and those who did not.

I did not have a barmitzvah as in 1940 things were very bad. There were 800 Jews in our town, and by 1940 when we were sent to the ghetto there were 360. In 1940 we were sent to Lodz Ghetto. It was very overcrowded and they only took in 120 of the 360 - the rest were sent away or shot. By 1942 I had lost everybody in the ghetto. Most of my family had died. I had buried my parents in Lodz ghetto.

I was working in the metal factory. In 1944 I was selected with 500 others for slave labour to Germany. When we left the ghetto we all knew this was the end of our journey. 2,800 of us arrived on the train at Auschwitz in thirty-five cattle trucks – the conditions were terrible, there was a shortage of water, etc. When we arrived many were dead, and those of us who were still alive went through selection. 500 of us who were metal workers were taken off and we stood by the railway. 2,300 were gassed and cremated. Things went from bad to worse. I prayed a lot in Auschwitz. In Lodz Ghetto I had found a prayer book that had been translated into Polish and this meant a lot to me. I used to recall every member of my family before my eyes to be with them.

We were then sent to Belsen in Germany, another concentration camp where the metal factory was supposed to have been. The people who were in slave outfits had quite a lot of hatred for us. When we marched to the factory in Belsen, I had never seen such a beautiful town in my life - it looked like the village in Fiddler on the Roof with beautiful mushroom-shaped houses. I kept telling myself I would survive. And I made myself a promise that if I did survive, I would become an architect.

On the 13th February 1945 the factory was hit by a bomb and they made us clean it all up afterwards. We could not work as it was quite damaged. We were taken on a death march. I heard two fellows planning an escape so I approached them. One was called Shweitzer. I was seventeen then and he was thirty. There was also Steier, another fellow aged thirty-one. I asked them to take me with them and they agreed. We escaped on the third night. From two in the morning we were supposed to make our way to Dresden. We managed to get to something like seven kilometres from Dresden. I knocked on the door of a house. A very nice German lady answered and I asked her to shelter us. She called her husband, they consulted one another and agreed. My colleagues could not believe this and thought they were lying. The couple, Mr and Mrs Foux, hid us for two months and we found a farmer to look after Shweitzer. I worked in the back garden in the greenhouse.

I next made my way to Prague as I felt it was too dangerous to return to Poland. I went to the Red Cross and told them I had an aunt living in Lausanne, Switzerland. I remembered the address that my father had told me. This woman's husband was a doctor and I had a bath there and they gave me clothes, and I slept under sheets. They asked what I was going to do now, as there was a place called Rejinstast where some of the Jewish people had ended up, including the people who had marched from Dresden. The doctor and his wife gave me various things to sell on the black market. I went to the station and travelled on the top of the train. When I arrived at Dresden I travelled another seven kilometers.

The first thing I wanted to do was to see the people who had hidden me and thank them. Apparently the SS had found out that Mr and Mrs Foux had hidden three Jews and had shot Mr Foux and shot Shweitzer. Steier managed to talk his way out and I found him forty years later in Israel. Mrs Foux is still alive and will be ninety-five in May. I write to her from time to time. I saw her last year when I had to do the coat of arms for the new Embassy in Berlin. I asked her why she sheltered us and she said she just felt she had to - a message from G-d.

When I was in Prague I met a few people from the Transport. There was a doctor there who sorted out the younger people. In 1945 they were brought to England and I came with them. They took us to Lake Windermere. I asked the doctor how I could put some meat on my bones and he said to eat whatever they give you. With the pocket money they gave me I smoked, and swam twice a day in the Lake.

When I came to London things were difficult, but eventually I managed to become apprentice to a firm of structural mechanical development engineers in Slough (they were an offshoot of an aircraft company). I found digs in Windsor and was apprenticed for three years. Most of the people who worked there were ex-servicemen. In fact one of the men was in Dresden on 13th February 1945 - he was a wing commander. I asked him and one of his colleagues if they could teach me English, so after work each day they would take it in turns to teach me. When I finished my apprenticeship I qualified to study architecture. I worked during the day and went to evening classes at night. Eventually I won a scholarship to the Professional School of Architects in Bedford Square, London.

At that time I was living in Belsize Park. After all that had happened in the past I did not feel that I wanted to change my religion. I had a loving family who were Jews and went back a long way.

My wife and I met at swimming training. We went to the Maccabiah together. I carried her gold medals and she advised me what to buy for my girlfriends and eventually we married. I studied architecture full-time. It was difficult as we had two children by then and my grant was very small. When I qualified I also taught architecture.

In 1974 I wanted to summarise my war experiences. I had an office in London and an office in Cambridge. In fact, the office in Cambridge is still there, as well as an office in Brighton employing about thirty-four people. I called my associates and told them that I was leaving. I then went to the Central School of Art & Design to study window design.

I joined the West London synagogue and was very friendly with Hugo Gryn because of our past experiences. I then joined Alyth.

***

I think my family had lived in Poland for four to five hundred years.
Why I think these terrible things happened to the Jews was because the
church taught that the Jews killed Christ. In our little town Jewish
people had wooden shutters, otherwise their windows would be
smashed. The Jewish people with the help of the rabbi made sure that
the priest moderated his speech and he was sent a present for
Christmas, as was the chief of police - this was the way of life. Poland
did not have a middle-class but Jews were the equivalent of their
middle-class people.

25   SUSAN HALTER

I was born in Budapest, Hungary, on 19th September 1927 in the Jewish quarter near to the Varosliegeg. My parents' names were Bertha Fisher and Otto Nador. My father, who was an ironmonger, was born in Vienna and went to Budapest with his parents. My mother's family came from the Austrian border - a place called Gunz. My parents were members of a synagogue which was between orthodox and reform. I have one sister Judy who lives in London and was born in 1923.

I went to elementary school in Budapest which was 75% Jewish. My secondary school was run by a nun. I studied Latin, German, English, physics, chemistry, etc. In our school we were divided into Catholics, Protestants and Jews and we had a separate class for Jewish education with a very good teacher.

I started swimming when I was fourteen. I was also interested in Hebrew studies at that time and was taking a special Hebrew class. I said that if I won a prize I would be able to pay my coach. I won many medals for swimming. I won my first medal in Hungary and then won another in 1992 in England for master swimming. I swam for Hungary in the 1948 Olympics doing backstroke and front crawl. I matriculated in Hungary and then went to University in Hungary. I then stayed with an uncle and aunt in London and carried on swimming with Mermaid Swimming Club. I then went to the Maccabiah.

Growing up as a teenager in Budapest we heard about Hitler and what was happening in Germany. Back in Hungary we all had to go to the work camp - there were big notices up on the walls. My sister and my best friend went there and it was pretty ghastly. After this they started walking us towards Vienna. They said if anyone tried to escape they would shoot us or hand us over to the Germans. Despite this I made up my mind that I was going to escape. So I paid somebody to look after my luggage. We were walking six in a row and I slipped out and made my way back to Budapest. I stayed with friends, applied for a working permit and swotted up about another town. My parents at this time were in the ghetto. My sister came back to Hungary much earlier with the help of a soldier to whom we gave money.

The Russians came to Budapest and there was a lot of shooting. After this the Hungarian government was set up and I went back to school and matriculated. I came to England in 1948. I belonged to two swimming clubs - the Bar Kochba Jewish swimming club and the Mermaid, which was more serious. I met Roman at the Maccabiah in the Bar Kochba swimming club. When I was in Israel in 1950 it was wonderful. The Maccabiah was more special than the Olympics. We went dancing in the Negev. I won a gold medal representing England. We also went to France and had a lovely time.

Roman and I got married in 1951 at Dollis Hill Synagogue. When we first got married we lived in Lancaster Grove and then we moved to Dickenson Road. We had two children: our eldest daughter Alona in 1954 who lives in Jerusalem, was assistant editor to Ariel and is now working freelance, and a son Ardyn two years later, who is an artist. They both went to Cambridge University. When I went to the next Maccabiah, Roman looked after the children.

I had many Jewish and non-Jewish Hungarian friends in Budapest. After the revolution people got scattered all over the place. I have a very good friend in Australia and one still in Hungary and I have been back several times.

When I came to England I went to a secretarial college in London. At the same time I was doing a correspondence course in English 0 level. After this I worked for the airline Air India for six years.

I will tell you about my teaching. One of the airline girls had a child, Aviva. She was born in 1964 and went to Camberwell Art College where she got a BA. I started teaching her swimming, as in the meantime I had done a swimming teaching diploma. I also did teacher training at Tottenham. First I was a supply teacher. I really liked St. Mary Magdalene in Islington. They wanted me to stay and I became a special needs teacher. In the meantime I had a job in a primary school in Westminster. When I qualified as a teacher my specialist subjects were English and Art. I decided not to take a full-time teaching job and I stayed at the school for twenty-one years. I am still a swimming teacher and I have been doing a Masters Degree.

26   ALFRED HAMMERSON

I was born on 2nd May 1910 in Carshalton, Surrey. I have a picture of my father's business - a furniture shop. This was sold and my next memory is when I was three years old coming back with my mother in 1913 from Montreal, Canada, to see all the family, then returning again before the First World War started. I had two older brothers - Lesley David and Alexander Harold. My mother died when I was three or four years old. On my mother's side we had three uncles living in Montreal. (I'm not sure where my parents' families came from).

After my mother died in Montreal it was difficult for my father to look after three boys in the house where my uncles also lived. We moved home a couple of times and eventually moved into a flat. My father needed a lady to look after us. After seeing a couple we were eventually introduced to a Jewish lady, Fanny Davies, who came out to Montreal soon after the war in 1919. Eventually my father married her. We came back to London in 1920 after father sold his business. He had to bring five people across the Atlantic, and buy all new clothes and presents for the family in London. He bought a new business lock, stock and barrel – I don't think he had a lot of money. The family all looked after us and different members gave us board and lodging.

I went to school in Hornsey Road, Holloway. The children made fun of me because I was dressed like a stranger. I wore knickerbockers or golf trousers, long stockings and boots. I had to fight back or run. I left school at fourteen and worked in my father's furniture shop - this was about 1928. I cannot remember having a barmitzvah. I had a Jewish education in Canada - a rabbi taught me to read Hebrew.

In England we went to shul occasionally. My father paid half a crown a week for the subscription to Finsbury Park Shul. A shamas came round to our house to collect money. We were quite unorthodox in our religion. My brothers and I worked Saturdays in my father's furniture shop in Seven Sisters Road, Finsbury Park, and my father worked most High Holydays.

At this stage there was a family conference as to my future. Also at this time the radio had been introduced. You had a little crystal with a 'cat's whisker' and it was finally decided that I should go into the radio business. The family knew somebody who had a friend manufacturing radios. I went for an interview with the manager at his factory just off Great Portland Street - it was not a radio factory but a light engineering business, light metal goods. I did not learn anything about radios but I did learn engineering and my identity card was marked 'engineering'. I stayed there about a year. I didn't like it very much. Then I went back to the furniture shop. In the meantime I was attending night school. I learnt bookkeeping and accounting and passed exams as an accountant. I did the books at the shop and ran that side of things.

At that time a Jewish tennis club had opened in Holloway. Sunday was the day we played tennis. I met a couple of Jewish families with local businesses who knew other Jewish boys and girls. There were also Jewish dances. They hired a hall and a band and advertised in the Jewish Chronicle. I met Augustus Rogers, one of the leading members of Alyth Gardens – a founder member. We went on holidays to Jersey together. One day Gussie managed to get two tickets for a cruise for £21 - Portugal, Lisbon, Gibraltar, Tunisia and the Canary Islands. The period was about 1935 when there was a recession, which badly affected the family business. I also took a holiday with Jack Leonard (Dyers & Cleaners family) to Belgium. Jack could only take two days but I took two weeks and friends came with us. We took this holiday in 1937. On the journey we met up with three Jewish girls, one of whom I eventually married a year later. Her name was Leah Wolf who came from Golders Green, and she had two sisters and one brother.

The wedding reception was at Hendon Hall Hotel. We went on honeymoon to Paignton, Devon. When we were first married we lived at 5 Beechwood Avenue in the ground floor flat of a converted house and the rent was five shillings a week. My wages in those days was £2 10s a week, but when I got married it was increased to £5.

My wife was a beautician and she ran the beauty shop in the Mayfair Hotel. In 1939 war came and we decided to start a family before we got killed. Charles, our eldest son, arrived the night the bombs dropped in London. At this time I volunteered my engineering skills. I was turned down a few times but eventually got a job using my knowledge at De Haviland, the aircraft factory in Burnt Oak. Therefore I did not have to fight, but was in the Home Guard and had to carry injured people on stretchers. I had a khaki uniform, steel hat and a gun.

We had another child during the war called David and got through all the traumas of the war. About 1943 we rented a house outside Reading with three acres of ground. We shared the house with Ernst Gombrich, who during the war was an interpreter, working at the listening station in Reading. He liked listening to the German programmes and had a couple of books printed on the History of Art at the end of the war. At this point I was working in an engineering factory in Reading and used to go by bike up and down hills.

After the war we came back to London. We then opened up a furniture business, again in Green Lanes, Haringey. We broke regulations to do this as we were not allowed to re-open businesses. People had to have coupons to buy furniture, which was very difficult. We bought a couple more shops in Archway and one in Reigate - the shops go under the name of Kings. Both boys went to good prep schools. Our oldest son went to a comprehensive school and our younger son went to Highgate. David became an accountant and Charles became a surveyor. Both boys were barmitzvah at Alyth Gardens, where we have been members for many years.

After Reading we bought a big house, which we sub-let. The house was too big and I had to carry a hundredweight of coal every day to keep the boiler going. That made me ill. We moved to a little flat in Lyttleton Road where we lived for a little while and then bought the one where we now live.

The businesses plodded along and in the 1950s we started buying properties with the support of bank managers who lent me money. Each time we opened up a limited company, and each time we sold the properties we made a nice profit. The success of my story is that I managed to buy up big old houses with big gardens in Reigate for about £200,000. The idea was to demolish them eventually and build a development. I managed to organise somebody from abroad to lend me a million pounds. I then got planning permission to demolish these houses and put up a big block.

I also set up an export business exporting anything to all over the world. My sons were also in the business. I travelled all over the world until there was a general slump as gold devalued. The foreign bank wanted their money back and the English banks, who were my guarantee paid them back. Then the English banks wanted some money from me and I could not pay and went bankrupt. I was asked to pay £12,000, which I couldn't. My solicitor advised me to appeal which the judge turned down and I was told to sell my land. However, I had two houses that were not included and they were my assets. I made a deal with the bank to sell these houses for the best price I could get and they accepted this.

After that I went back to work in furniture shops and now I just have the shop in Archway where I still work. I also still export and have three houses left. One son is in business with me and the other son runs the houses. My wife died six years ago.

Occasionally I used to go to services at Alyth but over the last twenty years I am no longer religious. Both sons are married, one with two children and the other has none. One grandson lives in Australia with his lady and the other in Hornsey with his lady. Both grandsons are solicitors.

27
JOAN HARRIS
CHRONICLES OF A TEENAGE REBEL

I was born in 1925, the eldest of two sisters and the product of a middle-class suburban environment. For the most part we lived in a semi-detached house in Golders Green and kept a massive white dog. I remember birthday parties in the garden, seaside holidays down in Clacton and Cliftonville, my dad's Flying Standard motorcar and his antiquated gramophone which played all the old His Masters Voice records, and mum's pedal-operated Singer sewing machine – a family heirloom since converted into a portable one, and still going strong.

From the age of ten I attended Henrietta Barnett School for four years and left in 1939. I then went on to Pitman College for about twelve months, where I developed an unexpected aptitude for shorthand and typing which was to prove a valuable asset to me over the years.

Growing up in war-torn Britain was not easy, what with shortages of everything, food rationing and other strict controls, but my sense of patriotism knew no bounds. I got involved with the British Red Cross as a regular blood donor and then went on to join the WVS (Women's Voluntary Service). I did various jobs for them including a shift at Liverpool Street Station serving tea to masses of troops passing through. I also sold government savings stamps from door-to-door, collected domestic tinfoil and waste paper, and manned a telephone in an Ambulance Depot.

The radio dominated every household. It bombarded us morning, noon and night with news bulletins, morale-boosting speeches, endless economy drives and major important public announcements. But best of all were the welcome sounds of Glen Miller's orchestra, Frank Sinatra and the Andrews Sisters, not forgetting the saucy humour of Tommy Trinder and Arthur Askey.

When the nightly air-raids first started we all rushed over to the shelter in Princes Park, not far from our own home. Conditions there were damp, cold and very cramped, but after one or two near misses when it threatened to cave in, the use of Hampstead underground station, the deepest one in London, seemed a good idea. Hundreds of families, clutching their blankets and other personal belongings, fought their way in to secure a small space for themselves – albeit on the stone stairways or draughty platforms – but feeling safe in the knowledge that the bombing would not affect them so far down below street level. One was aware of the camaraderie, which existed amongst a community united in crisis, especially in these circumstances.

The social life of a teenager during the war was obviously very restrictive. The synagogues, of course, did their best to provide a programme of suitable activities for those in our own age group but with so many young men being called up for National Service, the ratio between boys and girls was unbalanced. Once in a while we went dancing at Covent Garden's hugely popular ballroom, which gave us females the opportunity of dressing up in our best outfits – the 'make-do-and-mend' variety, and to wear those incredibly high-heeled platform shoes – smart but lethal if one was trying to 'jive' – a new American craze to hit the dance-floor at that time.

I was luckier than most because, once I was in the army, the Balfour Club in Portland Place was open to Jewish Servicemen and Women from all over the world. It had excellent facilities for meeting and making friends and they ran a well-stocked kosher refreshment room as an added bonus.

I enlisted in the ATS (Army Territorial Service) in 1942 with my best friend Trudy. We have known each other now for sixty-five years and are still very close. Our parents were none too happy about us leaving home, but the options were limited. It was either the army or a munitions factory, but with hindsight the latter would have been the better choice for me.

My initial training in Guildford was hampered by a rather strange phenomenon. Every night, when I was sleeping, my bed would gravitate towards the other side of the barrack room on its own accord, and I woke up to find myself in a different position from the allocated space I normally occupied. Since this occurred on a regular basis and defied any logical explanation, I had to file an official complaint. At first no-one really believed me, until it was discovered that shock-waves bouncing off heavy artillery about a mile away were shaking the very foundation beneath the floor of my corrugated iron hut and I just happened to be caught up (literally) in the line of fire!

To begin with my uniform made me appear so obviously like a new recruit that I decided to dip all my shirts, ties and stockings into a solution of bleach to give them a faded, washed-out look, more suited to a Territorial veteran. Unfortunately, the metamorphosis went disastrously wrong and the whole lot changed into an odd shade of khaki pink. I was issued with a replacement, the cost of which was deducted from my pay in weekly instalments.

I was then posted to an Ordnance depot somewhere in Sussex where I was picked up in an Army jeep from a small village station together with another ATS girl and taken to a formidable-looking Victorian building, which, apparently used to be a public school. As soon as we had both reported in, an escort bundled us into a cellar and kept the door locked for what seemed to be like hours. Just when we were near to panic, a sergeant came to let us out, apologising for the misunderstanding. The confusion arose because of our surnames – mine was Black and hers was White. One might be forgiven, therefore, in assuming it sounded like the brand name of a famous whiskey, which had, in fact, been ordered for the officers' mess. A 'case' of mistaken identity!

Our living quarters were infested with rats and one actually got caught up in my hair whilst I was lying down in my bunk. I became hysterical (naturally) and felt certain that my screams could well have been heard right across the English Channel. To make matters even worse I was so exhausted the next day that I fell asleep on duty – an act almost tantamount to treason – and was given a stretch of hard labour scrubbing out latrines.

Once my chores were done, I took part in a 'Salute the Soldier Week' campaign, striding along with other contingents in step to a military band. Right in the middle of the road, however, I dropped my handkerchief and bent down to pick it up, not thinking of the consequences. Bad move! The column marching behind me crashed into one another bringing the entire parade to a grinding halt. 'Here we go again!' This time I was assigned to dustbins and incinerator fatigues.

I tried to get home as often as possible, always bearing gifts. My pockets would bulge with cigarettes, chocolate, cheese and eggs and anything else I could scrounge from the canteen.

During a well-earned leave I went on a rowing trip down the river with some friends near Reading. Somehow our boat got stuck on a mud bank and the moment I tried to push it away from the edge, I fell headlong into the water. Up the creek without a paddle easily springs to mind here. A nearby working party of Italian prisoners-of-war quickly came to the rescue and fished me out. A few days later they turned up on my doorstep, complete with an armed escort, to enquire after their 'little river queen', the spectacle of which both my family and neighbours will never forget.

After my dad died tragically in 1944 I was posted back to London where I worked as a supplies clerk in the Royal Army Service Corps, responsible for distributing food and clothing to other units throughout the UK. Geography was never my forte and one can only guess how much of it went astray or fell off the back of a lorry, so to speak.

When Armistice was declared in 1945, I joined the crowds in Trafalgar Square bent on celebrating in timeless fashion by flag-waving and kissing everyone in sight. But as luck would have it I became a victim of some very dodgy 'champagne' bought from a shady shop in Wardour Street and found myself in Charing Cross Hospital being pumped out on a trolley in full view of the public in a packed Casualty Department. It was such a humiliating experience that I vowed never to touch another drop of alcohol ever again and I have kept my word. What a way to end my war!

I have deliberately refrained from recounting the more serious aspects of this War, which took place both over here and in Europe, in favour of a little light relief.

We cannot change any of those events, but, perhaps, there are lessons to be learnt from the past, which will benefit mankind in the future.

So many Castes, so many Creeds
So many paths that wind and wind,
While just the art of being kind
Is all this sad world needs.

28   BETTY HART

I was born in Vallance Road in the East End on 25th July 1911. My
father's name was Jacob Spearman and he had a furniture shop. My
mother's name was Rose. My parents came over from Warsaw,
Poland, when they were very young. I had three brothers and two
sisters. My eldest sister was Fanny, my oldest brother was Isaac, my
other sister was Hilda, then two younger brothers David and Morris. In
the First World War my father was called up to help with aeroplane
parts.

I went to Robert Montefiore School in Vallance Road and it is
still there. I was very bright and came top in everything. I was head
prefect. On my fourteenth birthday I got acute appendicitis and was
rushed to hospital and missed the date for taking my scholarship for
grammar school. I had to leave school at fourteen as my father died in
1922 and I had to go to work.

My eldest brother had a lot of friends and one of his friends
was in the men's hosiery business in Commercial Road, next door to
Frumkins - City Stylish Hosiery Company (Libby Frumkin's son is
Jonathan Sacks the Chief Rabbi). My brother told his friend that his
younger sister was leaving school and was good at arithmetic. The
man Libby married worked as stockroom manager. I got a position
there as cashier/book-keeper. I earned 12s 6d per week and had to give
my mother ten shillings, the 2s 6d paid for my fare, clothes, cinema,
etc. I worked there until I was about twenty.

I went to Hebrew classes at Buxton Street. Elsie Cohen, who
became Lady Janner, started it. Lady Janner also started the Brady
Girls' Club. My brother joined the boys' club in Brady Street. I went
to Lady Janner's engagement party. However I didn't have much of a
Jewish education as I had to go to work. My very first holiday was in a
group with Lady Janner somewhere in Kent. When I had saved up
some money I went for a walking tour in Europe.

My husband's name was Joseph Steinhart and when he was
articled in the City as a chartered accountant he changed his name to

Hart. I met my husband when we used to go hiking at weekends with friends – we got on a train at London Bridge and went to a little place called Gomshall where we stayed for weekends. One of the group had a cousin who joined us and that is how I met my husband. I used to meet him from lectures and we'd have a coffee. We got engaged when he qualified at twenty-four and we were married when I was twenty-two. We hired a hall at Manor House and an orthodox rabbi married us in April 1936. We had a flat in Manor House with an enormous lounge where we had all the rehearsals, as my husband was in amateur dramatics and he won many prizes.

At my husband's first job in the City he was offered £3.10s per week and decided to start up on his own. He used to work from the dining room. I used to help him as I was good at figures. I had changed my job by then and worked in Bond Street for a well-known family - Parnes - who had several ladies wear shops in town. You were paid a salary and worked on commission. I used to get home at 8 pm and then work with my husband. My mother-in-law used to send over food and sent help to do the housework.

My daughter Pamela was born in 1938 (she is now a retired lawyer, and a magistrate). When the war started my mother-in-law said we should live with her as she had an enormous house in Downs Park Road, Clapton. It was a seventeen-room house with a five-room flat, which we moved into because our flat was very difficult with a baby. We moved when I was in the nursing home having my daughter.

During the war my husband was in the civil action corps and reserved occupation. A little boy was very badly injured and he fought very hard to get him compensation. When we had the first bomb in Clapton we went to stay with our friends in Hemel Hempstead and my husband used to come at weekends. Pamela went to school in Hemel Hempstead. In 1944 John was born and we went to live in Woodside Park in a beautiful house where my son now lives. My husband carried on being an accountant and had an office in the house. We had a big Morrison shelter in the lounge, which we used when the doodlebugs came.

When the war ended my daughter went to North London Collegiate School. My son went to Hendon County and became articled to his father. My daughter wanted to do law and qualified at twenty-one. At seventeen she took an exam and was the top student of the year. She married at twenty-four and had a daughter and son. Pamela was the chairman of the Berkeley Group, which was the senior group of the West London Synagogue - she started the nursing home in Finchley. Her daughter, Sarah, is the director of the International Ski Federation, and is a British ski champion. She flies all over the world.

For many years my husband was a member of Oxford & St Georges, The Settlement and synagogue in East London, and did virtually everything including being treasurer. One day he met Dr Van der Zyl and asked if John could be barmitzvah at Alyth and he agreed. Shortly afterwards my husband was made a warden and later on treasurer. My daughter had her batmitzvah at the Settlement and wedding at north London, the ceremony being performed by Rabbi John Rayner.

Eventually my husband had offices in Ballards Lane, Finchley and then Canons Park where my son was articled. Unfortunately, my husband died very young of a sudden heart attack in 1969. After the funeral Dow came over every day and we had prayers at Alyth. Pamelas' family were all away in Spain at the time and Pamela had to come home. John then took over my husband's practice

My son was married at Alyth. After a time John met Judy. I said it was his father's wish that he had the house and I moved into a flat. When John's daughter Rachel was born they transferred from Alyth to Finchley Reform Synagogue where Rachel had her batmitzvah. I have two gorgeous great grandchildren – Alexei aged five and Rosanne aged three.

29   DR ALEXANDER HASENSON

I was born in Hamburg, Germany, on 16th December 1927. My parent's names were Rhoda and Joseph and they came from Russia. My mother's single name was Leibovitch. I had a sister who died when she was nine months old.

My grandfather, on my mother's side, was sent by his father from St. Petersburg to open a branch of their fruit business in Hamburg. On my father's side they went to Germany in 1922. They were living in Riga at the time and decided to go to Hamburg. My father had a wholesale fruit shop in Berlin and offices in Hamburg.

I was only in a Jewish school for about a term as we left in September 1934, a year after Hitler came to power. My father left a year before to go to England and when he had established himself he fetched us over. He was in the wholesale fruit business in Covent Garden. When my father arrived in England he could only speak Yiddish, German and Russian.

We first of all lived in a semi-detached house in Hendon and then moved to a block of flats in Vivian Avenue, where we had a first floor flat with four rooms. I lived there until I got married. I went to a number of schools. I started off at the local council school where I couldn't speak a word of English. Then I was taken away and sent to a private prep school in Hendon Lane. I don't know how my parents could afford it as we didn't have a penny and used packing cases for a dining table. I can only assume that my uncle helped out.

As far as my Jewish education was concerned I started cheder at Raleigh Close. I didn't like it and refused to go. I didn't have a barmitzvah, partly because of the war when I was evacuated to the Lake District. I first went with my prep school to Compton and Dundun in Somerset. They were twin villages. We lived in one and had lessons in the other.

My parents bought me back from Somerset before the Blitz started and when the bombs started dropping my mother and I were evacuated to the Lake District. I went to Kings School in Ambleside, a wonderful place. It was a private school run by an ex-army officer. We had lessons all morning, games all afternoon and lessons again in the evening. My mother and I lived in a flat in Windermere and I was a day boy. But after a time my mother went back to London to be with my father and I then became a boarder. I joined the army cadets but I didn't see very much of the war. My father was affected by the war, as he was right in the middle of it. He still worked in the fruit and vegetable business and in the Home Guard.

We didn't really have any family in Germany. My grandfather went to Palestine in the late twenties when his business folded so he had a British-Palestinian passport. He came back here just before the war and stayed with us. My grandmother came over to England with her daughter in the thirties. Unfortunately my grandparents split up, but we all ended up in England. The family was not naturalised until 1948.

I came back to London in 1944, just in time for the buzz bombs. I went to Ravensfield College and then I took my school certificate in London and matriculated. I had always wanted to do medicine. It took me several years to go to medical school as all the ex-servicemen were coming back and they had priority. In the meantime I tried my father's fruit business, which bored me stiff. Then I worked with my grandfather who had a factory in the Old Kent Road, grinding various powders into different grades.

Eventually, by my own efforts, I was accepted by the Royal College of Surgeons in Dublin. I was there for about a year. Unfortunately my mother had a stroke and I rushed back to London just before she died. She was forty-three. I returned to Dublin for a while, but my father was in such a state that I came back to London and managed to get into the Royal Free in Grays Inn Road where I stayed until I qualified. Although I volunteered before I went to medical school, I did not get called up for National Service.

I qualified as a doctor in 1959. I did three house jobs: the first in Bedford, the second in Amersham and the third in Catford where I was in obstetrics. I got paid doing these jobs. In Bedford I got £5 a week. When I finished my training I went straight into general practice in Stoke Newington.

I was extremely busy doing medicine and didn't have much opportunity to socialise although I met my wife Pat at a party. One night I had a party and somebody brought Pat and that was it. We were married in December 1957 at Alyth. The wedding reception was at the Mayfair Hotel.

Up until then I lived with my father in Vivian Avenue. Then Pat and I lived in a little flat in Fitzjohns Avenue. When I finished my house jobs my mother-in-law offered us her house in Blandford Close in the Suburb and she moved out. We had our daughter Ruth by then; she was born a year after we were married. We stayed in the house until we had five children. Unfortunately one of the children died. We moved to Linden Lea and stayed there for about thirty-eight years. Ruth was born in 1958, Janet in 1961, Ann in 1964 and then Peter fourteen months later. My children went to Whitefield School. Ruth became a nursery nurse and now teaches at Alyth. She is married and her surname is Weiner. Janet has a family and now lives in Canada - we try to see her once a year. Ann took a BA at Warwick University and Peter went into property and is married with two children. Pat has been a very steady influence over me. She is a rock in this family, and she is a most wonderful person.

I continued to work in general practice in Stoke Newington. I had many problems. For some years I worked in a lock-up shop. Eventually I had a group practice and worked with Dr Cheyne, who died after five years. I took on a new partner, Monty Clein, and managed to get into a new health centre. I did further training here and used to write down the minutes at meetings, quoting what everybody said, whether they liked hearing it or not. It was all quite interesting and this is where I broadened out into writing. I also attended an interesting course, since to be a trainer you have to go on a course for nine months. Every Wednesday afternoon I had to go to a centre in London. This course gave us an insight into dealing with our patients. We had a very good teacher, Peter Higgins, who was a professor of medicine at Guys. I used to write all this up and that really got my writing going.

I have always been interested in history. I have written a lot and been the editor of Centre and Crossfire, which is the magazine of the American Civil War, and Round Table in this country. I have built this up from a small newssheet into a 32-page magazine. I recently resigned as I felt that I had done as much as I can. At the same time I have written two books - The History of Dover Harbour and The History of the Golden Arrow. I have had over forty articles published, twenty medical and twenty military. As regards Alyth, I never had the time to be on any committees. I retired from full-time work in 1992 and from part-time in 1998.

* * *

My grandfather's brother stayed in Russia after his brother went to Hamburg and he was a colonel in the Russian Army Medical Service before the First World War. He won a gold medal in the Kharkov university medical school, which unfortunately got taken away from him because he objected to some anti-Semitic behaviour there. When war broke out he worked at the Chesma Military Institute, which is a home for old soldiers and a hospital. He was on duty the night they brought in the body of Rasputin and remembered seeing the Empress coming in and falling all over the body. My grandfather's daughter has written her own autobiography; she is still alive in her nineties. My grandfather's brother eventually left after the Russian Civil War. First they went to France where they had relatives, as his wife was French. He eventually came to London where he was offered a post and took an English medical degree at The London Hospital. He became a GP in West Hampstead.

My father also had Civil War adventures in Russia. Before the Great War my father had finished school and wanted to go to university. The main ones did not offer places to Jews so he had to go to Kazan, a very well-known town. My father studied engineering and really enjoyed being a student; cafes, girlfriends and he had a wonderful time until the war broke out.

In 1916 the Germans were advancing and most Jews were being kicked out of the frontier areas, so the family made their way to St. Petersburg. In 1918 my father was conscripted by the Czechs into one of the Russian regiments - the White Army. After the war the whole family went back to Kazan. He had many experiences and in 1920 he managed to make his way back to Kazan by foot and somehow found his family. They basically spoke Yiddish and Russian but they eventually dispersed, some of them going to Germany.

30   MARIANNE HASSECK

I was born on 16th October 1922 in Charlottenburg in Berlin, the only child of Walter and Suse Goldstein. My father and both my grandfathers were in the timber business. My father and my four grandparents came from Upper Silesia but my mother was a Berliner like me. My family was typical of Berlin Jews, middle class, assimilated and steeped in German culture. During the First World War my father, like most German Jews, fought in the German army and won an Iron Cross.

When I was four years old my parents divorced and eventually both remarried. I went to live with my mother, stepfather and my two half-brothers in Berlinchen, a pretty little town east of the river Oder which, since the end of World War Two, belongs to Poland. I attended my local primary and secondary schools until, in 1936, life became too unpleasant there for me as the only Jewish child.

The turning point in my education came when, as a result of the anti-Semitism, I was sent to live with my grandparents in Berlin to attend a private Jewish school. The teachers as well as the children in this school came from similar assimilated backgrounds as myself, but together we learned about Judaism and acquired a positive Jewish identity, which was to stand us in good stead as times for the Jews hardened.

On the 9th November 1938, known as Kristallnacht, my parents were warned off by one of the workmen in my stepfather's factory. They left home and we met up in Berlin where we were hidden in the flat of a very brave German authoress, together with five other Jewish men. Luckily we were able to leave Germany a few days later and, after a few days enforced stay in Holland, we arrived in England.

Materially life now became very hard; we had literally left without anything and in this country you could not get a work permit. We lived on the proceeds of a diamond ring and on what some relatives in the US could send us. My mother did some knitting and sewing for money. However, we were happy to be out of Nazi Germany where things took a turn for the worse. With the help of the Jewish Refugee Committee I got a scholarship to study horticulture at the Horticultural College in Swanley, Kent. This was a strange experience for me as the girls at college seemed young and unworldly and had no idea what was going on in the world. The food at an English educational establishment seemed more than odd to one who had grown up on the continent.

However, all this changed when war broke out in September 1939. We were glad because we thought it would soon be the end of Hitler. We were now allowed to work. My stepfather had luckily escaped internment, the fate of most male refugees, and he could now earn a bit of money. I went to work in a tomato nursery in the Lea Valley where I had to train Land Army girls who initiated me into the sort of English I had neither learned at school nor at Swanley College.

Later in London I joined the Free German Youth, a covert communist organisation, where I made many new friends. At the age of nineteen I married and a couple of years later my first daughter was born. When the war came to an end we learned that my father and his second wife, who had lived in Holland, had been deported and perished and that my paternal grandmother had died in Theresienstadt or had been sent east from there, a fate that had befallen six million Jews who had not been as lucky as us and not been able to get away.

The Free German Youth wanted us to go back to Germany to promote "Democracy" there. My husband, my three-year old daughter and I went to Berlin. This was a truly horrendous experience. The city was destroyed and there was a horrible smell of decaying bodies coming from the rubble. The people were poor and hungry and full of stories of how the Russian soldiers had treated them, and not a bit sorry for what they had done. We were sent to a small village in the East to build up a youth training school. A few months later my husband died of a thrombosis. I was twenty-five and homesick for my family and Britain, but it took me nearly four months to get permission to return.

Back in England I decided on a change of career and I was lucky enough to be accepted for teacher training at Trent Park where an emergency training programme had started to overcome the teacher shortage after the war. Here I had my big break and a wonderful year. All the other students, men and women had been through the war and were mature and I made many friends.

My first job was at a primary school in Holloway. The fierce and frightening headmistress taught me my craft; everyone was in awe of her for she was quick moving and tiny, but willing and able to do any job that came up. She was inspirational.

In 1953 I married Martin and later that year we went on a month's trip to Israel. I felt instantly at home there and we saw a lot. Martin said that in Haifa, amongst all the German Jews, he felt he had really married a "Yecke". On our return to England we started a family and by 1957 I was the mother of three daughters.

I continued teaching, with two breaks for maternity leave. In 1965 the Inner London Education Authority gave me a sabbatical year to obtain an academic diploma in education at the University of London. In 1970 I was appointed head of Jubilee School in Hackney. This was a large, inner city primary school with children ranging in age from three to eleven plus.

I spent a demanding, but very happy twelve years there. At the end of 1982 I retired. I joined the Association of Jewish Refugees and have been working for them, the Otto Schiff Housing Association and Jewish Care ever since.

Retirement for me has not meant slowing down. My day begins at 6.30 with a half mile swim and then either I go to one of the residential homes in the Bishop's Avenue where I run a book club for the residents of the three homes on the site, or give a talk on Jewish topics. On some days I do inspections of other homes for Jewish Care, as a lay assessor. I attend a weekly drama class and I belong to a group which studies Marcel Proust. Sometimes I have to do a little housework, and of course we travel.

Our three daughters are all married, with two children each, five boys and one girl, and we now have a great-granddaughter in

Chicago. One daughter is a teacher, one a pharmacist and one a painter.

I have visited Berlin a few times, but now it means no more to me than any other town. My home is in Britain which took me in at a crucial time and I will never forget it.

31 FREDA HEWSON

I was a twin and we were born on 14th March 1920 in a little nursing home where all the Jewish children were born. In those days they didn't know if you were expecting twins and it was a terrible shock to my mother. I was very tiny and had to be left at the nursing home until I was stronger. My parents made sure we always looked nice. My father was a tailor.

My father was born in London but had a Polish background. His name was Nathan Ballavon. I knew my grandfather (my father's father) but my grandmother died before I was born. My mother was Polish and came to England when she was sixteen years old. Her name was Rose Heffler. She had two sisters and a brother. They lived in Poland and when the pogroms started they sent my mother's sister and brother to England first. (I think their names were Max and Sarah.) Sarah went to America after coming to England. Max stayed here to welcome my mother who could not speak a word of English, only Yiddish. My mother stayed with her brother for a little while and went to work in a factory as a sewing hand (she sewed lining into coats). She then met my father and did not want to go to America and they eventually got married.

We all lived in Grafton Street in the East End. This was the same road where Lord Grade lived. My brother danced with the Grade brothers. Their mother was always in our house and often said she was short of money. I went to Stepney Jewish School with Lord Grade's sister and it was a fantastic school. My mother had to pay threepence a week for our Hebrew education. The headmistress was Miss Rose and we had to line up and make sure our hands were clean and shoes were polished. We even had a Batmitzvah ceremony in those days in a United Synagogue by Reverend Stern who was very keen on Jewish education for women. We had a lovely, lovely life in the East End. Our lives were lived in the street and in the school and we never thought we were hard up. My mother always made sure we had plenty to eat.

In the East End before the war we had problems with the Mosley mob. I can remember them marching along Whitechapel until they were stopped at Aldgate. There was a lot of anti-Semitism, but as we were at a Jewish school we didn't notice it so much.

When I reached the age of thirteen, I left school with my sister and we went to work in a gown shop. From the East End we had to get to Peckham, where we worked from 9 am to 8 pm every day and 9 am to 9 pm on Saturdays. I was taught window display and my sister was taught how to sell. The shop was called Wilsons. We earned five shillings a week and out of that my mother gave us two shillings pocket money.

When I was sixteen I met my husband. His name was Tony - his real name was Meyer Hewson. He came from Russia to England when he was six months old. Tony was eight years older than me and my parents liked him very much. He was very clever but because he was born in Russia he wasn't allowed to have a scholarship to go to Central school. During that time there was a safety-first essay that all youngsters went in for, and my husband won the top prize. Then a well-known family offered him a job as a journalist. He used to write articles for children. However, before the war he volunteered for the police.

I volunteered for the Land Army in Pwhelli, Wales. My sister and I had to go to a farm school where the farmers were educated and we had a lovely time, it was so beautiful. The Welsh people had such wonderful voices and sang from early morning until late at night. When the training was over the farmers were still not called up so they had no jobs for us. I went back to working as a window dresser and my sister as a saleslady.

At the beginning of the war in 1940, when I was twenty, Tony and I got married at a naval club in Piccadilly. We all had our photographs done by Boris – the most fashionable and popular photographer of the time. Even though it was wartime, my mother made sure I had a nice dress. We lived in Grafton Street with my mother as my husband and I had no money. My mother let off rooms in the house to make money and dad worked as a tailor in a factory making clothes.

When war was declared Tony was called up in the police force. He didn't like this as he was stationed at East India Docks. He took a course in physical training and became a physical training teacher.

In 1940 our house got bombed and we had nowhere to live. My father worked in the West End in Goodge Street and we were able to take shelter under his factory. So we took a furnished flat in the West End and slept in the shelter at night. My mother slept in the tube at Goodge Street station. Then it got very bad and was even more difficult as I now had children. My daughter was called Andrea and was born in 1943. After this the council requisitioned us a flat in Gordon Mansions next to University College Hospital. It was a four-bedroom flat for the whole family and it accommodated my husband and our daughter, my sister, her husband and child, my brother and my parents. My parents did not stay there for long and went to Leeds. My brother-in-law was discharged from the army and his family also went to Leeds and I was left on my own with a baby. It was horrendous. The bombs were hitting us from all sides and so my husband made us go to Leeds but I didn't stay there for long.

After this the council requisitioned for us two lovely flats in Holly Lodge Gardens in Highgate. My sister and I lived a couple of doors away from each other. My son Geoffrey was born in 1947.

The children were well educated. My daughter Andrea went to Camden School for Girls and my son Geoffrey, who was eight, went to St. Mary's School. Then he won a scholarship to the City of London School. Andrea became a secretary at John Lewis for nineteen years and suddenly decided she wanted to do counselling. She did a four-year course in Harrow and she got her degree at Middlesex University. She also does bereavement counselling for Jewish Care. Geoffrey went to Cambridge, but he was not happy there as they were mostly public school boys. After two years he decided to leave, but Cambridge wouldn't let him until he had taken his Part 1 because he got into Cambridge by gaining a scholarship. After this he wanted to work for Jewish Care but they wouldn't take him and told him he had to go back to Cambridge, and the Civil Service told him to go back. He returned to Cambridge, finished his social anthropology and got a second class honours degree. After this he went into computers and he became a systems analyst. Then he fell in love with a girl from Australia. They decided to get married and he is now in Australia. He is working for a very large firm and is a consultant in software.

We were offered the opportunity to buy the flats in Highgate but we did not have the money. I had some school friends who lived in Crooked Usage - they were builders. One day we had tea with them and said we were looking for a house. They said they had just the house for us. We borrowed from everywhere to buy this house - Jewish Care and the chairman of the Jewish Welfare Board were very fond of my husband at the time - Tony used to edit the Boy's Club magazine. For two years we lived on bare boards until we gradually got on our feet.

After the war there were no newspapers but they had to take my husband back. We had two children and wages were very low. His brother-in-law was a first class motor mechanic so he decided to go into business with him, but he had no idea and didn't do well. At sixty-five he sold up and I had to go out to work - we really didn't have much money – and I went to work at John Lewis. Tony applied for a job in a solicitor's office and worked there for fifteen years. We both played bridge and after this he took an '0' level in bridge and got a job at Barnet Council teaching bridge three days a week at the Sobell Centre, Montague Road, Hendon, and another place.

The reason we joined Alyth was when we went to live in Highgate we thought we would join the Archway United Synagogue and being religious we walked to Archway. When we got there it was Rosh Hashanah and they wouldn't let us in because we were not members. So we walked from Highgate to the synagogue in Alyth Gardens. They let us in and welcomed us with open arms. That was over fifty years ago. The rabbi then was Rabbi Dr Van der Zyl, then

Philip Cohen, then Dow Marmur. Geoffrey had his barmitzvah at Alyth and Philip Cohen was the minister at the time.

My husband started up the musicals and plays. They did 'Fiddler On The Roof' and 'The Black & White Minstrel Show'. David Kossof helped us at the beginning - he was the master of ceremonies. My husband and I were on most of the committees. Our whole lives have been with the synagogue and really enjoying it. We also started a group for the unattached. We asked the secretary of Alyth to give us names of all the single people in the local reform synagogues and we got them together. It was a tremendous success - everything was done by candlelight. We put on shows from the theatre group and we put on lectures.

My husband died nine years ago. I still play bridge and run the group every first Sunday in the month at Alyth Gardens - I don't know what I would do without it. Today, I am happy to be a great-grandmother.

32   JOY HOFFMAN

I was born in Luton on 31st December 1923, a little before midnight. In those days church bells rang out for half an hour before and after midnight to welcome in the New Year and were known as 'joybells'. The midwife told my mother that she should call me 'Joybell' (home deliveries were the norm) and my mother had the good sense to shorten it to Joy. I was also given a Hebrew name 'Yehudit' in memory of my paternal grandmother, but my maternal grandmother always called me 'Ukshun' – a description true to this day. She also tied a red ribbon to my wrist to ward off the Evil Eye whose powers she feared more than those of the Almighty.

I just about remember incandescent gas lamps but have clear memories of the wireless, powered by accumulators (wet batteries) which had to be recharged periodically, and of a series of flat irons heating on a hob on the kitchen coke fire. Coal and coke were delivered by the sackful and emptied into a cellar; logs were piled by a garden shed. One of my favourite memories is of the milkman with his pony and trap. I would take a jug and he would measure out one pint or two – fresh from the manufacturer who was contentedly chewing the cud in a field half a mile away. It was quite different from the fluid produced today on which no calf could be raised and which, in my opinion, defies the Trade Descriptions Act.

We had no refrigerator, although in summer blocks of ice could be bought at the door. If milk went sour it was put in a muslin bag to drip and convert itself into cream cheese. Muslin covers abounded, trimmed around the edges with coloured beads and placed over milk jugs and sugar bowls. Meat was kept in a meat safe in a cool pantry and seemed none the worse for that. We were surrounded by market gardens and small farms so that most dairy produce was farm-fresh.

As children we went to cheder twice a week after school and were taught our alef-bet and little else by a rabbinical student – later our minister – who supplemented his meagre salary by slaughtering chickens at a shilling a time! We were left to de-feather and eviscerate the still warm carcasses.

The headmistress of the grammar school where I went was a pioneer in girls' education. She was also a devout Christian who assured me that I was condemned to an eternal punishment as my forebears murdered Jesus.

Change was slow until the outbreak of war. So much changed during those years and the changes have accelerated since – some, but not all, for the better. But that is another subject.

33   JUNE JAY

I was born in Aberdeen on 1st June 1928 to Ernest and Sissy Bromberg. My father's family came from Lithuania, one or two generations before. He was a self-made businessman with his own dance hall and new cinema. My sister Audrey was three years younger. I lived in Aberdeen until I graduated at twenty-one. My mother was born in New York and returned to the UK when she was two and half. Her father was a jeweller from Vienna. I think my mother's mother was British born. My parents and all uncles and aunts have died.

My Jewish upbringing? Well, when I was young, the synagogue in Aberdeen was in the fish market. To me, religion smelled of fish. I have smelly memories of the prayer books and of the elderly gents who were part of the north of Scotland orthodox Jewry. I went to a fee-paying girls' school and took my Highers. Then on to University. At Aberdeen University I did a four-year course in three years because my parents were coming south and in 1949 it was felt that I should not be on my own in Aberdeen. I read economics because my father wanted me to go into the business (dance hall and cinema). I was not enamoured by that idea. Manipulative parents produce manipulative children. I was manipulative. I said 'All right, I'll read economics' because there was no such thing as business studies.

Father was born Broomberg in 1905. There were a lot of brothers. He dropped an 'o', whether it was to differentiate himself from his brothers or to sound more Anglicised, I know not. About 1920 he was employed to wind up grandfather clocks in large businesses in Edinburgh. He used to cycle around winding up all the grandfather clocks. One day he met a former school friend who looked as if he was doing well. He was carrying a case and my father asked what was in it. He opened it up and there were streamers and balloons. Daddy asked where he sold them and he replied 'To dance hall proprietors'. So my father thought, 'If a dance hall proprietor can afford to buy these things he must be doing well. Let's think of opening up a dance hall.'

My mother was not happy in Aberdeen. She found it cold and restrictive. Daddy was well-known. He became chairman of the synagogue Council and in the 1940s, after the war, the synagogue moved to a more salubrious part of Aberdeen.

During the war we felt we were at the receiving edge as a bombed smaller town, with large numbers of casualties. Because my father worked every evening we used to have some scary nights. I remember sleeping under the piano and being given brandy. I am not quite sure whether it was because I had period pains or because I was frightened of the bombs.

I left school in 1946, so I was very much part of wartime educated youth. It was taken for granted that if a girl went to a good school and did well, she went to university. If you did not go to university, you stayed at home. I did all those things. I was the only girl in the economics class and there were not a lot of people reading economics. While I was at university we had – from 1946 to 1949 – the best influx of continental and overseas students since the war, and a lot of returning ex-servicemen. Those of us who were metaphorically still in our gymslips were at a slight disadvantage. We started an international club that went well. I was active in it. Social life was with school friends.

There were few Jews, so we did not see a lot of Jewish people and most of my parents' friends were business friends. Daddy did a lot for the refugees. We had a raft of Austrians. One was a magnificent pastry cook. Daddy helped them to find jobs. Some worked as cooks and others as domestics with big local families. Among the Jewish refugees was Emil Falkenheim who attempted to teach Audrey and me Hebrew. It wasted both his and our time because we were not interested. We found it a struggle and his English was not good. We were rather snooty and he was three or four years older than we were. I met him recently and he said 'Ah yes, I can remember those two girls!' He had tried, but I came to

London not knowing any Hebrew, and not being able to read the prayer book.

I was brought up aware that I was Jewish but there was no kosher food at home. When she had married in 1927 my mother had started getting kosher food sent up from Glasgow. The meat was always rotten by the time it reached Aberdeen, so she gave up. We had no food problems during the war. There was still plenty of good fish. Fish was a staple diet of Scottish life. A nice little sideline during the war was to go into the country looking for eggs and visit a farm. We asked if they had eggs and often my mother would ask, 'Do you have a daughter who would like to come and work as a maid in Aberdeen?' If the daughter did come to Aberdeen as a maid she always ended up working on the buses, so perhaps they did an important wartime job.

I graduated with an MA as one did in Scotland in those days, MA Hons because I took one subject – economics and economic history. Whilst a student there were enough Israelis to be noticeable and they went out with the non-Jewish girls. I have met these Israelis recently in Israel. They really were not interested in Jewish girls. This may have been because to go out with a Jewish girl would have led to marriage, for which they were not ready.

My parents came to London with us. My father decided to give up his interest in his Palais and went into the London property business. My mother wanted to come to London to go back into the millinery business which she had been in before marriage. Incidentally, my mother and father were step-brother and sister in that my father's father married my mother's mother after they respectively had been born. They also wanted to come to London so that I would not 'marry out'. They lived in Prince Albert Road and then moved to Hampstead Garden Suburb. Later they built a house in Cragwell near Bognor. They still maintained their home in London and moved to a flat in Hans Crescent. My sister joined us in London although at that stage she was at university in Leicester.

I tried for a job in a personnel department. There was no advice about jobs given at university in those days, certainly not in Aberdeen. My father advised me to do a six-month secretarial course and although I hated every moment of it I am glad I took it. The course was at Marlborough Gate Secretariat in Bayswater. The owner was Mrs Moneypenny.

Through my parents I had met the Reverend Ephraim Levine of the New West Synagogue while they were having supper in a Jewish fish restaurant. He enabled me to meet a girl called Joyce Dangoor who took me to a junior committee meeting. There I met the man I was to marry – Alec Jay. He was active in Jewish affairs and had two younger sisters.

Alec had been in the Territorial Army before the war because he had seen the dangers. He wanted to go fight in Spain but his parents had not permitted this. Those were the days when boys usually did what their parents said. He had been to UCS and was fairly fluent in German and French, well read, and somewhat of a poet. His unit was stationed in the Kent Hop Fields, near Ashford. On 25th May 1940 they were told that they had to present themselves at Ashford Station to go over to France. They were a motorcycle division and had learned to drive these motorcycle convoys. The lads boarded the 'City of Canterbury' and went over to defend Calais. They knew they were going to do or die. They were not told that they were the diversion so that Dunkirk could happen.

Well, Alec was captured. He was on the dunes in Calais and a German came up to him, put his hand gun up his nostril and said 'Ich schiesse'. Alec knew enough German! He had various identities in the services because he said (and it is down on record in the Sunday Telegraph) that he would rather be buried as a Christian than thrown to the dogs as a Jew. So he put himself down as C of E. He had quite a dark complexion, lots of black hair, which he put down to his Spanish grandmother. He came from an Ashkenazi family.

Alec was a prisoner of war for the whole of the war. He attempted five escapes, four of which did not succeed, and the fifth was not considered to be an escape because the war ended. At least he came home alive. He lived within smelling distance of Auschwitz and knew what was happening. Because he was a fluent German-speaker they had made him the Dolmetscher – the interpreter – and he had the run of the town. Occasionally he fetched the bread, etc. He was once put in prison, within prison, for spreading alarm and despondency among the civilian population, which I like! He was tortured badly each time he was recaptured. He worked for the RAF Escaping Society, and tunnelled and did many things trying to escape. He had no 'sitzfleisch'. I know of prisoners of war who sat it out perfectly laudably and did courses. But that was not for Alec. He wanted to get out.

Eventually, toothless because some German guard had butted him with a rifle, and weighing just seven stone, he came home. He got home by devious ways. His last few days, just before VE-Day in May 1945, were spent in the hills above Prague because he got out through a farm gate, as he used to put it. It all sounds so simple. He had gone into the hills and fallen asleep. He had woken up with a pair of heavy boots beside him and thought 'Ah, ah, here we go again!' But it turned out to be partisans. He joined the partisans after they had cleared him and he used to go into Prague and shoot up a few Nazis.

On 8th May they all went into Prague and there is a very touching episode that he used to talk about. The doctor to the group of partisans was a Jew, married to a non-Jewish woman. She was the only one of four who did not divorce her husband, because they were encouraged to divorce their husbands. She came back to their flat on the 8th May and found her jewellery lying on the kitchen table. That could have meant that her husband had called in for the jewellery, or maybe somebody else had found the jewellery, or that her husband was dead. She just did not know.

Suddenly everybody came into Prague. The 8th May was a very full twenty-four hours. Alec remembered her and I met her later. We managed to trace her and prove that he had been there by showing her a handkerchief that she had given him and also by him remembering where a chest of drawers was. She said she had so many people coming into her house who were ex-prisoners of war or partisans.

Then he had the choice of going east to Russia or west. He was clued up because he read German newspapers most of the time which, of course, the camps did not like. He realised what was happening and knew the problems with the Russians. So he came west and then got home. He went to a reception camp where they were given cards. He had dreamed and told his family that he would send a card saying something to the effect that the prodigal son had returned or something that would be meaningful in a poetic way. He had to fill in his card. The authorities told him what he could and could not write – and it was not his poetic planned message.

Eventually he got himself to Paddington and wanted to take a taxi home to Dunstan Road where he lived. The taxi driver refused saying he was not going to Golders Green. There were cleaning ladies there who said, 'You take the young soldier'. So eventually he took the young soldier home. His father gave the taxi driver a huge tip which, of course, I did not think much of after the problems he had. Weighing no more than seven stone he was ushered into the house and sat in an armchair. The neighbours started coming in. There was no indication given to the parents of returning prisoners of war and of what might be the subtle way of treating them. They were full of joy and love. However unfortunately things went wrong the whole time. The champagne that had been kept for six years was flat. Then some woman turned up with a box of chocolate biscuits and said they were worth sixteen points. He did not have the faintest idea what sixteen points were and felt like throwing the chocolate biscuits back. (This must have happened countless times and this is what I know about returning POW's). He eventually had the remainder of his teeth extracted and got himself back into civilian life with few problems and returned to the Stock Exchange.

Alec had not gone to university because he was not allowed to by his parents. They said that since he was a sportsman and a runner, he would 'waste his time' on sports. Now Alec was twenty-six, so he was a good eight and half years older than me. My parents were worried that we wanted to get married. Whilst he was on the Stock Exchange he also drank beer, he played rugby and cricket. That was all very foreign to them. I had to remind them that he was Jewish.

Eventually we got married but not before we had an arbitrarily imposed cooling off period. We were told we had to wait until the autumn. In my pedantic way I asked 'When is the autumn?' Alec in his poetic way replied 'When the first autumn leaf falls.' So when that first autumn leaf fell on the bonnet of the car we presented it to my father and we were engaged. We were married eight months later on a Thursday, because that was deemed a desirable day. We did not want a Sunday, Friday or Saturday, and his friends were only able to come if it was between the end of the rugby season and beginning of the cricket. So I was blooded fairly well into rugby and cricket.

We were married in the West End and had the reception at the Savoy where Carol Gibbons played the piano for us. That was lovely. Our first home was in Chalk Farm in a flat that had belonged to his mother. We lived there for two years and then went to a delightful house in the Suburb. Our first daughter, Rebecca, was born in May 1955. Alec was still on the Stock Exchange with a small firm, but he was becoming very dissatisfied with working on the Stock Exchange. His wartime experiences had not laid the ground for a really successful post-war career and eventually he left the Stock Exchange in 1957, at the time that our first son, John was born, and went into business.

I had decided that I wanted to go back to work. I had had a few not very interesting jobs between graduating and getting married. I had met up with a woman called Louise Davies who is the well-known cookery author and dietician nutritionist. She needed somebody to stand in for her while she did a television programme. Apparently I could spin words together and had a voice that would be acceptable on the BBC. So I became her stand-in on a programme called 'Shopping List' which was part of the 'Today' programme in the days of Jack de Manio. I did that for ten years on and off on the radio – on the Home Service. I also used to take part in several programmes for parents and children as a supposedly articulate parent. It was not that easy to find them in those days. We used to talk to paediatricians about problems with children.

I had a third child, David, who was born in 1960 and we went to live in the country for six years in Ottershaw in Surrey. Then we came back to London so the children could go to a London school. Rebecca went to Camden School for Girls and the boys, as their father had done, went to UCS in Hampstead and did fairly well. I am really pleased for them. John is the business managing editor of the Business News of the Sunday Times. Rebecca runs her own design and marketing consultancy and David now lives in New Zealand. He is a filmmaker and teaches film and television studies. They are all on second marriages. Rebecca had a little boy four years ago. John got married the second time to Judy Bevan who was a fellow journalist and writes profiles of business and City people. They have adopted a little Chinese girl who is now five. David married a New Zealand girl and they have a daughter, Clarice, but they have split up.

In the mid-sixties Louise and her team were not considered zingy enough. Things changed at the start of advertising. So we were given the option of changing our presentation or leaving. It was difficult for the four of us to change our style with the same job. So we all left. I hoped I had become a whiz with the tape recorder but I was not always successful. I am now much better. So I joined various friends who were either in advertising, public relations or marketing and worked with them. Then I joined an opinion research organisation that I still work for as an executive interviewer, which I like.

My husband eventually started his own business in paper and packaging, then gave that up in the 1980s when the economy was down. He worked as a minicab driver and used to drive a Saab. He loved driving and was a very successful, much loved minicab driver.

He had a heart attack while he was in the car. It is a strenuous job being a cab driver and he drove at night, which he preferred. Alec died in 1993.

My synagogue history is from Aberdeen via the New West End Synagogue to Alyth Gardens. When we went to the country we went to Wimbledon Reform and became convinced and practising Reform Jews. The children all had a synagogue-based education. I don't know if it was that much family-based, but they all made successful and enthusiastic barmitzvah/batmitzvah candidates. By then we had returned to London; had left Wimbledon and moved on to Hendon where Rebecca used to help. But Hendon in those days was not very welcoming to the idea of women participating and so you had the problem for a girl of being an equal on the bimah when she was batmitzvah and then reduced to the ranks. That, and the fact that I suddenly realised with great hurt that I was not awarded the honour of carrying the Torah, so Alec and I left together with a group of women. We joined Hampstead Reform and I was with them for some years. Over the last years, because we have a lot of friends and acquaintances at Alyth, I felt drawn back there. During the thirty years we were members of Reform Synagogues we were both on Council at Hendon, I with particular interest in publications, education and youth. Then I was a member of the Executive for three years. We had synagogues for which we were executive representatives - I had Glasgow and Weybridge and one other. Alec and I felt strongly, discussed it and laid the foundations for this activity. We both gave our time and skills to Reform Judaism.

My grandchildren have not been brought up Jewish. Both Rebecca's husbands have been non-Jews, uninterested in their own religion let alone anybody else's. Rebecca is a festival Jew and brings James around. He knows that he is Jewish by virtue of having a Jewish mother and has been to synagogue with me but there is no Judaism in his home. John's wife is a committed member of her church. They live in Rotherhithe. Josephine was probably born

Buddhist but has been christened and knows about her Jewish heritage.

In New Zealand, David's ex-wife is a communicating member of her church. He stood as a labour party candidate at the last general election in New Zealand and his constituency contains both Auckland synagogues. He was invited to visit the Reform Synagogue, which we have in fact been to because I go out there every two years. We had just wandered in on a Friday night. He has become very much part of that synagogue and his daughter loves it. I don't know whether that means any more than socialising in a Jewish atmosphere on a Friday evening. Since it is not a labour-voting area, David was not elected although the labour vote increased. He found that one of the other candidates was acting in a somewhat Nazi way, and that some of his supporters were 'bully boys'. He issued a press release giving vent to his feelings and quoting his father's experience. This was considered to be an 'off-message' and we were asked to leave Auckland for two days. I was out there organising the social activity during the time of the election. So we left Auckland for a couple of days. By the time we got back it was accepted that what he had said was not necessarily politically incorrect. It was an 'off-message' in that they did not really want it to become a prime message but there was also truth in it and it is known apparently in New Zealand as the 'David Jacobs effect'. He has gone back to 'Jacobs' rather than 'Jay' mainly because his ex-wife, in her militant feminist way, was not going to take her husband's name. So they looked around for a name and came up with Jacobs, which after all was our original family name.

34   SOLOMON LIONEL KANTOR

My parents were born in Zagare in Lithuania. They came to London in 1911 and spent some months in a shelter. My father's name was Barnett and my mother was Liborazah-Lieber. My father was a dressmaker. They later went to South Africa where I was born on 30th April 1912 and where my father had a drapery business. I have a sister who is still alive and a brother who passed away at the very young age of twenty-eight. Their names were Rachel and Samuel.

When we lived in Cape Town we were not well off. I went to school near my home. Our district was a largely white, English-speaking area. At school I studied English and Afrikaans (which I can speak), maths, history and Latin. I mixed with white and black people. I used to learn Hebrew and translation after school. I then went to college and on to the University of Cape Town where I studied Civil Engineering for which my parents paid. I did not do much socially while at university – I spent most of my time studying.

In 1931 I had a job in a government department to do with irrigation and dealt with water. In 1932 my department sent me to country areas from scheme to scheme where water was required. In 1936 I returned to Cape Town for three years to do advisory work. In 1939 I was posted to a construction scheme. Then war broke out and I joined the engineering corps of the army in Pretoria and became a Second Lieutenant. After a year's training I was posted to Egypt. One weekend while on leave I visited an old university friend who lived in Johannesburg and he took me to Pretoria where I met my wife, Rose Merson. (Her mother came from a Lithuanian town. A few years ago my wife revisited this town.) She was a very devoted South African and worked for one of the government departments. We were married in April 1943 and my parents insisted on a shul wedding.

We eventually moved to Egypt for three months but when I was posted to Morocco I refused to go. In April 1944 I was posted to Italy to a works company engineering corps. My first job was to deliver surveys. I was then posted to a railway construction unit, repairing railway lines – it was quite an experience, which I enjoyed, although there was shooting going on all around us. Then I went off to a place called Optima where I stayed until the end of the war. I saw German trucks taking prisoners to prison camps.

One day we were posted to a textile town west of Florence. We were working on the Appenine Tunnel, which was 112 miles long. The army food was okay during the war. At the end of the war, in July 1945, I had to bring my unit down to the south of Rome. We returned to South Africa in 1945. During this time my wife stayed in South Africa and carried on with her job. I picked up my wife, and we went to Cape Town.

My Department of Water Affairs gave me more work. I did some canal construction for four years in the Orange Free State. Our eldest child, Ian, was born in 1946. Subsequently my wife developed a severe skin condition, which the local people couldn't treat. Our second child, Bernard, was born in September 1949 in Kimberley where I was working. In 1950 I was transferred to Pretoria for two years. I went from state to state during this time right up to the 1960s. I was very upset with the change of government in 1948 from United to Nationalists.

At this time I was working on a 100-foot high dam. I found a Masonic Lodge near to where I was working. I had Jewish relations in the Orange Free State. During the time I was travelling my wife stayed in accommodation from my first scheme. Our third child David was born in 1950. There was no school where we lived and I organised one to be built. Ian went to this school where they spoke Afrikaans with my employer's children. After this we sent him to an English orientated school. He had some Hebrew education. On Saturdays my wife took him to shul and on Sunday mornings to church.

I stayed at my job until 1960 and moved to Pretoria for a short while. I did various jobs in engineering until 1972. Then I worked for another engineering organisation for a number of years until I retired. Ian started senior school, spent one year at Union school, and then went on to the Pretoria Boys High School. He started an engineering degree at Pretoria University but changed his course to a management degree. He worked for a little while, got fed up, and went to Cape Town and bought his own bank with a colleague. There are now branches in Johannesburg, Pretoria, Durban and Cape Town. They sold the building and moved to Johannesburg. His bank was called Investec Bank. There are also branches in New York and Israel and a branch here in Gresham Street, near St Paul's Cathedral. He now lives in Amsterdam and has an accountancy qualification. Bernard lives in London and is in banking and commutes to Cape Town. David didn't go to university. He now works in Investic Bank.

I worked for the Armaments Corporation in South Africa doing engineering work. We took no part in politics. I got on very well with the black and coloured people in South Africa. One of the reasons Rose and I left Johannesburg was that we were mugged. They tore the skin off her nose, dragged her in heaps of rubble, broke her ribs, broke her hip. She was in hospital for two months and it upset her considerably.

My wife Rose passed away eighteen months ago – she had a very severe asthma condition. We were married for fifty-seven years.

35   MALLI KATZ

I was born Malli Hiebner in Berlin on 3rd March 1913, a date I have always liked and also my favourite number. I was the youngest of five children. My parents were Orthodox, my father a deeply religious man who provided a home background that was consciously Jewish, with Zionism playing a big part. So far as we were concerned, Herzl came only a small step below God.

Being the youngest I was very much loved and spoilt so that my childhood memories were happy ones; except perhaps for the doll's pram I always yearned for but never actually received. I suppose with five siblings to educate, nourish and clothe, money for such trivialities was simply not there. Although we lived modestly we all had a good schooling and there were always books in the house; and when the older of her children had grown sufficiently, mother would often take them to the theatre. Charity too played an important part in our family and there were money-boxes for all sorts of good causes scattered all over the house. I remember that my father frequently brought a guest home for Friday night dinner; I think he picked them up in the Synagogue and my mother would then fill their plates near to overflowing.

My brothers and sisters belonged to the youth movement 'Ezra', a junior branch of the Adath community, and whether they liked it or not they just had to take me to their meetings and gatherings. So it was that from early on I was already encouraged along the path to becoming an ardent member of various youth movements. First the 'Bund Deutsch-Judischer Mädchen', an innocent group of little girls, mainly singing 'Wanderlieder' while wandering around the beautiful woods in the neighbourhood of Berlin; later graduating to the Kadimah, the Zionist youth movement and finally into the Maccabi Hatzair, the educational branch of the sport organisation.

So far as my general schooling was concerned I was first sent to a Lyceum. At the age of ten years, being a very bright little girl and bringing home excellent school reports, my parents transferred me to a Gymnasium or grammar school in order to provide me with the very best of education. Alas, the bright little girl did not remain so for long and was soon swallowed up into a quagmire of mediocrity, naturally to my parents' sorrow, the youth movement having superseded both school and parental influence as far as I was concerned. The movement in fact had opened a door to a different world for me, first as a small chink, then a gap that widened more and more.

Outside of that however my world was still orthodox. On a Shabbat and Yom Tov everyone went first to synagogue and then for a sedate little walk in the park, later indulging in some reading, with Sunday activities much the same as the day before. The youth movement, though, brought me in touch with nature, real nature. On Sunday mornings we went into the woods with rucksacks on our backs, boiled cocoa over a wood fire, later on sleeping in tents or barns. We were always singing, always discussing, the subjects we talked about ranging from religion to nudity, from Communism to Zionism, from slavery to free love. Gradually for me the fences and barriers of orthodoxy began to fall. At one time I would walk several miles to and from school and never write on Shabbat. I would then pin my handkerchief to my dress so as not to carry anything. Later I saw no harm in at least carrying a book. In time too, I began to eat in my friends' homes without enquiring too deeply into the question of kashrut. All in all the youth movement took precedence over school and to a certain degree the parental home, but we also learnt a lot. We studied Jewish history, we read Dubnow, Achad Ha'am and Graetz, we studied the history of Palestine, we learnt modern Hebrew and even tried to sharpen our brains by learning the Tanach.

After the hurdle in my old school of the 'Einjaehrige' (pupils who had reached the equivalent of our 0-Levels), we now had three years in which to study for the Abitur, an exam rather like the old matriculation, only higher. I feared that my new class teacher would be the most boring, the dullest and most reactionary teacher known in the school. The prospect was horrific. At the same time, however, there were rumours, in the Youth Movement of course, that elsewhere in the city there was the 'Erste Staedtische Studienanstalt', another name for a particular Gymnasium, functioning on more progressive, freer and more modern lines. Pupils there were addressed as 'Fraulein' with family name added, taken on visits to theatres and concerts whilst at the same time one could also voluntarily take part in afternoon classes on subjects of ones own choice. Best of all, in summer the school moved to the 'Woods' on the outskirts of Berlin to Eichkamp, adjoining the famous, beautiful Grunewald, a heavenly prospect for us.

One morning my school friend Hilde and I played truant from classes and boarded a train to Eichkamp, taking no notice of the gentleman seated opposite us. We discussed how we would present the negative and old fashioned aspects of our present teachers and their methods; whose names we would include as we talked to the Director of our chosen school; how to convince him of the benefits we would derive from his own wonderful and modern place; not least also how to face our parents with our secret plan and the request for a possible transfer.

Leaving the station we approached the school with thumping hearts and were at last ushered into the Director's office. As we entered something dreadful clicked in my brain. The gentleman opposite us in the train was the Director of this desirable school, but fortunately for us he had a great sense of humour. After scolding us for being so indiscreet he examined our school reports, whereupon he then accepted us with the proviso that our parents agreed to this transfer, which fortunately they did. School life now improved more and more, the teachers were younger, the subjects more relevant and up to date, whilst on a social level friendships were formed, one of which, in my case, lasted throughout our life until her death in the Seventies. What I liked best of all was that in summer our classes were held outside in the open with all pupils sitting on the grass in a circle, whilst in winter we were up in the mountains skiing in the morning and studying in the afternoons and evenings. I do not know whether we learnt any more in this particular school than we would have anywhere else but we were certainly very happy.

I sat my Abitur in February 1932. At that time Hitler was only on the periphery of Jewish consciousness, but I was already a convinced Zionist and determined to go to Palestine. I could not see myself clearing fields of rocks there or drying swamps, as the earlier pioneers had done, but I did want to do something constructive, so I chose to study architecture. In order to be accepted as a student at the technical high school it was necessary first to undergo six months of practical work, in my case on a building site. It was 1932 however and Germany was in a deep economic depression. Where on earth would there be an opening for a mere girl in such a purely masculine profession? Help, however, came from my friend Lotte, an apprentice in a commercial pottery who was already herself preparing for Palestine. She had managed to find a job in Hamelin, the famous rat catcher town, and now talked the owner of a furniture factory into accepting me as a volunteer worker for six months. It turned out he was the Master of the Cabinet Makers Guild in Hamelin and also a very kind man; how otherwise would he have accepted a Jewish girl seeing that the town was already so infested with Nazis?

My parents at that time could barely afford to support me after I left home, but even so managed to send me a modest sum each month. However it was really only with the help of Lotte and her parents that I actually survived. Lotte and I shared a room and all the money we had, but not being used to hard work I was always hungry. Lunch consisted of a big bowl of thick soup costing 50 pfennig eaten in a workman's cafe. It was ambrosia for me but still could not entirely fill the big empty hole in my stomach. If only I had had another 5 pfennig for a bread roll!

At work I carried big planks of wood and learnt to plane and polish. In time I also made simple drawers and eventually was able to copy detailed plans for the more complicated pieces of furniture.

There were only a few Jewish families in Hamelin but luckily for us amongst them was a young lawyer, a locum for the absent Jewish doctor, and a student from the technical weaving school. All three were Zionists destined for Palestine and so, otherwise starved of young Jewish friends, we had a wonderful time together. Even before Hitler became Chancellor, the streets of Hamelin would echo at certain times of the day to the jackboots of Nazi troopers singing their bloodthirsty songs. From the pitched gables of the beautiful medieval houses the party banners with their Nazi swastikas were hanging down to the ground so that it was difficult to pass by without brushing against them. We were not particularly comfortable in this situation but we were never afraid. We had an inner conviction that we did not belong here and that we would soon be elsewhere, giving us the backbone and strength to come through.

In the autumn of 1932 I returned home and enrolled in the school for furniture making and interior design. I was the only girl amongst all the students and the only Jewish one at that. Right from the beginning I made it quite clear that I was a Zionist and that I would eventually leave Germany and go to Palestine. Although there were a number of Nazis in the college even at that early stage, never once did I hear an anti-Semitic remark, either directly or indirectly. It was almost as if an invisible wall had been thrown around me with nobody ever stepping inside. Whilst it gave me a feeling of safety it was nevertheless a little lonely. In fact only one student ever befriended me, the son of a teacher who was a member of the Social Democrat Party. Even though he lived at the opposite end of town he would walk me home every afternoon, an hour-long stroll. We walked and talked, about the present, the future, about him, myself, our hopes, dreams and anxieties. It was such a pure friendship. Later, during the war years, I would sometimes think of him, wondering where he was, what he was doing. Was he a solider in Rommel's army in North Africa or perhaps fighting in Russia? Did he know about Auschwitz and Dachau and did he still remember me?

I eventually left the college in Hamelin when I finally realised that my professor was deliberately ignoring me and my work. Whenever he passed my work table he would look furtively in the other direction so that the plans I was working on were never viewed, corrected or commented upon. Obviously he did not feel very comfortable in my presence but then neither did I in his. By now it was the end of the term anyway and it seemed as good a time as any to quit.

I returned to Berlin where I was again roped into the Zionist youth movement, now more tightly than ever. In 1932 the idea of a youth Aliyah was born. It was Recha Freier, the wife of an Orthodox Rabbi in Berlin, who was the mother of this Aliyah and not Henrietta Szold as so many others maintain. It was Recha who approached the Maccabi Hatzair leadership to ask them to let her have a number of young girls who could help in choosing the most suitable children to be prepared for the Aliyah.

Although I was one of these chosen helpers I hated the task. Whilst my parents were not affluent, living in a lower middle class neighbourhood not too far away from the poorest district, I was until then totally unaware of the poverty in which some Jewish families lived. The myth that 'Jews are rich' exploded around me. Parents came with their twelve to fifteen year old children in tow, fathers without work, mothers in ill health, begging me to accept their child on the way to salvation, meaning Palestine, education and work. Little did they know that I was only a minor tool in this process, merely filling in a questionnaire and sometimes adding a personal observation. They thought I had only to say yea or nay, reminding me of the prayer that we say on Yom Kippur 'Who will be and Who will not.' I was very unhappy about this but fortunately I was soon released from this honourable but painful task as the certificate for my own entry into Palestine had now arrived.

I remember a large brown cabin trunk standing in my room being packed with books, photographs and clothing, most of the items quite unsuitable for a Chaluzah - linen blankets and, to my horror, a pair of large silver Grecian style candlesticks. These were only used for the High Holy Days and I really disliked them. They were far too large and ostentatious for me so I took them out of my trunk. My parents, however, put them back again, so once more I took them out until eventually my parents won by sheer persistence and the candlesticks came with me to Palestine.

I do not remember the number of people there were in this particular group of Chaluzim and Chaluzoth I travelled with, but I do remember the scene on the platform of the Anhalter Bahnhof, the place of departure. A seething noisy mass of people; travellers and well-wishers, those who were on their way and those who hoped to be in the next group. There was laughter and tears, kissing and back-slapping, firm hand shakes and above all songs, Hebrew mainly, as well as loud shouts of 'See you in Tel Aviv!' Had there been a bit more space on the platform then I am sure we would also have danced the Horah. In the eyes of the railway employees we saw amusement, astonishment and yes, even respect.

I cannot recollect any of our journey by sea from Trieste to Jaffa. The Mediterranean in November can be cruel and seasickness wiped out all memory. Even our arrival was an anticlimax, with no feeling of elation, no falling down and kissing the ground; only my friend Lotte from Hamelin standing there waving and waiting.

With all formalities out of the way, I was taken by Lotte to a friend's house in Tel Aviv where I spent my first two days in Palestine, having been warned beforehand of possible unwanted attention from the friend's husband! It was customary on Friday night to walk along Allenby Street to meet and greet old friends and generally see who was where. It was also the rule to go on 'Tiyul' as soon as possible, that is to see the country and to try and find one's direction, if not already affiliated to a particular Kibbutz. Since this did not apply to me I went to the Emek Yisroel where some older Kibbutzim were already established.

In Ein Harod I found two friends who were already members of this Kibbutz and they invited me to stay for a while. It was harvest time for the cauliflowers and it was my friend's job to hammer together the wooden crates for transporting this particular vegetable to the markets of Haifa and Tel Aviv and so I helped in this work. Even to this day, however, whenever I eat this pleasant dish I remember this friend of mine saying "I like cauliflower but not to the extent of having to eat it for two long months two or three times a day in various shapes and guises!"

Afterwards I moved on across the valley to Hefzibah, a Kibbutz founded by Czech Chalutzim. It seems hard to believe but the first wooden hut I encountered contained the entire Kibbutz's carpentry. The carpenter, Gavriel, a tall and handsome man, worked on his own and after I had told him my story he introduced me to the Kibbutz secretary. Thereafter it was decided amongst the various kibbutzniks that I would be allowed to stay as a guest and work in carpentry for up to six months. After that I could decide for myself whether to become a member or to move on, those being the rules at the time.

As far as I was concerned fate had spoken and I now became a carpenter in a Kibbutz. By nailing together two short and two long planks of wood and screwing in a connecting rod, hey presto we had made ourselves a wardrobe. When put against the wall and adorned with a length of cotton material in front it served its purpose admirably. Whoever said it had to be of polished walnut with a bevelled mirror and fancy fittings as in Hamelin? We also built school desks, which was quite a difficult job, and playpens for the babies, or lullim as they were known in Hebrew.

I was very lucky in having a so-called 'room' of my own in a long wooden hut containing four or five other rooms similar to mine. The planks on the floor were poorly laid and fitted badly together so that dropping a small item such as a pin or button meant they were lost forever. Worse, the partition walls only reached three quarters of the way up to the ceiling, leaving an open space above through which all sounds were carried from one end of the hut to the other, but who cared? We had a door, one we could shut and even lock, quarters that were certainly preferable to sharing or living in a tent as was still customary in some Kibbutzim.

Food at breakfast time was awful, just green tomatoes, small unpitted olives, salt herring, a sickly sweet grape jam and a dreadful kind of fat flavoured with roast onions. At least the bread was good and there were also lots and lots of big mugs of delicious tea.

It is not my intention to discuss the ethos and philosophy of Kibbutz life or its practical applications, but two relatively minor things still stick in my mind. One was the feeling of total bliss when handing in my dirty clothes before Shabbat and receiving in return a parcel of clean ones, freshly laundered and ironed. The other was the ever-present danger of slipping on bits of soap left lying on the floor of a shower house which some members had not bothered to pick up, since it was only too easy to get a fresh supply.

At first I had no idea that Gavriel, the Kibbutz carpenter, was also the Kibbutz Casanova and although he had a beautiful young wife I did not always feel comfortable working near him and I certainly did not want to become one of his conquests. I also realised that being an unattached female I could not remain unattached for long. As I did not see anybody around me to whom I wanted to attach myself, I soon thought it best to move on.

Again I was lucky. A member of the Kibbutz, an older woman, had befriended me and she understood the situation I was in. Her friend happened to be married to the well-known architect and town planner, Richard Kauffmann, in Jerusalem. Although I was only a quarter trained draughtswoman she nevertheless managed to get me a job in his office in the spring of 1934.

I cannot honestly say that on arrival in that historic city I felt any great sense of elation. The ascent which gave such a splendid view of the place and which has already been described a thousand times, touched no raw nerve of awe, veneration or humility - I just didn't feel anything. Jaffa Road, the place of entry, was flanked by roughly cut stone houses with some rusty ironwork, everything looking dusty and neglected, whilst the shops had low lying entrance doors and even lower windows displaying a variety of inferior goods. By comparison, the grand department stores of Herman Tietz and Wertheims in Berlin were altogether on a different planet. It is with some shame that I have to admit being struck by the beauty of Jerusalem only very much later, but then at least with some force.

Kauffmann's office was situated in an old Arab house, the rooms placed around a large atrium, beautifully cool in the summer and hellishly cold in winter. Nevertheless, I found the work interesting and under the tutelage of Kauffmann's first assistant I was put to work making detailed plans of all the woodwork, windows, doors and built-in cupboards, my work supervised by another newly arrived Oleh who was most helpful whenever I had any problems. The Oleh, himself, a gifted, even brilliant architect, had some minimalist ideas however which were not always suitable for Palestine or its climate. Many times I either witnessed, or was caught in the middle of, a heated argument between architect and builder.

Kauffmann though was a very gifted and innovative architect, introducing many new ideas, particularly with respect to kibbutz housing. He was also a town planner, responsible for most of the designs of the settlements of that period, including the original one for Nahal, the birthplace of Moshe Dayan. In all his work, the interests of Kauffmann's clients came first and no builder, plumber or electrician could ever reckon on getting a backhander from him. I admired the man very much.

As time went by I got to know at least some parts of Jerusalem - the Jaffa Gate, David's Tower and the Old City, which at first I found to be without charm. There were all those people pushing and shoving, so many smelly donkeys with large boxes on their backs, cats scuttling about, excrement which had to be avoided and then the butcher's stalls with their carcasses of sheep and goats impaled on iron hooks, with huge flies swarming over them. At least the fruit and vegetable stalls were lovely, full of exotic and unknown offerings, also the stalls displaying hundreds of strange spices.

My greatest disappointment turned out to be the Wailing Wall. The narrow path that led to it merely passed into another narrow space where old men stood next to a stone wall swaying back and forth, praying, crying out, beating their heads against the large stone blocks and sticking little pieces of paper into the crevices. All the while beggars were huddled on the ground, stretching out clawed hands and demanding 'Tzedaka' or charity, an armed British soldier watching overall. Could this, I wondered, really be the place generations of religious Jews throughout the centuries have yearned and died for?

There were compensations though. Together with some friends, we walked through the quiet and lovely suburbs of Rehavia. We usually went on foot, and when we had money we hired donkeys, in this way discovering the beauties of the Judean Desert in a leisurely manner. Sometimes too, we took the autobus down to the shores of the Dead Sea, and even bathed in the oily, salty water.

Other events are also prominent in my mind. I remember Toscanini conducting the first concert of the Palestine Symphony Orchestra at an evening performance. The majority of members had been expelled from various prominent European Orchestras and Toscanini was showing his defiance of both Hitler and Mussolini by his gesture in making a political point through his music. Another musical event I remember vividly was one that took place by the light of the full moon in the amphitheatre of the Hebrew University campus on Mount Scopus, the Dead Sea spread out like a silver cloth far below us.

Another time Richard Kauffmann with a friend, his wife and myself in tow, attempted to reach Petra in a clapped out old Opel on a day trip. We were accompanied by the minimalist architect on his powerful Zundapp, a motor cycle which he had brought from Germany rather than cash which would have been far more useful. Although we left Jerusalem at dawn we never did reach our goal. Rather like Moses and the Promised Land we only got as far as looking across the valley towards where we perceived Petra to be. Even now, I can still feel the sense of disappointment, but my elders considered it unwise to proceed further into largely uncharted and not always friendly territory and refused to go any further. On another occasion we made a boat trip across the Red Sea in order to visit a cave. Half way across an unusual and fierce storm arose. We almost managed to reach the other side but were then unable to land, similar to an experience I had many years later on the lake of Zurich. The Red Sea did not contain the fresh sweet waters of the Swiss rivers however, and heavy salty waves crashed into the little boat, burning my skin and, even worse, my eyes.

We survived, but not so my new leather jacket, a present just received from my parents. When I took off the salty water-soaked garment it stood stiffly upright. No desalination or cleaning process was effective and so I had no option but to throw away this cherished garment of mine.

At the time of which I am speaking, a group of immigrants from Germany known as the Histadruth Olei Germania, many of whom had brought the means to buy, started building small cottages on Keren Kayemet soil, each with about half a dunam of land. Eventually I was able to do likewise.

Ever since I left Berlin my parents had been sending me small amounts of money through friends, though whether legally or not I never found out. Contrary to some reports of Jews stealing and misusing such monies, I have to say in all honesty that I personally received every penny my parents forwarded through these channels. It was because of this that I at length found I had sufficient money to qualify for one of these Histradruth-built houses. Of course being in the trade helped and soon I purchased a good corner plot on the site of the future settlement of Kiriat Bialik. A plan for the house to be built there was already in existence and more or less of a similar design to all the others, but being in the profession I put in my own changes for all the wooden fitments, so that when my parents arrived in September 1936 they had only to purchase beds and, together with all the household goods they had brought with them, were soon comfortably settled.

The actual process of building Kiriat Bialik took quite a long time of course and ideally I wanted to be on site as much as possible in order to supervise. This was difficult living in Jerusalem, so when eventually the arrival of my parents was imminent I very reluctantly left Richard Kauffmann's employ and moved instead to Haifa. There I began work for two new bosses, both gifted architects who had migrated from Hungary and Rumania respectively. Their Zionist connections in the latter two countries meant that they received commissions to build apartment houses on Carmel. It was my job to produce small-scale plans of these buildings and to submit them to the Municipality for approval. Since I spoke rather better English than my bosses I also had to write all official letters. I still wonder sometimes what the recipients made of my jumble.

Petty cash was another charge of mine which to my embarrassment was sometimes simply not available. I then had to supply my own coins for such things as buying stamps. Everything else was, of course, simply bought 'on the book' as was the general custom here.

In Haifa I had many friends and lived in lovely Bat Galim, meaning 'daughter of the waves', a suburb of the city on the seashore. In those days Bat Galim had a fabulous swimming pool built out into the Mediterranean where strong waves would come crashing in. Being a Pisces I made good use of the pool every morning, a short walk along the shore in the early morning sun seeming to me almost like paradise.

By 1937 the political situation in Palestine was deteriorating markedly with the Arabs rioting and protesting violently against the continued Jewish immigration. Building activities came practically to a standstill, as did our activities in the office. There was no work and no money. I was put on half days, my bosses unable to pay me even the miserably small salary to which I was entitled, and not unnaturally I was becoming depressed. Then my mother had a brilliant idea. Her sister and family had also left Germany and were now in Paris. At mother's suggestion I would pay them a visit and at the same time enjoy the World Exhibition which was being held there. What better opportunity for a visit! Money was a problem but I just managed to scrape up the fare for the fourth class passage from Haifa to Marseilles on the Felix Roussel, a beautiful ship which the Germans sank later on in the War.

Once on board I was shown to a bed in a vast hold already filled with a mass of humanity: men, women, hundreds of children packed together with all their many boxes, crates and sacks. The air was filled with smoke from pipes, cigarettes and goodness knows what else. There was constant noise and the whole scene was reminiscent of a souk transplanted on board our ship. I looked around, tried to breathe the non-existent air and then simply ran out on deck where I remained for the next two days and nights. Not surprisingly perhaps I became ill, which in a way was quite lucky for me. Having developed a cold, high temperature and a tummy bug I was put into the ship's hospital on the upper deck and isolated. Fate was kind to me, for I had fresh air, a clean bed, good nursing and delicious food. Then, when I had recovered, the nursing staff literally closed their eyes and allowed me to stay in this clean, orderly place for the rest of the voyage.

Another lucky coincidence contributed to the success of this memorable trip. I discovered that an old school friend of mine was also on board ship, only in glorified first class rather than my humble fourth. Her parents had sent her the ticket from Holland and now that I had recuperated she invited me to join her for tea in the first class lounge. Thanks to her I could also use their luxurious swimming pool, provided of course we went together.

As we approached Italy the ship was due to sail through the straits of Messina, just at a time when Mussolini decided to hold his naval exercises in the area. We were therefore forced to wait and so in the meanwhile anchored opposite Taormina, off Sicily. An armada of little ships came off shore to meet us, offering their wares and shouting greetings. To me the scene was sheer magic, with the Roman Amphitheatre as an outstanding picturesque backdrop.

Of course, Mussolini's exercises played havoc with our arrival time in Paris. My aunt and uncle, not knowing when to expect me, had left for the country with their small children to escape the heat of Paris, which in August can be unbearable, but had at least left the key to the apartment with the concierge. This was of no help to me when I arrived at the Gare de Lyon around midnight, for there was no-one to meet me. So here I was on my first visit to Paris quite alone and soon, considering the late hour, practically the only person left on the station. Frightened and miserable, I took a taxi to my uncle's address and quickly realised that we were driving through a poor and dingy district. There was no one about and the dark windows of even darker houses stared at me in a most unfriendly manner.

At last we stopped but there were no lights to be seen and I wondered what to do? The friendly taxi driver, however, who knew the customs of the country, merely pressed the concierge's bell and soon the door opened and the sleepy woman appeared. 'Oui bien sûr,' she said. 'M et Mme Strauch are expecting their niece and here is the key to the apartment.' I was saved, though not quite. The apartment I now entered was ghost-like, cold, stale and ever so empty. More to the point I was tired and hungry as I had not eaten all day. Perhaps I would find something in the kitchen, a crust of bread, a biscuit or a bit of sugar. Never had I seen a dwelling place with quite such bare shelves. There was just nothing at all. They had even taken the salt and pepper with them to their country place. I thought this a significant pointer to their financial circumstances.

I crawled into bed on an empty stomach but still managed to sleep well and only woke next morning to the sound of keys turning in the lock. It was my uncle who had returned with a fresh baguette and many regrets. After I had eaten he took me back to his little country place to be warmly welcomed by my aunt and her little children.

Soon after I was back in the City, in enchanting, intoxicating pre-war Paris. The wide boulevards, shaded by tall trees, often radiating from eye-catching viewpoints, convinced me that Mr Haussman, too, came next to God. I was overwhelmed by the stained glass windows of Notre Dame and particularly of those in the Sainte Chapelle, hidden away in the courtyard of the Palais de Justice. I 'discovered' Rodin and his statues which made me cry, as they touched an inner core within me hitherto unknown. As for the Quartier Latin, this was an enchanting new world; all those young and not so young people sitting at the pavement cafés seemingly without a care in the world. There were no thoughts of World War, Hitler, the Jewish refugees or Arab riots, only the gossip of the little bistros. One could sit here for many hours nursing a delicious coffee for a whole franc and help oneself to one or more of the mouth watering croissants, provided of course that the patron did not notice just how many. These wonderful baked delicacies brought back to life many of the taste buds which had so nearly died of neglect under the drab Palestinian cuisine.

None of these little cafés or bistros ever seemed to close. At night there was music and dancing everywhere, lots of laughter and red wine, all of which brings me back to the subject of food - French food. The markets to which I accompanied my aunt were a delight to the eye as well as to the nose. The smell of French cheeses nearly knocked me over and even today I still have a strong attachment to ripe Camembert. What makes French food so special, you may wonder, at least in those days before the invasion of American fast food ideas? Everything seemed to taste so pure, so specific; butter tasted buttery, bread had the smell of wheat or rye, potatoes tasted like spring or summer, whilst fruit carried a whiff of a benign summer, not too hot, just warm, bringing out its very own flavour. But 'Der Mensch Lebt Nicht von Brot Allein' (man does not live by bread alone) and I for one grabbed all that Paris had to offer that was going free.

There were the parks, the Place du Theâtre and its many artists, the delightful Jeu de Paume with its magnificent impressionists and of course the Louvre, which actually disappointed me greatly. In those days the Louvre for me meant Da Vinci's Mona Lisa and there she was in the red-clad overstuffed room, the lady with a mysterious smile surrounded by all the other paintings, next to her, on top of her, even below her, all overshadowing her completely. Poor Madonna, she deserved a better fate I thought. Still the statue of the Winged Victory made a very deep impression. There she stood at the head of those magnificent stairs ready to take off through the roof and soaring high - into what I wonder? I only wished I knew. Many years later my then son-in-law made a similar although abstract sculpture. I call it my Winged Victory.

I fell in love with the City and also with a beautiful, gifted, impoverished and sick student. I was quite prepared to throw my lot in with his, but was saved by the wisdom of my aunt and uncle. They dragged me to their house doctor who explained that a man suffering from diabetes at such a young age would in all probability never be able to have children. I still have his beautiful poems.

Not long after, in November 1937, I left for South Africa to stay with my sister, a polio victim who was expecting her first child. I was reluctant to leave Paris at first, but a handkerchief decided my fate (which is another story in itself) and so I made my way south, sailing from Marseilles for Cape Town on December 4th. I stayed in that lovely city for the next twenty-four years, in time marrying Walter, a fellow refugee from Berlin and a past member of our Youth Movement. We had two children, Tamara and Judy. The beauty of the country, however, was becoming soured for us by the harshness of the politicians. Apartheid was an oppressive law with which all white people were expected to conform. However, Walter and I felt that as refugees from a dictatorship which had enacted such cruel laws against the Jews we could hardly behave in similar fashion to other ethnic groups. It troubled our consciences. The Sharpeville massacre in March 1960 settled matters for us. We packed up our home and came to England, where we settled permanently in London.

Often in quiet moments I still wonder where I would have ended had I stayed in Paris and not heeded my sister's call.

36   JERZY LANDO

I was born near Lodz, Poland in 1922. I was born in Polugniowl
Street. I had a brother, Michael, who was four years older than me.
My father's name was Yakov Hirsch and my mother's name was
Gustawa. My parents go a long way back in Poland - my mother's
family goes back to the late 1700s. My father was a textile
manufacturer.

I went to school in Lodz. I started school at six years old. A
teacher came to my house for my Jewish education and I had a little
religious education at school. I had no problems with the Christian
children at that time. I was barmitzvah at thirteen. Near the school I
had a job translating into Polish, which was called the School of the
Society of Merchants of Lodz. This was a grammar school. I remained
at the gymnasium until war broke out in 1939. I wrote a book that was
published about those years.

When I was growing up I was aware of what was going on in
Germany. Things were particularly bad in 1938/39 when Germany was
demanding large chunks of Polish territory. My mother used to visit
Vienna and witnessed several bad incidents. My parents and I tried to
get out of Lodz. Before the war my brother was studying in Manchester
but unfortunately came back to Lodz just as the war broke out. He
stayed for three weeks and then decided to try and get back to England,
which he did, although I don't know how he managed to do this. He
went through the German and Russian lines. My mother, father and
myself got into the car and tried to escape to Rumania, but we had to go
back to Lodz. This was in 1939 when Lodz became part of Germany.
When we lived in Lodz during the war we found the German officers
quite friendly and used to talk to them.

At that time the Germans started expelling lawyers and
industrialists from Lodz. We found ourselves in a transport going out
of Lodz, through Krakow. We were lucky as my father had some
customers in Krakow and we stayed there until May 1940. When we

were expelled to Krakow, we spent the night in a concentration camp and a German soldier pulled me out as I was wearing a Star of David and looked like a Christian. Then the Germans forced all the Jews out of Krakow so we decided to go to Warsaw.

By September 1940 we were forced into the area that was the Ghetto. We lived in the Warsaw Ghetto through the first two months of occupation until September 1942. Before the war my father was wealthy. He had jewellery, which we could sell for food. My father also had money which he repaid people after the war. During the last year in the Ghetto my father set up a partnership with a Gentile acquaintance and they made leather goods. Therefore materially our family was never short of money.

During the first months of the occupation of the Warsaw Ghetto more than 300,000 people out of the 400,000 who lived there were shipped to Treblinka gas chambers. Therefore there were about 80,000 survivors. I was in the Ghetto for two years and left in August 1944. I was the first of the three of us to escape from the Ghetto. I was then nineteen.

First of all I went to Krakow and tried to find some people to help me. However this was difficult and I finally found myself living in Warsaw as a Christian because of my Christian appearance. I found a Gentile to employ me, even though he knew I was Jewish. My father also lived in Warsaw, but never ventured out into the street. My mother ventured outside with her sister.

I joined the Polish Underground in June 1944. When the Polish riots started in August 1944 I joined the Polish Resistance and led a small group of people. I was wounded. I found my father in hospital as he had also been wounded. Two months after the Polish uprising the situation became hopeless; most of the city was destroyed, several hundred thousand people were killed. The Germans treated us not as partisans but as prisoners of war. I was then marched with other Polish ex-soldiers into general captivity and I stayed in Lanz, one of the larger prisoner-of-war camps, until December 1944 when the Russians shipped us to another camp in Bremen, northern Germany. We were liberated in April by the British.

In the meantime my father found himself in hospital outside the Ghetto. My mother had escaped with her sister and they lived with some Christian peasants and managed to get away after three months. My father was still very ill. About a week before the war ended in Poland my mother came to visit him and was told that the German police had come to take away my father's belongings.

In 1944 I lived in Warsaw and worked for a company that specialised in metals. We used to get wagonloads of clothes from people in concentration camps and when they had been sorted they were recycled and shipped to Germany. It was my job to prepare a monthly report. I became quite friendly with a German official who did not know I was Jewish. I asked him to write a certificate to say how important I was to the German war effort, which he did. I showed this to my boss and he asked if he would do the same for his two sons, which the German official did.

After I was liberated I couldn't go back to Poland as I had belonged to the Polish underground. I was considered the enemy of commoners and if we went back we would be transported to Siberia. I went to Germany and for a few months, until April 1946, I was an interpreter. At that time my mother who was in Lodz said it was safe, but I did not like it there. My brother died in June 1946. In July 1946 my mother and I then got permission to go to London for compassionate reasons.

I first of all went to Salford where my brother had studied before the war and got a diploma. I lived in Manchester and started working there. My father's family who were in the textile industry and lived in Brazil asked us to emigrate there. We went to the consulate in Liverpool but were advised to go to the consulate in Paris, which my mother and I did. We bought a one-way ticket to Paris and the next day we went to the consulate. When we said we were Jewish we were told it was not possible to go to Brazil. However we managed to find in the telephone directory my mother's boyfriend when she was eighteen. We contacted him and he remembered my mother. A half an hour later there was a big car with a chauffeur outside our hotel and we were taken to his chateau. My mother's old boyfriend took us to the Home Office and we had a year's permission to stay. He gave me a job in his textile factory and said he was going to make me a manager of his factory in the South of France.

However in 1950 I met an English girl called Angela who became my wife six months later. We got married at a United Synagogue in the West End and the reception was at the Porchester Hall.

I then went to Manchester to work for a textile company as a manager. My father-in-law suggested I should work for myself and he lent me some money to start my own textile business. I started this from nothing and by 1972 I employed about 150 people. I had a factory in Leicester where I employed 100 people and a very large warehouse in London.

After Angela and I married we lived in Southgate and then I built a house in Cockfosters. I had two daughters from this marriage. Karen was born in 1951 and Jeanette in 1953. In 1970 my marriage was on the rocks. We separated and started thinking about a divorce.

Soon after this I met Iris, the lady who was to become my second wife. She came from Berlin and was Christian but converted to Judaism and we then got married. I have a daughter, Nicola, from my second marriage. She went to North London Collegiate School and is now studying engineering at Cambridge. We first lived in Northwood, where we belonged to the Liberal Synagogue and then we moved to our present house in January 1988. When we first moved here we belonged to the West London Synagogue and in 1981 we joined Alyth. However I have not been very involved in Alyth.

In late 1970 the textile business became extremely difficult. I found that I was losing money and gradually started moving out of it. I realised that I had to do something else. I was fifty-four years old when I started learning computing. I started out in software in my own business, specialising in writing software for the textile industry. I built up quite a big business, one in Margaret Street and one in Nottingham. My company was called Cambridge Data. In 1987 I sold the business to a public company and became a computer consultant under the Department of Trade and worked from home. I was on a subsidised scheme assisting companies in computerisation. I became a member of the Computer Society. Then somebody passed my name to the British Know-how Fund, which was subsidising consultants behind the Iron Curtain at the end of the Cold War. I then got a number of assignments going back to where I started with Polish companies. This involved me travelling to Poland for four years, staying a week at a time. However, four years ago I found the travelling too much and then concentrated on doing work for SAGE.

In the meantime I have put together a manuscript of my biography. I had to learn to write properly. When I was semi-retired I took a course in creative writing at the Hampstead Institute, and within a year I completely re-wrote the manuscript. The London Jewish Cultural Centre published it.

37   HAROLD LANGDON

I was born on 22nd April 1916 and, according to my birth certificate, in Bromley by Bow. My father's name was Abraham and my mother's was Selina. My mother's single name was Glassman. They were both born in England. I think my mother's parents were from Poland but I don't know where my father's parents were born. I knew my paternal grandfather very vaguely because when I was very young we would go to his home on Seder nights. I can also remember my maternal grandmother and we would go to Hendon Synagogue together.

A year or two after I was born we moved to New Street, which was a small turning opposite (what was) the New Theatre, which is now the Albery Theatre in St. Martin's Lane. Our house had three floors; my parents had the drapery shop on the ground floor and I was in the top room. We had a housekeeper who looked after my sister and me. When we lived in New Street I went to a primary school called St. Martin in the Fields, down the bottom of St. Martin's Lane.

My sister Ruth was four years older than me. She was very active in the synagogue and Russian Jewry and was one of the first to go to Russia. Ruth died thirteen years ago.

When I was about nine my parents gave up the drapery shop and my mother opened a millinery shop in New Street. My father went into garment manufacture. We moved to Bristol House, a block of flats in Southampton Row, and my ambition then was to be a lift man as we were not allowed to use the lift all the time. I went to a school in Bloomsbury where I was extremely unhappy, so I went back to St. Martin in the Fields. After St. Martin's I won a foundation scholarship given by Westminster City School and my fees were paid. This was a grammar school although I think of it as a minor public school. I matriculated at sixteen, which was like '0' levels, and then took my 'A' levels in Economics, History and Geography. I stayed there until I was eighteen.

When I was eleven or twelve we moved to Golders Green and have lived there ever since. I continued to travel to Westminster City School. I went to Hebrew classes at the Western Synagogue in Alfred Place and was in Hebrew classes with the two daughters of Reverend Livingstone, who also taught me my barmitzvah at his house. (Many years later Reverend Livingstone proposed me as a member of Hendon Rotary Club to which he belonged.) I used to go to Hendon Synagogue. I often used to find the tenth man for the minyan, which would not happen today as it is a very big synagogue.

After leaving school I went to The London School of Economics for three years from 1934-1937. In the first year I did not do very much and took the intermediate exams. I became very good at table tennis, became secretary of the banking society and a member of the Israel Society. I took a banking and accountancy degree for which I got honours. I came across Rockefeller at LSE and also Harold Laski and Lionel Robins. I was very active in deputations to parliament and in the India League.

When I graduated in 1937 the situation economically was not good. Technically I was equipped to go into one of the banks. However I didn't get any replies to the applications I sent in. On the application form you had to state your religion, so this did not help me. My first job was in a market research company - a well-known advertising firm. I did not stay there very long. I applied to go on the Marks & Spencer graduate scheme. I had a letter back telling me to go to four or five stores and write about them. I did this and got a second interview. In the meantime, I got a job with Petmar Mitchell, accountants. I was secretary of the trade association of construction engineers based in Westminster, just by St. James's Park Station.

It was now 1939 and the situation was such that I felt I had to do something, so I joined the Territorial Army - 75th Middlesex in the Royal Artillery. My sister arranged this as she worked for MGM. I was mainly with people who worked in the studios. We used enormous speakers, which were searchlights, and we followed the aeroplanes. We were in Purfleet Marshes in detachments of four or five people with a phone and hut. We had a rifle and were waiting for the Germans to come down in parachutes.

Before the war I lived in Golders Manor Drive, Golders Green. My mother died of cancer at the end of 1938 at the age of fifty. My father carried on his business at the garment factory. He built up his business and at one time made army uniforms. During the war he lived in St. James Mansions, a ground floor flat in a big old-fashioned block in West End Lane. All the neighbours came to our flat when there were air raids.

I was called up on 24th August 1939, before war was declared on 3rd September 1939. During the war my sister was evacuated to Leeds with her company who were carpet manufacturers, as they were bombed out in the City. I used to travel to Leeds to see my sister and that is where I met my wife, Esther Cramer. We were married in Leeds in 1943. After we were married my wife came to London and worked as a civilian in the War Office, just off Whitehall.

I basically spent the war in the British Isles and I was a sergeant. I had been on the guns during the blitz at Primrose Hill, Gunnersbury Park and Finsbury Park. I didn't mind the guns - they were more of a morale booster than anything. Incidentally, I am still in contact with my old CO who retired as a colonel. He is ninety-one now and has celebrated his diamond wedding. I got on very well with my fellow soldiers, particularly with the girls. The early part of the war during the blitz was pretty grim but otherwise okay. Towards the end of the war I was transferred to the educational force and visited sites.

In 1945 at the end of the war, we moved from St. James Mansions to Hoop Lane. My father came with us but then he remarried and he lived in Edgware.

At this time I became quite disillusioned with my synagogue and somebody suggested I go and see Dr. Ramsen who was the rabbi of Alyth. He told me to come along to a few services and I felt very much at home. I became one of three wardens. During the war there was a Mr. A L Kaye who was a German refugee and ran the services.

After the war I went into the administration side of my father's business. I was also on the council and executive at the synagogue and became chairman in 1960. I then went on the RSGB committee and in 1964 I became honorary secretary for three years. During that time we took on a general secretary, as we didn't have one.

I was still working with my father. In 1954 my daughter Selina was born and she went to Channing School. She is now a doctor, married and has two daughters. My wife worked part-time in my father's business. When my father retired I carried on the business for a while, but didn't like it. I eventually sold the business to a property company.

About this time RSGB was expanding and was very influential. Many of its members were very active in communal work and it was felt we should have a greater voice nationally. A committee was set up on relationships within Anglo-Jewry. Albert Friedlander is the joint-president with the Archbishop, a moderator and the current Chief Rabbi of the United Hebrew congregations.

I spent time helping the Board to recognise our rabbis as an ecclesiastical authority. This led to a great deal of work involving Rabbi Sidney Brichto and there were many negotiations which eventually succeeded at the end of 1971. We also established an advisory committee of the Chief Rabbi, which met in the home of Rabbi Jakobovits and dealt with issues concerning the Council of Christians and Jews.

I joined the Board of Deputies in 1970 after I resigned as chairman of RSGB. I was elected to the executive in 1974. I was re-elected each term and then resigned in 1991. Even in the early days we made an impression. When the United Synagogue had its 100 years celebration in a hotel where the Queen and Prince Philip attended, this was only on condition that all sections of the Jewish community were invited, although it was a United Synagogue function. The President of the Board presented us to the Queen by name and said, 'We like to feel we are free-thinkers of our religion.'

173

Another time I was at a reception at St. James's Palace and again I was presented to the Queen with three other people. I was also presented to Prince Charles and the late Princess of Wales at Hampton Court.

From the beginning I was also involved in the Leo Baeck College. We allowed members from the Liberal movement to join. I was on the Council from its inception and became Chairman from 1975-1978. I am still a life governor of the College.

As far as Israel is concerned I was a member of the Zionist Federation in 1967 when I was chairman. I have been to Israel several times. My sister organised the RSGB trips to Israel with the Board when we had the Iraq business. I went with a deputation from the Board to Eilat to show that it was safe to go and to encourage other people to go. I also talked to the Israelis who still didn't think we were doing enough.

I have now handed over the reins to others. I have enjoyed my involvement in the community. I hope that in a very, very small way I have been able to contribute towards a positive and revitalised Jewish life.

38   PROFESSOR LEDERMANN

I come from Berlin where I was born in 1911, son of parents also born in that city. Likewise too I believe my maternal grandfather was born there, in contrast to my father's family who came from the eastern part of the country. As for my paternal grandfather, Jakob Lederman, he was originally an elementary school teacher in a part of Germany that was later taken over by Poland after the First World War. Most of the children at the school spoke Polish even then and my grandfather was necessarily fluent in both languages, amongst others. Later he gave up his post and came to Berlin in 1865, where he worked in a secretarial capacity for a Jewish banker by the name of Bleichroeder, who was himself personal banker to Bismark. He earned his secretarial title by virtue of being able to write shorthand, which was quite a novel idea then.

Apart from Jakob's secretarial work however, he was also used as a courier, once apparently even being sent on a secret spying mission. I say that because he is actually mentioned in a book published by an American historian wherein the author states that he was a secret agent working on behalf of Bleichroeder and therefore also for Bismarck himself. In addition Jakob was a linguist with a working knowledge of many languages, including English. Perhaps for this reason he was sent to England at one stage, though for what reason I am not certain. Quite possibly it may have had something to do with the opening of the Suez Canal in 1870. As you no doubt know, the waterway was constructed by France, which did not suit the British who were very anxious to gain overall control. This was still possible by the acquisition of a sufficient number of shares, and though these were available it was apparently an awkward moment for the purchase. Nevertheless the money for it had still to be made available to the British Government at very short notice. In the end most of the finance came from Jewish Bankers, Rothschild in particular. To facilitate the transaction, it is quite possible that my grandfather was sent to

England to persuade Lord Rothschild to make this money available. The end result was that Britain was able to acquire 51% of the shares, in this way gaining majority control of the Suez Canal.

This had been my grandfather's one and only trip to England and he was enchanted. He said afterwards to my grandmother, who was then about to give birth to my father, that 'we should really live in England - it is a country where you will be respected, where there is freedom for the Jews and no persecution'.

Oddly enough, my own father had a very English sounding first name, William. I believe that herein lies the reason for my father's first name. In his enthusiasm for all things English, Jakob called his newborn son William - not Willie or Wilhelm you understand, but William. In a way it was all rather odd, especially as he could speak little English himself, but when he eventually came to live in this country many thought that he was at least partly British in view of the name.

My father was a general practitioner, living and working in a very poor district in the eastern part of the city, looking after patients who were too poor even to pay for their own health insurance and therefore in receipt of government support. Though a pauper's doctor, he was nevertheless popular and happy in his work. Everyone knew him when he was out on the street, well-wishers doffing their hats and greeting him with a cheery "Good morning doctor!"

I was the second of four children, having an older brother and two younger sisters. We all grew up in Berlin where we lived on the first floor of a corner house, in a very large apartment of some eight or nine rooms divided into a medical practice on one side and living quarters on the other.

My mother Charlotte, William's wife, came from a very different background. Her family were very assimilated, with no interest in Judaism whatsoever. The family name was Apt and her father's first name Sigismund, all very Germanic and sounding like something out of a Wagnerian Opera. It was typical of many German Jews then, all falling over backwards to become purer German than the Germans. Even my own first name is very Germanic. Be that as it may, Charlotte was proud to be Jewish though hardly ever going to Synagogue, whereas my father, who had been brought up in an Orthodox fashion, still said his prayers and went to synagogue on High Holydays.

My childhood was reasonably happy apart from my health. I was asthmatic from quite early on and rather a sickly child. For instance, when I was nine years old, I remember being taken out of school for an entire term because of my physical disability.

In August 1914 my younger sister was born. I was just three years and my older brother six years old. We remained in Berlin throughout the course of the war, except for my father who was called up halfway through to become a medical officer in the German army. Given the rank of Captain he was sent to the Front in France where he cared for the sick and wounded of both sides helped along by his reasonable knowledge of French as well as his own mother language. Perhaps it was the stress of the war but my father's health eventually began to deteriorate, in the course of which he developed an illness of some kind that left him in poor physical shape in the post-war years, although he did at least live for many more years.

Life for our family was hard during those war years. There was hunger and deprivation and I still had my asthma. To help me recover I was sent away from Berlin for three months towards the end of the war to a farm where I could enjoy better food and breathe the fresh country air.

To this day I still remember at least part of the war; the defeat of the Russians in the East and their great revolution; also the fact that much the same kind of thing nearly happened in Germany, only in this case it was suppressed by the army. Still, it was not exactly the best of times to be walking along the streets to school. Often we had to hide in nearby houses when fighting suddenly erupted between the revolutionaries and the army and machine guns began to fire all about us

However, once in school I did at least have an easier time of it, that is apart from my asthma. Otherwise I learnt very quickly, especially mathematics. I found I had a particular aptitude for the subject from my first lesson. In later years this became my chosen profession.

My particular school in Berlin was the Leibniz Gymnasium (or Grammar School), named after the famous German philosopher Gottfried Wilhelm Leibniz. It was for boys only, four hundred strong, with the emphasis on Latin, and the total exclusion of all women. Certainly I never saw one anywhere near the place. I studied Latin for nine years at the Gymnasium and towards the end of that time could read it almost as fluently as my native German. I remember once the Headmaster coming to take our class when our own form teacher was off sick. He spoke to us throughout in Latin, choosing as his subject various fables, all of which I found I was perfectly able to understand.

Classical Greek was another subject on our timetable, spread over a six-year course. Here too I found that at the end of that time I was sufficiently knowledgeable in the language that I was able to read quite easily the wonderful literature of that era. On the other hand we learnt very much less French, and English hardly at all, just two hours a week for two years. Alternatively, we could have spent that time on Hebrew of all things, which I found rather odd. I learnt later that there was a valid reason for this and it concerned the Lutheran Church. Candidates for ordination were required to be highly educated in certain subjects such as Hebrew and Greek in order to be able to read the Old and New Testaments in the original script. Speaking for myself I opted for English, just so that I could at least read it after a fashion, basically all I could manage.

Anti-Semitism was rampant in the decades both before and after the First World War. Innocent people were often assaulted in the street, insults commonly hurled about as well as many instances of young boys refusing to play with Jewish kids. Perhaps I was more fortunate than most in this respect since I hardly ever encountered any such problems at school. This may have been due to the fact that there were so few of us Jewish boys, only about three in my class of eighteen. In fact I even enjoyed a measure of popularity, being a rather small boy who presumably needed looking after. This was made clear to me one day at school when a lad from another class collared me in the playground and started to become offensive and physically abusive. I was only saved when another boy, huge in stature and non-Jewish like my tormentor, intervened and beat him up in turn.

Despite the general anti-Semitism my school nevertheless had two or three Jewish teachers on the staff prior to the coming to power of the Nazis, one of them our own Latin master. However, none of us, teachers and pupils alike, had any illusions about the future for the Jews in Germany. I had read the hateful Nazi literature and, unlike my father, was convinced that Hitler would not simply go away but come and do as he had threatened. The man may well have got some of his perverted ideas from Martin Luther, the great reformer of five hundred years ago. In one of his pamphlets Luther had already advocated the Holocaust, saying that Jews should all be locked up in their synagogues and then set on fire. Certainly I did not feel safe in Germany and neither did my two young sisters who soon turned to Zionism, joining the Zionist Youth Movement, learning Hebrew and later migrating to Palestine where they married and had families.

I found University was not much better than anywhere else so far as anti-Semitism was concerned. It did not affect me too much personally and I was able to apply myself to work. One memorable day I even had the privilege of attending a lecture given by the great Einstein himself. Even so it was almost impossible for a Jewish academic, no matter how distinguished he was in his field, to be given a full professorship, although an exception was occasionally made for someone who had converted to Christianity. Quite surprisingly therefore, one of my mathematics professors, Issai Schur, a great Jewish scholar, stayed true to his religion and in consequence later suffered terribly. The same discrimination of course also applied to medicine. In my university in Berlin not one of the many distinguished doctors was ever offered a Chair. It was simply not done and not only in Germany. Switzerland too had its little foibles.

My wife-to-be's father, Franz Stadler, was an academic, an Associate Professor of the History of Art at Zurich University, a post incidentally that involved him in commuting between the University in Switzerland and his home in Munich on a regular basis. Time and again the Swiss Minister of Education, whom he knew personally, together with some others of like mind, would propose Franz for a full Chair in Zurich, only to see it blocked by the Senate, which objected to his religion. Under these circumstances, therefore, the advent of Hitler as Chancellor of Germany early in 1933 came as no surprise to us.

It was fortunate that I had by then all but completed my studies at the university, a circumstance due mainly to the fact that I had done sufficiently well at school for the authorities to allow me to take the German equivalent of present day 'A' levels six months early. This was a lifesaver for me since I could now attend university at the age of just seventeen and thus get most of my qualifications shortly before Hitler came to power. I was actually in my finals at the time but nevertheless decided to leave Germany immediately. My brother, who had earlier qualified in medicine, had already left for England in 1933, courtesy of one of my father's patients, a Banker with overseas funds who offered finance to help get him over. Alas however, when it was my time to leave, no such funds were available, the Nazis by then having put a stop to all such transactions.

Nevertheless, luck did not desert me and it was all due to my brother. One day whilst in Edinburgh my brother heard by chance that the University of St. Andrews were about to institute two scholarships for refugees in danger of persecution either for their professional or political affiliations, one intended for a Jewish refugee and one for a non-Jew, the bursaries to be administered by the International Student Service in Switzerland. Of course I applied at once and thankfully was successful. I arrived in St. Andrews shortly thereafter, in January 1934, the only Jew there so far as I knew. A few days later I was joined by the other successful applicant, a man who had been associated with the Social Democrat party in Germany.

Although my brother and I had now left Germany, my father still seemed unable to believe what was coming and had no wish to leave the country. For a long while he remained ever the optimist, always maintaining that Germany would get another government soon.

'This man Hitler' he used to say 'won't last forever'. Alas for his naivety. My mother on the other hand saw only too clearly what was going to happen. When in 1938 the opportunity arose to leave, she acted accordingly. Funnily enough it was my father who provided the catalyst. He had been knocked down in the street by a car one day, suffered broken legs and taken to hospital. Away from her husband's influence on the household my mother then simply packed everything up. It was a fait accompli. When all was ready, she took my father out of hospital, the two of them then making their way to England, my father tottering about on crutches - literally a 'broken' man.

Two years earlier, prior to my parent's arrival, I had already gained my Ph.D at St. Andrews and thereafter held a series of posts in Scotland and England, as well as doing a brief spell in Edinburgh pursuing some postgraduate studies. Of course, my academic appointments in this country were all in mathematics. I was successively assistant lecturer, then lecturer at St. Andrews, lecturer and senior lecturer at Manchester University where I remained for sixteen years, then finally first Reader, then Professor of Mathematics at Sussex University, a period that spanned four decades from 1938 to 1978.

In 1940, while still at St. Andrews, I became a British subject and together with my brother was also now better able to care for our parents. (At one stage during the war, when it became possible, we took over part of a house for them in Muswell Hill, north London, not far from where I live now.) At the same time I became friendly with the Professor of Astronomy at St. Andrews, a man much older than myself who could so easily have been my father. We had a lot in common, the link between astronomy and mathematics being very close; and also his wife was Jewish. His mother was a Scottish lady, originally a Finlay and his father a German national by the name of Freundlich. Prior to Hitler, he and his wife had lived and worked in both Germany and Czechoslovakia. Professor Freundlich had been an active collaborator in the past with Albert Einstein, the same great person whose lecture I had attended in my university in Berlin some years before.

Professor Freundlich was hospitable to a degree and I was in and out of his house in St. Andrews throughout the war. I was still quite young then and unmarried. Not until peace was declared in 1945 did my mentor emerge from his study one day to pronounce on a subject that he had never before mentioned - my marital status. 'Look here Ledermann' he said to me, (we were rather formal!) 'You ought to get married now that the war is finished'. What could I say to that? Only that 'You are right Professor Freundlich, but it takes two to get married.' It was then that I was informed that he happened to know just the right person for me, a girl called Rushi, a young lady born in Munich of a German mother and an Austro-Hungarian father, both of them Jewish. The Professor had met Rushi one time whilst in Czechoslovakia and had been suitably impressed. Now he concocted a way in which we could both innocently meet.

I happened to be visiting my parents in Muswell Hill soon after when Rushi Stadler appeared at the door one day bearing the draft of a scientific paper that the Professor and I had previously been working on together. He wanted my opinion, though whether on the paper or on Rushi was perhaps a moot point. Whatever the reason, Rushi and I were married the following year in Epsom in the house of some of her Czech relatives; good business people who had been in the wool trade before the war and had managed to bring much of their wealth out of the country with them. With the money they had bought this lovely place in Surrey.

Long before the war, Rushi's parents had left Germany for Switzerland and had lived there for many years, her father a Professor of Art in Zurich University who in his earlier years lived in Munich and commuted regularly to and from Zurich before fleeing the Nazis. The uncertainties of post-war travel unfortunately prevented them from attending the wedding, though one sister did manage to come from Paris.

We had the civil wedding in the local registry office then, since we knew of no synagogue in Epsom, and had a religious ceremony in the house, performed by a German- speaking rabbi.

When we first met, Rushi was already a trained psychiatric social worker working in a child guidance clinic. However, with little opportunities for her in St. Andrews we decided that there would be more scope working in a big city, so we moved to Manchester where I took up the position of lecturer in mathematics, later becoming senior lecturer. Rushi for her part continued in practice as a social worker, later being promoted to train others in her chosen field. It was also during our time in Manchester that our only child Jonathan was born.

As the years passed, Rushi became eager to branch out of social work and to train as an analytical psychologist. This was only possible in London, so we decided to move south. I liked Manchester. We had many friends there and the atmosphere was stimulating, but I felt that my wife's professional career was as important as my own. We ended up in Sussex, in Hove, and on our exploration of the countryside were intrigued to find builders hard at work, digging up a part of the lovely Sussex Downs, a restricted area for such activities if ever there was one. This particular work though did at least have official sanction, for it transpired that here was to be the site of the new Sussex University. I immediately applied for a position in the mathematics department and happily was accepted, thus becoming one the five founder members of the university, in 1965 being awarded Chair of Mathematics.

We stayed in Sussex for thirty-five years. When I retired three years ago we went to live near our son in Highgate. Jonathan too is a doctor, like so many of our family, and is presently Reader in Medical Oncology at University College Hospital as well as consultant in oncology to the Whittington and Royal Free Hospitals. Sarah, his wife, is also a doctor, a paediatrician at Great Ormond Street, specialising in renal disease. They have four children.

Rushi stopped working at the age of eighty, but my brother still practices at the age of ninety-two, whilst I still give the occasional lecture in Sussex, in my beloved university there. Considering the past, I dislike going to Germany and Austria and try to keep away. An exception once was an International Congress of Mathematicians in Berlin in 1998. Somewhat to my surprise Rushi and I were officially invited, with all expenses paid. It was an interesting experience with a great deal of hospitality, but we were still not happy there and would both much rather go to Switzerland instead, where the German language does not hold the same feeling of menace for us as it does in Germany or Austria. Much happier still are our trips to Israel, to the families of my late sisters. How much different life might have been, I sometimes wonder, if only Israel had existed in the 1930s.

39　　　　　　LUDWIG LEVY

I was born seventy-five years ago in December 1924, in Berlin. It has been said that I was a beautiful baby though I have changed a bit since then. My father was by profession a lawyer, and looking back on my early childhood I realise that ours was a reasonably secure and comfortable lifestyle. My mother sadly died of cancer when I was nine years old. This was in the early years of the Hitler regime and I still remember when my father was called to my school to be told in no uncertain terms to remove his son because no Jewish children would be allowed there in future.

In 1936 my father decided that my sister and I should go and live with his sister's family, who had already emigrated earlier to Spain and were living in Barcelona. Unfortunately, soon after our arrival the Spanish Civil war broke out, and I well remember the fighting in the streets at the time. My uncle consequently decided to leave Spain. I ended up in a boarding school for German Jewish refugee children near Merano in the so-called 'South Tyrol', which is a mainly German speaking part of northern Italy, having been part of Austria before World War I.

The Italian authorities decided to close the school in late 1938 and my father, who was then still living in Berlin, came to visit me at that time. During his stay the Kristallnacht took place in Germany when several Synagogues were burnt down and many Jews arrested. I recall when he telephoned a friend at home who warned him that on no account should he return to Germany. My father was consequently stranded in Italy having left behind all his worldly possessions. He eventually managed to obtain a visa for Ecuador in South America where he spent the war years. At that time he was frantically trying to get an immigration visa for me to come to England.

I finally obtained a permit to live in England in February 1939, through the kindness of a Christian gentleman and his sister, who were ready to help in providing me with a home and education. I was fourteen at the time and, as we were living in a little village near Cambridge, I attended school in that city. I recall that each Saturday morning were religious lessons, and all the Jewish boys were excused, but only on condition that they attended the Shabbat synagogue service. The only way I could get there was by bicycle from my home five miles away in the country. The first morning I left my bike near the synagogue entrance, much to the horror of the other boys who all lived locally within walking distance. Following this I parked it around the corner, and everybody seemed happy after that.

After leaving school I moved to London in order to make my own way for the first time. I shared a room with five other Jewish refugee youths in a cheap boarding house. I took various temporary jobs such as washing plates at Lyons Corner House, working as a junior hotel porter, etc., before learning welding in a Government Training Centre. This meant I could now do essential war work.

During this period my friends took me along to a Club for Jewish refugees called The Austrian Centre, where I asked a beautiful young girl, who subsequently became my wife, to dance. We are still together after having been happily married for fifty-five years. Incidentally, the ceremony took place at Alyth Gardens Synagogue - where else? She had come previously from Nuremberg on one of the Kindertransports, but that is another story.

When the war ended, I wanted to learn a trade and became an apprentice to a furrier who also made stuffed toys as a sideline. It had always been my ambition to have my own business. When this firm suddenly folded I took the plunge and, after offering to supply his former customers, spent most of my life's savings on buying an industrial sewing machine. While my wife still kept her job in the garment trade, I achieved my dream with a staff of one part time machinist and a couple of home workers. Soon my wife joined the firm and there followed a long stressful struggle of building the business. But there were also many happy moments.

We have now been retired for several years. Fifty-three years have gone by since those early days and, as our business grew, so did our standard of living, changing from one furnished room to two, and from a small flat to our little bungalow. Compared with today those were indeed hard times, but they never seemed so then. This was an exciting period in our lives and served to make us appreciate more fully the comforts we take for granted these days. I shall always feel grateful to the people of this country for having given me a refuge when I needed it and the chance to make my life here – also to my dear wife for having put up with me all these years.

40
SYLVIA LEWIN
JOTTINGS FROM A LIFETIME

I am having an interesting, fulfilling, wonderful life.

Having been born in South Africa, I soon realised that all was not well in the social mores of my country. At the age of ten I went into a shop and was amazed to be served first, before two waiting African black people. As I grew up we joined the Progressive Party in a small effort to correct the wrongs being perpetrated. Maybe it was the coward's choice, but once I had completed my studies at the University of Witwatersrand, Johannesburg, gaining a BA Honours degree in Speech and Language Therapy, I emigrated to London. I returned only once in 1971 when things were as grim as ever for the non-White population. I was lucky that my parents realised that both their daughters would leave the homeland. I had emigrated a year earlier and had a lovely flat and home waiting for me.

I joined B'nai B'rith, which appealed to me as much for its cultural and social programmes as for its welfare activities. I quickly made friends and became Secretary of the Lodge and began to feel very much at home in the company of British Jewish compatriots. B'nai B'rith has given me so much and I have given B'nai B'rith much of my free time, thought and care. It yielded me a wonderful husband, David, who I met there and married in 1966. I worked actively at all levels and in 1982 I was elected as National President of B'nai B'rith in Great Britain and Ireland. Those six years proved to be a most amazing challenge and gave me enormous confidence in public speaking, organisation and creation of new projects. In my time as President, B'nai B'rith's membership grew; we created an Employment Service which later became the B'nai B'rith Jobs Club; we set up the by now enormously successful Jewish Music Festival, which has recently graduated to become a Jewish Music Institute at the School for Oriental and African Studies (SOAS). Through B'nai B'rith David and I made friends all over the world and our home has always been open to people from everywhere who felt comfortable when staying with us or coming for a meal.

My voluntary work has been fulfilling and rewarding. Fortunately my paid work has been varied and interesting as well. I have worked as a speech therapist at Akiva School since its inception twenty years ago. I had been David's secretary when he created his own cable business. I did the testing for a career advisory service. I ran job clubs for the Employment Service, helping long-term unemployed people to reassess their situation, become more motivated, and regain their self-esteem and their jobs. David and I also ran a business employing fifteen people who also ran various Employment Service programmes on behalf of our company.

Four years ago I took a post-graduate diploma course in special needs teaching and have enjoyed the past years particularly as a combined speech language and dyslexia therapist.

The highlight of my life? My three children – Danielle, Karen and Michael. Danielle, a special needs co-ordinator, now lives with her doctor husband, Daniel, in Sheffield. Karen, a music therapist, lives with her computing husband, Dean, in Reading and Michael is studying Mathematics at Queens College, Cambridge. They are my pride and joy, my best friends, and my hope for the future. They are aware of the need to be considerate of others, to give everyone a fair chance, to help those who are not as fortunate as they are, and to be open-minded. Basically we are so lucky that our children have taken on all the mores which we held so dear.

41
BERTIE MANN
WARTIME EXPERIENCES

O ne of my earliest experiences in the Army was a wild, anti-Semitic diatribe, so brutal and bitter, that I asked to be excused and left the Mess for my bedroom. Ten minutes later the Adjutant arrived with an apology from the Commanding Officer for his appalling verbal conduct, inviting me to return to the Mess. The C.O. had relented a little and, somewhat reluctantly, realised that he had overstepped 'reasonable bounds' by taking advantage of his superior rank and age. One reflected that this senior officer's conduct was no better than that encountered in Germany or Austria at the hands of the Nazis, and here we were engaged in a life and death struggle against Fascism and anti-Semitism. We nursed the illusion that as English, Scots or Welshmen we were every bit as good as our non-Jewish peer group, but at the first test of the strength of this assumption we found we had been living in a world of make-believe. War or no war, we remained second-class citizens.

I can well recall 'swanning' around Europe in the U.S. sector. I sent one of my junior officers to find out who were the occupants of a large adjacent stone building. It was found to be occupied by a solitary British Officer. The culprit proved to be Vivian Herzog (a British Officer in the Intelligence Corps, one of the sons of the late Ashkenazi Chief Rabbi of Palestine). We talked about the future of a Jewish State into the early hours. Alas, I have never had the opportunity of renewing our acquaintance.

Disembarking from a landing craft was no picnic. We were laden with heavy equipment, strafed from the air and shelled by guns. We seemed vulnerable prey. Our landing craft was scratching and grating the floor of the Channel. Another moment and we raced ashore, took cover and crept into some abandoned dugouts. We lay there for what seemed an eternity and attended to a few trifling medical problems. Cold, wet and plagued by bouts of uncontrollable shivering, not one of my men developed pneumonia or even a trivial cold.

We pushed on to Bayeux and Arromanches in France. The former was damaged, but not beyond repair. This was the memorable spot where my first parcel arrived from England. It was a humble pair of khaki woollen gloves knitted for me by my wife Betty. The only problem was the multiple deformities the design revealed. The fourth and fifth fingers were displaced backwards and clearly there were multiple 'fractures' and 'dislocations'. But there was more to come - the package also contained a tin of biscuits. This was the same hard tack we had been living on for the past fourteen days - inedible fare.

At long last we had surmounted the many obstacles and victory seemed within our grasp. Brussels was now in our clutches and after the reception accorded the allied troops on entry into Paris the future looked rosy indeed. And so it was. We were truly feted. The girls and women covered us with flowers and kisses. The men fished out flasks of spirit, which they had kept hidden for five years for just such a memorable occasion. Tanks and armoured vehicles modelled their tracks 'in approval' at our achievement. Dance halls were full. Men were drunk with success and beer. Then followed the disastrous defeat in the Ardennes. War looked so simple when conducted with a map and little coloured flags.

We edged a little closer to the Rhine and there was a knock on the door of my beautiful captured caravan. The interruption was none other than my brother-in-law, Major Ellis Birk, who had arrived to lay down a smoke screen for our sector of the front. But now there was chaos - a motley band of German troops, Volksturm and Hitler Jugend. They had no right to be out after 9pm. We were witnessing a historic moment - the decomposition of a once great army.

A message came down from Division. I was to report on hygiene and medical conditions in Buchenwald. I hared into the American Sector and arrived exhausted at Buchenwald. There I found corpses in open pits, prisoners as emaciated as skeletons and, wrapped in a few inadequate rags, my cousin a shadow of his former self. The smell of putrefying corpses drifted downwards. There were scores of such camps. There had been about 15,000 in the camp, mainly Red Army personnel of whom around 10,000 had perished, not so much from wounds as from gastro-enteritis, exposure, dehydration and starvation.

I lamented to a British general about the inhumanity of the scene, but he had to report on the damage and carnage of battle and had no wish to moralise. To my surprise the Senior Russian Officer in this large POW camp was Jewish and we conducted a restricted, refracted and limited discussion in my very imperfect Yiddish. The Brigadier turned to me and said 'Mann, you didn't tell me you spoke such fluent Russian!'

42   ALEC MARMOT
AN EXPERIENCE OF ALIYAH

I was born at home in Harford Street, Hackney on 13th November 1921. My parents had come over from Russia about twenty years earlier, having already married and had two sons in Kiev. Sadly, I never knew my father - he died six weeks before I was born. My mother was left with nine children (seven boys and two girls) under the age of seventeen. My eldest brother had to take over running the family grocery shop which supplied us with our living, though not a very handsome one. Times were difficult back then.

When I was about twelve my mother sold the shop and we moved to Leytonstone. We were very orthodox at that time; every Shabbat morning we all trooped off for the 20-minute walk to our nearest shul, Forest Gate Synagogue, and I had my barmitzvah there. I also joined Habonim around this time and so was inculcated with Zionism from an early age.

At thirteen I won a scholarship to Leyton Technical College but after eighteen months there and without reference to anyone in the family, I decided to leave and get a job. I was unhappy, not only because there was anti-Semitism at the school, but also because of our poverty. I was often sent to borrow a few shillings from a neighbour so we could have something special - fish or chicken - for the Shabbat meal. By this time two of my brothers had gone off to China to seek their fortunes - and I also wanted to start contributing to the family.

I got a clerical job with a scrap iron and steel merchants for the princely sum of 12s 6d a week. I continued there until 1939. When the war started, I volunteered for air crew duties in the RAF and some of my brothers joined the Army. We all wanted to do our bit in the battle against Hitler. I didn't actually get called up until 1942 because of my job in the steel business which was crucial for arms production.

We had ITW (Initial Training Wing) near Torquay. We were given twelve hours flying practice to see if we were any good as a pilot. I was hopeless but they took me on as a navigator which turned out to be a lucky move. Those lads who were even worse at flying than me were assigned as air gunners - a role which had a very high fatality rate. We were based in Lincolnshire mainly; I was a wireless operator for Mosquito and Beaufighter fighter bombers. I did not suffer a lot of danger although quite a few of my friends there were killed on missions.

When I was demobbed in 1946 I visited a Zionist training farm in Maidstone, Kent and it was there that I met my wife Myra.

In early 1947 I decided to go on Aliyah. At that time there was only one way to do this - by Aliyah Bet - illegally - because the British were only allowing a very small quota of Jews into Palestine. So I was sent with about fifteen others to south-west France. I started working in a camp providing food and other aid for the refugees flooding into France from Germany, Poland, Romania and Hungary. Meanwhile some of the group headed off for Palestine from Marseilles, a hazardous journey in decrepit little fishing boats, having bribed the port officials to turn a blind eye.

I met up with them again shortly afterwards as they got caught by the British and sent back to Marseilles on a ship which became known as the Exodus. I remember they anchored about half a mile offshore and a party of us took out supplies of water and tinned fruit in a landing craft. It was a dangerous mission as the waves came crashing over the craft, nearly drowning us as we tried to pass the crates of food up to the ship.

I stayed on at the camp for a year and then, as a thank-you for giving up my passport for fellow Jews to use to travel across Europe, I was allowed to go on Aliyah Daled, which meant a proper ship going to Haifa, with a passport (though of course not my own!).

We landed in Haifa in January 1948 and the British let us in without a hitch. I went straight to Hadera, where my Habonim friends had already settled. It was really no more than a village, and I helped pick oranges and rear trout in the trout farms. I soon found myself sent out to the desert as we expected an attack from Iraq. I spent some weeks there, digging trenches and waiting for something to happen. Nothing did - and then the Syrians launched an attack from the north.

So I volunteered to defend Kibbutz Negev, at the foot of the Golan Heights. Every morning at 1am the Syrians used to shell us. It did not last long - a quarter of an hour, half an hour - you could set your watch by it. We were hopelessly out-armed and out-numbered by the Syrians, but luckily they were either poorly trained or demotivated because we managed to hold out against them.

In May 1948, when the British left and the State of Israel was declared, the attacks intensified. Four of us from the kibbutz went up to the Syrian border, to a place in the hills called Mansura overlooking Jordan. We still did not have anything worthwhile to defend ourselves with or attack the enemy. For example, I only had a rifle. It was a bare and horrible stony region - we had to dig our trenches with pneumatic drills. It was also full of scorpions hiding among the rocks, one of which stung me on the backside (which is only funny in retrospect!) There was of course no electricity and no water; our water was brought to us in a tanker. This tanker had previously been used to transport paraffin; consequently all our food and water always tasted of paraffin. It was awful.

Years later in Jerusalem, I visited an ex-kibbutznik, Rosie, who had been at Mansura with us. "Do you know, you saved my life?" she said, and I really did not know what she meant but she reminded me of an incident I had long forgotten. We had been walking towards the water tanker to fetch some containers of water when a plane passed overhead. It was not an Israeli one - ours were few and far between then - and I suddenly saw it release two bombs. I thought, they're going to hit us, so I grabbed hold of Rosie and carried, pushed, dragged her into the nearest trench and we both jumped in. I fell on top of her and the bombs crashed down on the water tank, just 10 or so yards away, blowing it to pieces.

At one time, Myra, who had come to Israel in July 1948, came up to Mansura from the kibbutz at Hedera. Within days she went down with malaria and, as we did not have proper medicine there, she soon became delirious. We called an ambulance from the nearest medical point to come and pick her up. I was not allowed to go with her, as we had a place to defend. Just as the ambulance started off with her inside on a wheeled stretcher, I saw the doors fly open. I went hurtling towards it and managed to catch the stretcher as it was about to roll out, and shouted to the driver to stop. These heroics must have impressed Myra because the next year we got married in Tiberius - on the rooftop of what we understood to be the oldest shul in the world.

As the immediate threat of war receded, we were moved from Mansura to a new place about a mile away. Here, on slightly easier ground, we built a kibbutz. We moved from tents to wooden huts and I became the kibbutz carpenter. We lived there for two years and then moved to Haifa. We left Israel in 1952 and did not return for seventeen years. But when I did eventually go back to the kibbutz, it was as if I had been there the day before. I took up with my close friends in exactly the same way, and I visited thereafter at least once every year, and we kept up our nice friendships until eventually they died one by one.

When Myra and I moved to Haifa, we had a bed and £7 which was our parting gift from the kibbutz. She took up secretarial work and I got a job as a labourer on building sites. We worked hard that first year, saving like crazy to buy a flat. Eventually, somebody got us a flat above the Haifa slaughterhouse. It was really quiet, nice and comfortable - when it did not stink to high heaven from the burning of carcasses below.

From working on the construction of the Blue Band margarine building I got a job as a lorry driver with the company, and then I got a white-collar job showing American companies around areas for new projects, trying to get them to invest in Israel.

Life was by no means easy in the young State. Our staple diet in Haifa was frozen cod from Iceland, with eggs and meat rationed. The worst part of it was the inflation. When we started saving it cost £400 to buy a flat; by the time we got that amount it had gone up to £700, and then £1200 and so it went on. We decided therefore to return to England.

We started off in New Cross and eventually made enough to buy a house in Colindale. We had no furniture, other than a bed and orange boxes to sit on. I went into the insurance business and worked my way up to make a good living. I eventually set up my own business. Myra and I have three grown-up daughters, and now live in Hampstead Garden Suburb.

***

FROM GODFATHER ALEC TO GODSON ANDRE ON HIS 3RD BIRTHDAY, SEPTEMBER 1985

M y dear Andre, I have the feeling that this letter is a year early. You are, after all, only three and commonsense tells me that you would need to be about four before I could expect you to know and understand about our Jewish people, their history and the facets of the Jewish problem. The thought came to me when we were all together in Sydney at a Friday night party to celebrate the 50th Wedding Anniversary of your Grandparents Nat and Alice, coupled with Nat's 80th birthday. You, Andre, and your Mummy and Daddy, had come from London, Uncle Woolf and Helene had come from Paris, Woolf's daughter Anne and her baby had come from America, their daughter Clare and her three children from Israel.

Myra and I were born in London and your Grandpa Nat was born in Russia and came to London as a young boy, even younger than you, and then eventually went to Australia to bring up your Daddy and Uncle Allan and Paul. Meanwhile, your Grandparents, Bernard and Lotke, had escaped from the Nazis and went to Australia to start a new life in a country where to be Jewish was not a crime. They then brought up their daughters, who are your Mummy and Aunty Felicia and Aunty Renee, who are also living in different parts of the world.

So they call us the 'Wandering Jews', because it is a habit we have acquired by necessity - the necessity to survive. For more than five thousand years Jews have been forced to leave country after

197

country. If we take the recent examples of your Grandparents - then Grandpa Nat and his Mummy and Daddy had to leave Russia, because from 1880 to 1910 the impositions forced upon Jews made the survival of the Jews very hard. All Jewish boys who reached the age of thirteen were sent away to do twenty-five years military service and most of them died during their first year in the Army because of harsh conditions and marches through the snows. So, many Jews, like Nat and his parents, escaped to other countries.

The Nazis were a German political party who were in Government from 1933 to 1945 and they were determined to get rid of all the Jews. Bernard and Lotke had to escape to Russia, where they had a hard and uncomfortable life, and they were frequently very hungry and very cold because they didn't have enough food and clothes.

Fortunately we are divorced from the periodic onslaughts made on the Jewish people in different parts of the world, because we live in a country of temperate climate and temperate political attitudes. Let me just say that I believe we are very lucky to be Jews, because there is a richness in our heritage which is to be envied. We love life because we don't take living for granted. Every day is precious, so we see and appreciate the birds and the sky and the flowers, and smell the fresh air. We know and understand the importance of the written word, because our religion is based on reading and learning. So we read and discuss and we write and encourage the theatre. We love music, and there is so much music in our Synagogue services. We are taught from early days to believe in Charity - that is, to spare time and money for people less fortunate than ourselves.

Finally, because I don't expect to return to the Jewish theme for some years to come, I take the liberty of enclosing a short talk I gave, which also shows a facet of our Jewishness.

I wish you many happy returns, I wish you a happy and healthy year, and when you get to about five, we will discuss more serious topics.

Lots of love.

43   DONALD JULIAN MARTIN

(The Living Testament by David Martin, son, with added testimony by Annabella Martin.)

Dad is dead, we are bereft
A void has opened in all our lives
Sarah, Simon and I have lost our beloved father, our anchor
Annie, Jonathan and Rachel have lost their devoted father in law
Joshua, Joseph, Naomi, Samuel, Ben, Estie and Ruthie have lost their
adored grandpa
But most of all our mother has lost her cherished life partner

Our parents, Donald and Annabella, Annabella and Donald: for forty-four years they went together like the birds of a feather they undoubtedly were. Each provided the other a degree of support, companionship and love that has become a model for all of our marriages. Their joint interests in art history, music and travel, but most of all in the lives of their growing family, were powerful forces that melded them together. They were inseparable. Whatever great distances have separated us physically over the past years, we have always been a close-knit family, thanks to their constant support and unconditional love.

Our father's life was a remarkable Twentieth Century odyssey, even when we take into account the enormous dislocations of that unstable century. Donald Julian Moses was born in Berlin in 1931. He was an only child. His father, Martin Moses, a Prussian Jewish First World War veteran had remarkably survived gas gangrene and the loss of a leg in the trenches at the age of seventeen. He won the Iron Cross for gallantry, fighting for the Fatherland he loved. He was an employee of a very big department store in Berlin called Tietz and rose to become a departmental manager.

The family lived comfortably, in denial of the developing Nazism - Martin Moses was a decorated war hero! - until circumstances forced the recognition that something had to be done.

Dad was sent to England on the Kindertransport at the age of seven. This amazing evacuation of children from Germany in 1938 successfully saved many lives and is an enormous tribute to British Jewry. My father remembered saying goodbye to his parents at the train station in Berlin thinking he was going on holiday to Denmark where he had gone the previous year with a group of children He did not understand why his mother was sobbing uncontrollably. He was not to see her again until he was sixteen, by which time his mother had already contracted the cancer, which was to eventually kill her.

(In January 1939 his parents realised that they had to get out of Germany and managed to obtain a forged visa for Lourenco Marques (Mozambique). Never having heard of the place they tried to find it in an atlas - as they were looking in South America it took them some time to find it.)

He was taken in by Charles and Lily Hall, who were close friends of British business associates of his father. They had a boy three years older than Donald and they treated him as their own son. Alan and Donald were close brothers until Alan's untimely death a few months ago. They lived in Sunderland and my father was sent to school the first week he was in England.

What must it have been like for a seven-year old boy to be taken from his family and all his familiar surroundings in this way? I believe it was the emotional trauma of this formative experience that motivated his later commitment to the importance of family relationships above all others. There was never a day in his life that he did not think of his relatives who perished in the Holocaust. He particularly remembered an uncle who the family ransomed from Dachau early in the 1930s who sat crying in the corner all the time, only to be slaughtered later on with all the rest of the family who remained after 1939.

What must it have been like for a seven-year old boy from an enemy country to be sent to school understanding nothing of the language? Donald Moses rapidly became Donald Martin. He learnt the King's English in two weeks and never spoke with a hint of a German accent. Twenty-five years later he told us that he was unable to speak his mother tongue. What must it have like for an only son, used to the warmth of his mother's embrace and the comforts of home, to be sent to a northern English boarding school? He played rugby and squash and along with the rest of the school community dug for victory. He was given responsibility early on to care for the chickens and collect the eggs.

He returned only recently to Berlin with mother and it was clear that his mental map of the early years was intact, because he was immediately able to find the apartment building where his family had lived.

At the age of sixteen he flew for the first time in his life to Mozambique where his parents had settled; this was still the pioneering era of commercial flight and many refuelling stops were required before reaching Johannesburg. As he boarded the plane a man said: 'Sit next to me son. Don't want some woman sitting here being sick.' My father vomited his way to Africa!

Although he spent some months in Mozambique and returned again to visit his parents in the early 1950s it was clear that there was no future for him there. It is difficult to imagine the problems of meeting parents he barely remembered. He found this a very traumatic time, particularly as his father was a real Prussian: Donald assisted him in the office and woe-betide him if the stamp was not stuck on a letter at exactly right angles. The plan was for him to find work in Johannesburg, but as South Africa had not signed a peace treaty with Germany (Donald had travelled on a Nansen passport) he had to return to England - not unwillingly.

He was now a British subject and he returned to London to become an articled clerk with his brother Alan. He always regretted the straightened circumstances and the need for employment that prevented him from obtaining a university education. Nevertheless, he passed all the examinations first time round (remarkable in those days) and became a chartered accountant. It was decided that he should be articled to a firm of Chartered Accountants (both Alan and one of his uncles were Chartered Accountants). Donald went for an interview to a very large, well-known firm. The interview went well until the end, when Donald said he presumed it would be all right if he took time off for the Jewish Holidays. The answer was a frosty refusal. Of course he did find another more accommodating firm.

Donald met Annabella in 1951 before she went up to Cambridge and their relationship survived the stresses of her university education. They were married in 1955. As a husband and father myself I speak from experience when I say he set the standard as a devoted and loving husband. Nothing was more important than being with mum and the kids; he hated business travel and made it his business to be home for dinner every night. At a time when gender roles were more rigidly defined he taught us that men could contribute much to family life at home. He flipped pancakes and washed dishes, as well as performing many traditionally female functions with nothing more than a simple happiness and gratitude that he had a *family!*

What sort of man was he? What made him tick? I believe it can be summed up in three words: Family, Generosity and Duty.

The family was the prime focus of his life. When we consider his disrupted upbringing, the mere existence of our family, to say nothing of the strength and closeness of our relationships, is truly a miraculous achievement of his that I still cannot fully comprehend.

Evidence of this treasured sense of family can be gleaned from the way in which Donald overcame his repugnance at his father's return to the Germany that, in spite of everything, he still loved. Both he and Annabella, and his grandchildren, frequently visited him as he spent his last days in Wurzburg in a Jewish old-peoples home.

We lived in the same house during our childhood with stable parental support based on mutual trust and respect. He welcomed his daughters-in-law into our family with characteristic enthusiasm and love. He was truly the rock of Muswell Hill.

He was generous with both time and money. No conversation with him was complete without him asking if we had enough money or if we needed anything - and he really meant it! Nothing was too much trouble and he never said 'no' to anyone! When asked for advice, whether personal or professional, he would give his undivided and ongoing attention.

This commitment earned him enormous respect from his professional colleagues, as well as from those in the community. He was constantly being drafted, elected or co-opted to school or other community committees where he gave his time and expertise most generously, usually in the capacity of Treasurer. One of my most enduring memories of him from my childhood is sitting with him at the kitchen table counting the money into large piles of very small change raised from school fairs or jumble sales three or four times a year.

In recent years life became harder for dad. Because of developing physical frailty he found everyday tasks progressively difficult, and things that he had previously done easily became a lot of effort. Nevertheless he refused to give up and only three weeks ago was at Covent Garden with mum enjoying the opera.

He was prematurely taken from us by a short but very unpleasant illness which burden he bore with characteristic concern to protect mother from worry. He suffers no more, but we are left to deal with the severe pain of his loss.

44

EVA MEYER
PASSION AND PREJUDICE

I first became aware of myself in Majorca. I was born in 1931 and my parents had emigrated to Majorca from Germany in 1933, after my father found himself banned from practising as an accountant in Cologne because, despite his atheist family background, he was Jewish by descent. My parents had chosen Majorca because it was known as the Island of Peace - it had not had a war for a hundred years. There my father tried, unsuccessfully, to work as a photographer and my mother ran a boarding house. For me it was a happy time.

By an ironic twist of fate the Spanish Civil War broke out in Majorca in 1936 - no peacetime! My parents wanted to leave for England but were forced instead to return to Germany, first via a German warship and then in the locked compartment of a train. On arrival my father was immediately arrested for being a Jew. He was given the option of going to a concentration camp or leaving the next day for Italy, with nothing but a one-way ticket for himself, my mother and me.

Our life was hard in Milan. With Mussolini as leader all the Jews were trying to get out of Italy. That same year, 1936, we left Italy bound for South Africa, where my father had cousins. Our fare was paid by a Jewish aid agency.

In South Africa my father got a job as an accountant with Westinghouse, but in 1939, when war broke out, he was classed as an enemy alien and immediately lost his job. He had great difficulty finding work and tried several types of employment. I can remember clearly one of these jobs was as a waiter – he worked for just one night, but he felt so insulted that he gave it up straightaway. Eventually my father's uncle, (a wealthy South African resident), lent my parents the money to buy a fish and chip shop, but he demanded 7½% interest. My parents slaved in this shop for five years. It was in a poor white area outside Johannesburg - most of the clientele came in drunk. My father found this very hard to tolerate. In the evenings he built up his own accountancy practice. By 1945 when the war was over my parents were able to sell the shop and my father started to work full-time as an accountant, with my mother helping with the bookkeeping. By then he had developed cancer - undiagnosed for two years – and died soon after. After my father's death, my mother started accountancy from scratch. She was very successful and built up quite a large practice in Johannesburg.

At that time my mother's best friend, living in Switzerland, sent her a bundle of letters from my mother's parents and her younger sister who had stayed behind in Germany. First they had been sent to Theresienstadt concentration camp, where my mother's parents had died. My aunt then went to Auschwitz. There is quite a lot of correspondence. They were very matter-of-fact letters because they were careful not to say anything too emotional. But they are also horrific, because we know where they had been and what had happened to them. Later there were just postcards which my aunt wrote with a blunt pencil which was obviously all she had and always stamped across it was 'Answer in German' on an open postcard. My aunt just disappeared.

Whilst still a child I developed a passion for music. I studied the piano and violin. Music was my passion and I did not want to do anything other than music. I took a degree in music, coming top of the class and winning a scholarship to study with Max Rostal at the Guildhall School of Music here in England. I begged my mother to join me in England because I was so against apartheid (which separated blacks and whites in South Africa) but my mother simply could not face uprooting herself yet again and insisted I return to South Africa when my studies were completed. She worked very long hours, was desperately lonely and had made huge sacrifices for me. So back I went in September 1956.

On my return I played with the SABC (South African Broadcasting Corporation) Symphony Orchestra. I also performed in a trio, which was invited to perform, unpaid, for black South Africans.

Following this, the black leader of the musical society invited me to mass and to have lunch with his wife in Sofia Town, a black township. This was during the implementation of the Group Areas Act and I knew feelings between blacks and whites were running high. The act segregated black and white living areas and blacks were being moved out of their houses into townships far outside Johannesburg. So I said I would love to come but requested that the music society leader, Michael Rantor, meet me at a garage so I would not be driving alone in the car to Sofia Town. He sat in the front with me - the normal thing to do.

Two days later I was told that my contract with the government run SABC would not be renewed. That was like getting the sack. My champions in the orchestra demanded to know why. The management would only confirm it was nothing to do with my playing. The truth came out by accident. Father Mathew, a family friend of Michael Rantor, invited me to play in another black township and happened to mention that Michael had told him that when we were in the car driving to Sofia Town, Michael and I had been followed by Special Branch. I nearly jumped out of my skin! 'Why did Michael tell you and not me?' 'He was embarrassed,' said Father Matthew. 'Why embarrassed?'

Father Matthew explained it was not usual for a white woman and a black man to sit together in the front of a car. Special Branch suspected we were contravening the Immorality Act which outlawed sexual relations between blacks and whites. When we went to mass they gave up the chase. I was eventually reinstated by the SABC, but I turned it down because I had a job in Durban.

In 1960 my mother went on a world tour to visit surviving members of her family and friends. While she was away the Sharpeville massacre occurred. The blacks were demonstrating peacefully against the Pass Laws, which meant they always had to carry a passbook. If they did not they would be arrested and quite often taken for slave labour on a farm, and some were never seen again. It was terribly iniquitous. A huge number of unarmed blacks went up to Sharpeville police station to hand in their passes as a protest. The police panicked because they were outnumbered, and killed and wounded hundreds, including children. There was a world outcry. This, together with my mother's trip which opened her eyes, made her decide that we would leave for England. This was what I had been waiting years for.

I was lucky to have accompanied the English Royal Ballet on its tour of South Africa and when one of its leaders heard I wanted to leave South Africa because of its racial irregularity he promised me a job with the Royal Ballet Touring Orchestra if I came over (I had hoped for one with the Royal Opera House but he told me they had a men only policy). I toured with the Royal Ballet Touring Orchestra for about two years and then decided to base myself in London and try for a London job.

As a first step I got private pupils, then a job teaching at South Hampstead High School for Girls, plus freelance work with the BBC Symphony Orchestra and then the Royal Philharmonic - the first of the big London orchestras to accept women. I also worked in some West End musicals, not really what I wanted, but I ended up leading the orchestra and playing solos. This proved fortunate as one of the people who ran the English Chamber Orchestra was in the audience one night and offered me extra work with them. I enjoyed that enormously.

In April 1966 my mother, having survived a really serious car accident, decided life would be easier in a ground floor flat, so we found one in Golders Green. This led to a major change in my life when a new neighbour arrived in August 1966. She was also a German Jew, so we felt very much at home with her. I was standing at her kitchen sink showing her how to use her waste disposal when in walked her tall, dark and handsome brother, Henry Meyer. And that's how I met my husband. On New Year's Eve he asked me to marry him and we married in March 1967. Henry was working as a social worker and I subsequently worked with the English National Opera for thirty years. I had to retire when I turned sixty-five, but my musical career did not end there. I still get asked to play with them, now and then, and it is very nice to keep my hand in, to feel wanted.

45   HENRY MEYER
ROOTS AND RESOLUTIONS

I was born in Berlin in 1925. I can trace my family roots right back to 1685. I know that the maternal side of my family lived in a house in Waldstein which is on the Rhine, opposite Koblenz. (Eight years ago I went with my wife Eva to visit it.)

My father was born in Vienna in 1888, served in the Austrian army in the First World War and acquired a couple of Austrian medals, a Turkish medal and, believe it or not, a German Iron Cross (2nd Class). Returning to Vienna after the war he found he was quite unable to obtain any employment because he was a Jew, so he finished up by travelling to Berlin. Although trained as a merchant he was, in fact, a natural inventor and his claim to fame was that he invented the first tubular electric lamp (in the days before neon and fluorescent lights). It was a tubular lamp with a filament.

In 1933 when Hitler came to power, he left his lamp-making factory in Berlin and travelled first to the USA and then to the UK. Here, on the strength of his expertise with lamps, he offered to start a factory which would create employment and so was given permission to immigrate.

His next step was to return to Berlin to collect us. We got out by a rather devious method. My father put about a story that we were moving from our flat to a new house, but we would be temporarily staying in a Berlin hotel as our new house was not yet ready. In fact, we did move into a hotel, but from there got on a train, ostensibly to take a holiday in Holland (which was still possible for Jews). Instead, we hopped on board a ferry which took us from the Hook of Holland to Harwich.

I was sent to a small school in Brick Lane with my younger sister, and there began to learn English. I went on to win a scholarship to UCS in Hampstead.

Our family went through the Second World War as so-called enemy aliens and, at one point, my father was even interned. He rang home on the day of his release only to find a policeman answering his phone and to be greeted with the news that our house in Woodstock Road had been bombed.

My school stayed open throughout the Blitz. My first experience of someone actually dying was a school friend who had travelled home with me the night before on the bus. The morning after I passed where his house should have been on the Finchley Road. It was no longer there. Apparently what was left of him was found stuck up the chimney of the bombed house.

When I turned thirteen, my father decided I had better get barmitzvah'd, but I didn't think much of the idea and managed to divert my Hebrew lessons into being taken rowing on Regent's Park lake. This was the beginning of my interest in maritime matters.

School finished in 1942 and I began looking for ship industry apprenticeships throughout the country. No success, until one arrived from Portsmouth, of all places! This was the most restricted area of all where even the native English had to get a special pass.

A fortnight after starting my apprenticeship I received an unexpected invitation – to have dinner with none other than the Company Chairman, retired Admiral of the Fleet, Sir George Shepherd and his wife. This was one of the most bizarre experiences of my life. There was I, a junior apprentice and an enemy alien to boot, dining with Sir George while the Blitz was going on and we were being bombed by Germans overhead. In fact, both Sir George and his wife spoke excellent German and they simply wanted someone to practise on!

My first career in the ship industry took me to many far-flung places – India, Singapore, Malaya and Nigeria – as well as many parts of Europe. Of the many years I worked abroad there is one thing of which I am particularly proud. I was very aware that the companies I worked with treated native managers as unequals. I had immediately formed friendships with the natives, and when I left India the only person able to take over my job was an Indian. Much the same thing happened in Africa where, once again, the only person able to take over my job – mainly because I had trained him up to it - was Nigerian.

My first marriage had by this time ended in divorce, with a sad tale of many court actions in attempts to maintain my relationship with my son.

Now, back in England, I discovered a strong religious faith for the first time in my life. During some of this period I considered myself to be a Christian. I knew far more about Christianity than I did about Judaism at this stage. It was only gradually that I discovered that what attracted me to Christianity was the ethics behind it which were, of course, Jewish in origin.

I decided to stay in the UK and become a social worker, and several years later I became a mental health officer.

It was during this time that I moved into the block of flats in Golders Green where I still live, and there I met my second wife, Eva. It was my second mother-in-law who sensed there was something missing in my life and persuaded me to find out about Alyth. I met the present rabbi, Charles Emanuel, at my mother-in-law's funeral service and he gave me an open invitation and I found out that, yes, I like Alyth. Although my religious conscience is pretty shaky, and still is today, in due course we joined Alyth and have been members ever since.

There have been many journeys in my life, but the most important one is the one that proved a spiritual as well as a physical journey.

46   NORMAN MYERS

M y life began in the East End of London, where I was born on 8th November 1920 in what was then known as The London Hospital (now the Royal London), the third son of Phillip and Leah Myers.

My father came from Manchester, where he was born in 1875, later coming to London with his parents. As a young man after leaving school he was apprenticed to a cobbler, but when he married mother he took up a position as Secretary and Collector to four small Jewish Friendly Societies under the aegis of the 'Achei Brith', a post that paid him the grand salary of £2 a week with which he was expected to provide for his growing family. How we all managed in Brady Street I still do not know to this day. We only had two bedrooms, one living room, no bathroom and just one outside toilet for the six of us. Nevertheless, I do remember that despite the lack of amenities we were all happy, clean and respectable.

We lived on the third floor of Brady Street Buildings in Whitechapel until I was fifteen, thereafter moving to a similar flat in Navarino Mansions, Hackney in 1936. We were a family that included three brothers and a sister born in 1927. She was later to marry and bear a son, only then to die tragically young in 1957.

My own school days began in Underwood Street, in Whitechapel, followed by the Robert Montefiore School in Vallance Road, as well as six months at the Jewish Free School in Bell Lane (Frying Pan Alley). I thereby continued a family tradition since I was following in my father's footsteps where, towards the end of the century, one of his teachers had been Israel Zangwill. In the 1970s the tradition continued when my own son and daughter attended the school.

At the age of eleven I won a scholarship to the Raines Foundation Grammar School in Arbour Square, Stepney. I greatly enjoyed my time there, with art and literature among my best subjects and rugby my best sport. Unfortunately though, this cost money and when I reached the age of fourteen my parents found that they could no longer afford to keep me at school, so I left to look for work.

I scouted around the City of London and managed to find a job as an office boy at a solicitor's office in Fenchurch Street, at a salary of ten shillings (or 50p) a week, rising after a year to twelve shillings and sixpence (or 62½p).

In my spare time I spent most of my youth at the Brady Boys' Club in Brady Street, Whitechapel, where I thrived. I discovered that I had an organising ability, one that would stand me in good stead in the war to come and then later in the peace that followed.

I joined the Local Defence Volunteers (later the Home Guard) at the time of Dunkirk, serving until called up in October 1940. Six months later, after army training, I was sent to Blackpool where I learnt the morse code and graduated to become a wireless operator in the RAF. In June 1942 I was posted overseas, first to Suez in Egypt, later to Libya, thereafter mainly to Bahrain in the Persian Gulf, where my organising ability came to the fore.

Although I was only an LAC or Leading Aircraftman, the lowest of the low, I nevertheless organised concerts every week for officers, NCOs and ordinary ranks - all this done with the aid of a record player and some records indented from the RAF, and putting on classical concerts very much in the manner of the Proms at the Royal Albert Hall in London.

At the same time, I also formed the Bahrain Cricket Club, strictly according to MCC rules (and of which great institution I was later to be a member for some thirty years). We played several matches against employees of such concerns as British Petroleum, Cable & Wireless and various other companies, and had a thoroughly enjoyable time for almost two years. The war over at last, I came back to England in October 1945 and was demobbed in May 1946.

The following year I married Pat and we now have a son Geoffrey, a daughter Jennifer and two grandchildren, Daniel (presently on a gap year with the Federation of Zionist Youth in Israel) and Mark who attends Mill Hill school.

In 1945 however, my career still lay before me and I first went back to work in my old job in the solicitor's office. But this was not a path I wished to pursue. What I really wanted was to work in films. So in 1949 I started my own Company, Greville Films. It was not named after Greville Janner as you might perhaps suppose, but after the place where Pat and I lived when we were first married - Greville Hall in Maida Vale. In time Greville Films began showing movies after tea at children's parties. This in turn eventually led to my becoming a full-time party entertainer in the 1950s, by which time we were already living in Golders Green.

As my clientele built up I even started entertaining Royalty, Prince Andrew being amongst the first. One newspaper article once headlined me as 'The Royal Court Jester' though not, I hasten to say, on the front page.

In quieter moments I continued my love of sport, playing golf at Finchley Golf Club and watching cricket at the MCC grounds at Lords in St John's Wood.

I am now in my eightieth year, fifty of them spent entertaining children. However, I have still not stopped work entirely for I still perform at the odd party when asked. I have also just written my autobiography, for which I was interviewed on television. The title of the autobiography, 'Uncle Magic - The Life and times of Norman Myers,' is due to be published this coming autumn. Lord Hanson, who first gave me the name Uncle Magic, has kindly written a forward.

With so many interests, who knows what else I shall be doing when I get to be ninety? One way or another, it has all been a most exciting and enjoyable life.

47   MARIA ALICE PHILLIPS

I am an early Edwardian by birth, having just missed the Victorian era by some eight months. I was born in Stoke Newington on 17th September 1901, my mother Catherina van Moppes of Dutch Jewish extraction, my father Ben Westell from a Church of England background. Ben's father, my grandfather also Ben, was an assessor with the Inland Revenue covering the Preston area. My father was educated at Manchester Grammar School. When he left he became a civil servant in the Post Office and was sent to London, where he lived in a boarding house in Crouch End. It was here that a family friend introduced him to his future wife, my mother Catherina.

My mother left school at thirteen when the family came to London. Her father Levie was a diamond cutter who came to London in 1893 looking for better economic opportunities. The diamond trade at the time was experiencing a slump and many of our family left to set up elsewhere. My grandfather Levie, or Louis as he later called himself, was encouraged to come to England by one of his customers. His other brothers went variously to Antwerp, Paris and New York.

Louis, his wife Eugenie (née Rose) and Catherina settled in London in Seven Sisters Road, N7. Eventually, after Catherina met and married my father they lived for a while with her parents in Seven Sisters Road where I was born. My parents later moved into a little house in Hornsey where my brother Louis was born. When the underground opened we moved to Golders Green and lived there until I got married at the age of twenty-five.

My first school was in Childs Hill. From there I went to South Hampstead where I was Head Girl and stayed until I had matriculated. Toward the end of the First World War I was encouraged to go to work to help with the war effort, and for a time I worked in the India Office as a clerk. I also took part in some amateur dramatics at South Hampstead after I left school. I always had to play men's parts in the school plays because I was tall and had a deep voice.

During the First World War I can mostly remember the anti-aircraft guns on Hampstead Heath firing on the German Zeppelins. We carried on fairly normally and I went to the shul in Dennington Park Road on Shabbat with my brother Louis. He went to Haberdashers School and was a very good linguist with a remarkable mind, winning many school prizes. He had a lot to offer but sadly never made much of a success of his life.

It was always intended Louis should go to university and not surprisingly, as far as the family was concerned, he won an Exhibition to one of the colleges in Cambridge. My father couldn't afford to send Louis to university - in those days you had to pay and there were no scholarships. However my uncles, who were in the diamond trade and had their own business called L.M. Van Moppes & Sons near Holborn Viaduct, offered to help financially. My brother was thrown out of Cambridge after a year, although I don't know why – I think it may have been because of his gambling. I believe that the early death of our mother in January 1922 at the age of forty-two did not help. Louis was a young teenager at the time and it affected him deeply.

Despite his recent failure, my uncles Mike and Sol stepped in once more to help, this time with the assistance of Rabbi A.A. Green of Hampstead Synagogue. Between them they made sure that Louis successfully completed his studies as an accountant and after qualifying he went to work in Nottingham. He later joined the army, learnt Italian and should have been posted to the Intelligence Corps but caught tuberculosis instead and was invalided out.

Prior to the First World War my father Ben had risen to become second clerk to Bow Street Magistrates Court. Then, when hostilities broke out, he went to work for MI5, although he never told the family about this. However, records recently released at the Public Records Office in Kew clearly show his name as having been a serving member. When peace came he returned to his old job as clerk to Bow Street Magistrates Court, this time with an MBE after his name.

I had left school by then and father suggested that I train as a barrister, to which I had no objections. I was a student for three years at Middle Temple. In those days you had to pay about £200 to the barrister and £100 to his clerk to become a pupil in the barrister's chambers. In fact I was one of the first women barristers in this country.

I met my future husband, Lewis Phillips, at Dennington Park Road Synagogue. He had had a hard war - an officer in the Royal Horse Artillery awarded the Military Cross for bravery. After demobilisation he went to Imperial College and studied chemical engineering. We were married in Hampstead Synagogue in Dennington Park Road in July 1925. The reception was in my father's house, 7 Heath Close, Golders Green. He had arranged a family party in the garden and afterwards we went to Switzerland for our honeymoon.

After that, my legal career ended and we went to live in Tonbridge, Kent and then in Southborough, where Lewis worked for a record company as a chemical engineer. He was required to make the correct mixture to physically produce the records. When this job ended he bought into a small factory in Ealing, and we then moved into a new home in Holders Hill Road, Hendon. This suited me quite well, as I found life in Southborough rather boring apart, that is, from amateur dramatics which my husband and I both enjoyed.

We had two children, Robert born in London and Patricia born in Southborough. Robert later attended Haberdashers, like his father, and also became a chemical engineer. Pat went to South Hampstead as I did. She became hockey captain and after leaving school went to a teacher's training college in Newcastle where she obtained her teaching qualifications, becoming a teacher with special responsibility for Geography and Physical Training; in later life working also with children with learning difficulties.

As the Thirties went by the threat of Hitler's Germany, to Jews in particular, became all too real. We were members of Kinloss at that time and with the support of Rabbi Dr Porush, the Minister, Rabbi Cyril Harris and other leading rabbis we all worked amicably together to find homes for Jewish children rescued from the Nazis. I was their secretary and got on well with all of them, our sole object to help rescue Jewish youngsters from Hitler's Europe by means of raising money and finding sponsors. In Croydon we even opened one of our own homes for the boys. They were mostly sixteen and much harder to place than the girls.

In the late 1930s, during the Second World War, Lewis was employed by the Admiralty as part of the war effort to make gun sights for them in his factory. He also used to work at night in the garage sizing fine industrial diamond powder for his cousins. They were so pleased with him that after the war they offered him a job running their own diamond powder department, and he stayed there for the rest of his life.

During the Second World War I had my first experience of anti-Semitism. I was a member of the WVS in Finchley. There was a vacancy in the office for deputy chairman and my name was proposed. Both the chairman and deputy secretary wanted me, but some of the others said no as I was Jewish. Lady Reading heard about this through a Jewish friend who worked with her. She sent her to Finchley to interview me and asked me if I would like to work instead in Tothill Street, Westminster, giving advice on legal matters. I said I couldn't do it every day as I had a family to look after but I would come twice a week. This was accepted.

We were in touch with my grandfather's sister before the war and also my mother's cousin with whom she used to correspond. The war took a fearful toll of the more distant Dutch members of my family, many being sent off to concentration camps. With a few exceptions I never knew much about them, but a long time after the war I suddenly received a cheque for £50 from my cousin Lewis van Moppes. Enclosed with it was a note to the effect that he had received this money from a solicitor who had obtained money from the estate of Dutch relatives sent to the concentration camps.

Towards the end of my grandfather's life he and his wife Eugenie bought a house in Monte Carlo and they used to live there for half of the year. Soon after my mother died - I was eighteen - I was invited to Monte Carlo with my aunt (my father's sister) who had nursed my mother all through her illness. We stayed the night in Paris and visited my great aunt. We took her a bunch of lilac. She laughed and said that was what you gave to an engaged lady. All this was about seventy years ago. We went to the South. It was empty of people in the summer and very full in the winter. My grandmother lost all her money there gambling - my brother inherited this gambling trait from her.

I continued working at the WVS for quite some time after the war, in fact, until my husband died in 1953 when he was only fifty-six. At this time we were living in the suburb - we had moved to Hilltop and had a large house. I had to get rid of this house because the garden was too big, so we moved into a smaller house in nearby Blandford Close.

My son married Helga and he went to live near the van Moppes factory in Basingstoke, having taken over his father's old job. They have three sons, Lewis, David and Robin. Both Lewis and Robin have families. Robert is now retired and lives in Miami with Joan, his second wife.

In 1957 Pat married Alec, a medical student. They have four children, Ruth, Janet, Anne and Peter, all now married with families of their own. She lived in a flat in Fitzjohn's Avenue and when she had a baby she moved back to the house and I moved into a flat in Belsize Park. I then came to live in a flat in Charlton Lodge, Temple Fortune Lane. It had the convenience of a lift, was near to shops, not far from the station and was also very near Alyth Gardens shul, all of which suited me very well.

I have been very active for a long time at Alyth. I used to take the children to Kinloss every Saturday and Robert had to sit by himself. After his barmitzvah, which he had to do by post as he was evacuated at that time, he announced he wasn't going to Kinloss anymore as the men did nothing but talk Yiddish and he had to sit by himself. Therefore at Robert's instigation the family decided to join

Alyth.   My husband became the Hon Secretary of Alyth and unfortunately he died soon after.

I was the second woman to be elected on to the council. The first woman was Ray Bran. I was also the first woman to be made Chatan Torah. I had various kinds of jobs including being treasurer on the Women's Guild. I was on the council until I broke my leg and couldn't come to council meetings. I am good at breaking bones - I have broken both hips. I remember when I broke my arm I had my whole arm in plaster for nine weeks and had to live with my daughter. I have been twice to Israel on tours, but don't feel particularly Zionistic. I can remember going to Massada and Haifa.

I always liked knitting and sewing but I don't like cooking. I have never liked cooking and refused to learn when I was a child. We always had a maid at home who did some of the cooking, but my mother did most of it.

I shall soon have my 100th birthday and count my blessings that I have two children, seven grandchildren and twelve great grandchildren, with another imminently due. I intend to celebrate with as many of them as I can on the London Eye.

48

ANITA RAPP
A REFUGEE'S STORY

I was born in Essen, Germany, on 7th February 1925. My father was a businessman in textiles (although his real forte was cooking) and my mother was a housewife. I had a twin sister and an older sister. We first lived in quite a nice district and went to a nice little primary school. Then, when Hitler came to power, things rapidly got worse and worse. The school decided they did not want Jews anymore, and my sister and I were kicked out. My family moved to a poorer neighbourhood and we started at another school.

Like lots of German Jews we were aware that we were Jews, but did not keep a Jewish home. We thought of ourselves as German first and then Jewish. But now we had to go to a Jews-only school. At first we had good teachers and a pleasant building but things soon deteriorated and we were moved from one derelict building to another, and the standard of teachers went down. All the people who were still quite capable of anything were already emigrating and we were left with all sorts of people who were not really fit to teach children. Then after Kristallnacht in 1938, when I saw so many of Essen's beautiful synagogues burning, I think Jews basically did not go to school any more. I was thirteen.

My mother had a sister, Else Heilbron, who had married an English Jew after the First World War and they lived in Manchester. My elder sister Hanne had already been to school in England, so the plan was for all of us to get out to England, being vouched for by my aunt. My twin and I came to England in March 1939 on the Kindertransport, and went to live with Aunt Else. My parents would join us later.

When we came to Manchester we could not speak a word of English. We all spoke German in the house, and we started at school where the teachers also spoke to us in German. Thanks largely to my aunt's Scottish maid who used to chat to me I gradually picked up the language (possibly with a slight Scottish brogue).

When the war started, my aunt asked us whether we wanted to carry on at school. You shouldn't ask this of fourteen year olds – of course, we said no! We wanted to go to work and earn money.

I became a dressmaking apprentice, a job I absolutely hated because, unlike my sisters, I was dreadful at needlework. I worked for a very posh dress shop, but the manageress was very anti-Semitic saying Hitler should kill all the Jews and that sort of thing. Another Jewish employee and I complained to the bosses about the manageress but they told us to ignore her.

At that time, I knew my parents were in a concentration camp. In the beginning I received Red Cross letters from them – you know, twenty-five words every hundred years – but basically I did not know what was happening to them. It was only later that we found out that my parents had died in 1942, in the concentration camp at Theresienstadt.

When I was sixteen I decided sewing was not for me, and I got my second job doing bookkeeping in a department store called Henry's Stores. The owner, Leonard Cohen, was a very nice man and employed about twenty refugees. The only thing was he rather took advantage of our situation and paid us practically nothing.

When I was eighteen I was called up for war work. As I was not yet naturalised I could do either nursing or domestic work in the ATS (which I didn't fancy) or work in a factory, so I chose this. To start with I worked as a capstan operator making parts for aeroplanes. Unfortunately, I am not mechanically minded – I think all the planes that came down must have been the ones I had a hand in constructing! Then I worked in a bakelite factory making clocks, which was very hard work, I also worked in the office at Courtaulds textile company for a while, and then as a secretary for a very frum man – he used to say his prayers while he was dictating letters.

In 1942 my sister married a fellow Jewish refugee she had met in Manchester and they emigrated to join the rest of his family in the States. I went out to join them in 1949. We lived together in New York where I worked as a maid. It was here I met my husband, Henry.

Funnily enough, he was originally from Dusseldorf, very near my hometown, but we met thousands of miles away. He had been a GI during the war. Things moved fast – we met in June 1950 and got married in November.

We returned to England the following year, and Henry joined his father's firm. Both his parents had got out of Germany and his father had set up a business trading in metal. We lived in Cricklewood. In 1953 my son David was born and I became a full-time housewife. My daughter Nicola was born in 1959. We later moved to the Pennine estate off Hendon Way, and then to Hendon. We came to Alyth through Jerome Karet. Henry knew his father who was also in the metal business, and when we met on a cruise Jerome persuaded us to join the synagogue.

It was through Alyth that I finally discovered that, despite my messed-up education, I had a talent for voluntary social work. To begin with Henry and I were on the social and functions committee helping raise funds to build the Youth Centre. Then I started helping at the Friendship Club, and from that I started the Alyth Social Club. Twice a week, we provided talks, recitals and card games with a light lunch for elderly people. I also made a point of keeping in touch with members, particularly if they didn't have family, and making sure they were okay if they were ill. I was chairman of the Club for some twenty-six years and then went on the Synagogue Council, being active on security and hospitality, helping to set up and run the chavurah suppers on Friday nights. Sadly, we decided to close the Club last year, when the original 'customers' had either passed away or were too frail to come. I think I found it rewarding to discover I could do something to help the elderly members of the synagogue, maybe because I had been unable to help my own parents.

Both my children married out, although my daughter is keen to bring up her children as Jewish. She says this is also a way of maintaining the link with her grandparents and proving they did not die in vain.

AUBREY ROSE CBE
49 MEMOIR OF THE OLD EAST END
AND BUILDING BRIDGES

I am a real Cockney – born literally within the sound of Bow Bells – albeit to Polish Jewish immigrants. My journey from the cramped streets of Stepney, where I spent my first eleven years, to leafy Hadley Wood where I now live, has been very interesting and rewarding.

I recall my childhood in the East End with affection, a certain kind of longing and, according to my wife, with an element of make-believe and wishful thinking! The adults around me may have been tortured by shortage of money and other worries, by all the desires and frustrations of economic man and woman, but I knew nothing of these problems. My world was full of security, parents, family, friends, adventure and fun.

My children may not remember now but when they were very young, six or seven, they loved to hear stories of when I was very young. They never tired of these tales, however often I told them. 'Tell us', they cried, 'about the time you were a little boy.' They curled up on their beds before going to sleep and listened attentively while I repeated familiar stories of my upbringing in London's East End. Perhaps the material poverty, the constant sense of adventure, freedom of the streets, the extraordinary characters involved, contrasted vividly with the heavy respectability and bourgeois order of suburban Highgate in the sixties.

For years I have sought time to put pen to paper and re-create that never-to-be-forgotten world. Like Citizen Kane, I have always felt a part of me has remained in that old world of my childhood, that I lost something when we moved away, something never restored to me, something forever missed and lacking. Impressions on the unblotted, uncluttered mind of a child remain stark and vivid, especially if those early years were as happy as mine.

I was a real wild child, (a "vilde bria" in Yiddish). I roamed the streets daily. I climbed something daily, a tree, a lamppost, a wall. I played games daily in the school playground or in the street.

Every day I was involved in being a Jew. Each afternoon I left school, came home, had tea and then wandered off to the local Hebrew classes at Redman's Road Talmud Torah. We went there too on Sunday mornings, but not on Friday nights, and Shabbat when we attended Jubilee Street Zionist Great Synagogue close to our home, where my grandfather had been involved and where Rabbi Levene gave his sermons in Yiddish, bringing a flood of tears to all the women's gallery. Every day I was involved in being a Jew, learning Hebrew, praying in Hebrew. It was the natural way.

After a big mid-day Shabbat lunch we would stroll up and down Mile End Waste, meeting, talking, gesticulating, gossiping – my father, a tailor, knew so many people that we had to keep stopping to chat. I knew the ghetto within the ghetto in which I lived like the back of my hand. In Dempsey Street, E.1, now truncated and town-planned half out of existence, I knew who lived in every house. I practically lived in every house, constantly darting in and out of every house with my friends. There was no privacy.

I started my learning career at five in Dempsey Street School. A teacher played a piano as we danced about. When she stopped we all lay down on little camp beds. I went right through several camp beds onto the floor. We learned nothing as far as I recall, maybe the alphabet, a few words, a few sums. The teachers were wise. We were bursting with energy and they let us run it off. The school still stands.

I grew older, seven, and was whisked away to another school in Redmans Road, a street or two away. Everything was within walking distance. I joined the boys' section. Girls had their own section. We did not think much of girls, apart from those in our street. The new school was a joy. It had a secure playground in which I could spend hours at cricket and football, the chief joys of my life. Normally we played these games in the middle of the street, suspending play only when a car or horse and cart rumbled by, and certainly when a policeman hove in sight up the road. The wicket was the black drain cover in the middle of the road. We made up many other games, usually involving tin cans and tennis balls. We broke many windows in Dempsey Street houses, but when the householder came angrily to the front door we had fled. In time I became known as the chief offender. My mother kept the local glaziers in business restoring windowpanes broken by our footballs in winter and cricket balls in summer, whilst she consoled and pacified irate neighbours. She was a peacemaker.

My parents had lived next door to each other in Oxford Street, close to Dempsey Street. They married in 1906, and celebrated their golden wedding. I believe it must have been an arranged marriage, quite common in those days, since they had such different outlooks. Not that I understood or perceived any of this until I grew up, (although I retain doubts whether I am yet grown up). It was said that my father and his family were on their way from Poland to America, but like so many never got further than England. Some of those who settled in England for quite a time believed they were actually in America, the Goldene Medinah.

At night when I went to sleep, the sound of the Singer sewing machine whirred away in the workshop next to my bedroom. When I awoke in the morning I heard the same busy sound. The Singer sewing machine was my lullaby at night and my alarm clock at dawn. My father worked fifteen or more hours a day making waistcoats for the fashionable City of London retail tailors. People had their suits made in those days. Off-the-peg suits were in their infancy, at least in our world, especially as every other person seemed to be a tailor.

Sometimes I accompanied my father on his rounds, delivering the completed waistcoats to Chappells near Gresham Street, Silvers close to Cannon Street, Nymans and Vuillermoz, across the river in Westminster Bridge Road. I was proud of my father, a craftsman, always so well received by these smart, tailoring establishments. That home workshop where production never ceased was a small room on the first floor front. In fact, it *was* the first floor front. Two machines stitched up the cloth and linings, which my father had cut from brown paper patterns that hung on the wall. Around a small table sat two women, sometimes accompanied by my mother, sewing buttonholes all by hand. Opposite my father, with a long table dividing them, was a presser. He had his heavy hand irons - really heavy, I used to try them, - constantly heated by gas flames. He laid a garment on his pressing frame, covered it with a damp canvas, then ran the hot iron over the lot. Steam soared into the air, the presser coughed and coughed, then took out and lit another cigarette. What his lungs were like I never knew, but in hindsight he was coughing, steaming, and smoking himself into the world-to-come. I used to earn pocket money pulling out stitches with an ivory implement at a halfpenny a waistcoat.

Not a bad income resulted, as with a halfpenny we could buy a full bag of sweets. Groups of us - we invariably moved in groups - wild youngsters, used to crowd into a sweet shop. Someone asked for a halfpenny worth of sweets from a jar high up in the corner of the shop. The woman owner climbed up a ladder and turned her back on us. As she performed this operation several of the boys used to stuff chocolates from the nearby counter into their pockets. Whilst I never did this, I never said or did anything about it. Thus are delinquents and criminals born. If the woman ever caught any of us at this calculated theft she swore at us, often in Yiddish, and chased us out of the shop. Had a policeman been called, he would have given us all a clout and we would never have done anything like it again. We were wild kids, street kids.

As children we lived in our own little world, part real, part fantasy. We were lucky not to be aware of the terrible things happening in Europe. We heard the names Hitler and Stalin. We gathered there was some sympathy for the Revolution in Russia since our families had fled from the poverty and anti-Semitism of pre-First World War East Europe. Fortunately, we kids of the street had not the faintest idea of the racist Holocaust of Hitler ahead, and the existing ideological Holocaust of Stalin that engulfed the world. I realise now that parts of our families must have perished in one or the other, and only by luck had we ourselves escaped. But these are later thoughts. At the time we knew nothing of impending disaster.

The nearest we got to politics was to chase round the street at election time in the 1930s chanting, 'Vote, vote, vote for Danny Frankel. Punch old Donovan in the eye.' Frankel was the Labour candidate. We, as under-dogs, identified with him. Donovan was the Conservative, and somehow there was a feeling that his party contained too many anti-Semites. As I write this years later, revelation has just been made of the shameful bloc of Conservatives and aristocrats who were prepared to do a deal with Hitler and who violently opposed Winston Churchill, then in his political wilderness. As children we saw some of the refugees from Nazi Germany. It did not make much sense to me. I particularly noticed that many of them wore long heavy overcoats, almost to their ankles.

As I write, memories return. The pen is a catalyst, a key that turns locks and opens doors. I know I could never get such light on the past from a typewriter, (an almost defunct animal), or a word processor, the new wonder of the age. My friendly pen, however, traces, describes and revives light and memories. I recall Whitechapel High Street one weekend, packed with shouting people. 'They shall not pass!' echoed. Shop windows were smashed, and I stood in one of them watching, without understanding, as some battle seemed to sway back and forth. Later I learned it was the fight to prevent Oswald Mosley's Blackshirts from marching through Jewish areas.

Years later, when I had some communal responsibility for Jewish defence, I witnessed similar efforts by the heirs of those Nazis, the National Front, who adopted the same tactics of marching through immigrant areas to provoke and intimidate, exhibiting the brutal chauvinism of the inadequate, often illiterate, bully-boys of this world.

Also in those far-off days I heard of a group called the Jarrow marchers. They were walking from the north of England to London to protest against unemployment. To a child this meant little, some incomprehensible issue swirling high above our heads. But it became reality for me when many of the marchers lodged in Smith Street School, a minute from my home. I saw them daily. I spoke to them daily. Everyone sympathised with them. The men wore peaked caps, behaved well and were helped by the locals. Then one day they all disappeared and the school returned to normal. This was a boon to me as one of my routes to my own school, when I did not feel like walking, was by climbing. I clambered up and over part of Smith Street School, outbuildings, walls, railings, and let myself down into the neighbouring playground of my own school. All my life I have continued to climb. In the 1970s my daughter Esther and I spent many happy hours climbing the highest trees in Kenwood. It all begins way back. We don't change as much as we think.

I was a practical child, but also a dreamer. I adored sport. My love of football, nurtured in the streets, continued throughout my life. I played continually until my mid-twenties. At the age of sixty - what an age, other people become sixty, not me! - I played a full match in aid of Jewish Students Rag Week, and we oldies beat the students 11-6. I was proud to be top scorer with 4 goals to my credit, the last goal as good as any scored in my teens, as my family heard continually from me. All this emerged, like climbing, from my early years.

Often I crept out of the house at 7.30 in the morning, waited in the street outside the school playground door and then played a solid hour's football before classes began. My mother, concerned that I might waste away from starvation, often rushed round to the playground with the breakfast I had forgotten to eat. I was consumed with the sport, lived for it. I played for the school, and was never prouder than when Mr. Goldstein, our Headmaster, announced in assembly how we had beaten neighbouring schools, mentioning the goals I had scored.

In the later Thirties when I did not go to synagogue, I accompanied my uncles, whom I adored, to Lea Bridge Road where we cheered on Clapton Orient, the 'Os', later known as Leyton Orient. They were not the world's greatest but they were our team. Often too I went to see Arsenal play at Highbury, where home and visiting supporters mingled together, good-naturedly, with never a hint of violence.

Football came into my dreams, and my dreams became confused with reality. Each week I memorised the results of every match in the Football League's four divisions, and thus learned more about geography then I did at school. As I lay in bed, to the background of the grinding sewing machine, my fantasies were all about football, imagining myself as some Superman centre-forward scoring goal after goal, re-creating the moves that led to the brilliant shot or header I placed in the far corner of the net, away from the despairing fingers of a defeated goalkeeper.

My room was tiny, dominated by an enormous mahogany cupboard. On the wall were some prints of Venice, which must have accounted for my later love of the painter Turner. On hot nights - there seemed so many of them - the window was wide open. I listened to the ships in the nearby docks, hooting and steaming, blasting and blaring. It gave me a link with an unknown far-away world.

My fantasies went beyond football. I dreamed about King Kong and Tarzan. I could not get out of my mind Robert Donat playing a ghost in 'A Ghost Goes West', and how he passed right through a wall. I used to repeat chunks of dialogue from films, seen in our local Cameo or Troxy. And as I lay in bed, often awake late because of the noise, I imagined, as others surely have done, that I could float through the sky. I did this by donning a special waistcoat and inserting some secret metal in the pockets which negated the force of gravity, and so I floated above the earth and swooped and zoomed everywhere, helping, rescuing, soaring about like a bird.

My most delightful visions were not fantasies at all. As I lay quiet in the dark, brilliant colours and shapes shot before my mind's eye, wonderful patterns, squares, circles, concentric movements, patterns replacing patterns as in some illuminated kaleidoscope. It was like a glimpse of another world. If only I could somehow capture permanently those patterns and colours that came to me so easily, one replacing another with constant clarity and luminosity. It was my own private picture gallery, far more real and vivid than any picture gallery I visited in later life. This facility stayed with me for many years, but gradually dimmed as I grew older and became immersed in the practical world of earning a living, the triumph of dull necessity over glowing imagination.

We children lived in our own fantastical world. Along the road lived my friends Cyril and Miriam. I was in their house daily. Their father was always in bed. This seemed strange to me, whose father never seemed to go to bed at all but was always working. My friends explained that their father worked all night in a bakery and slept all day, so we had to be quiet and not wake him.

Further along the street was a Welsh dairy. The East End was full of Welsh dairymen who had opened little dairies in London, the milk-world of the Joneses and the Morgans. Frequently my mother gave me a pitcher and I and my friends wandered to the dairy where a cow was kept and milked. I returned home, the pitcher full of hot, fresh milk, straight from the cow. Somehow we survived without pasteurisation, homogenisation, skimmed, semi-skimmed, full cream, half-cream. I adored milk. Often I picked up a pint bottle - it also came the usual way - and drank the lot. My father used to tell me of his early years in his Polish village, when he and his elder brother Philip lay down under cows and drank the warm milk straight from the udders. He also told me that his father, grandfather Abraham, used to swim the width of the Vistula river with my father on his back. Can I believe such tales? They must be right as my father was the most honest person I ever met throughout my life, congenitally incapable of telling a lie.

My other daily friends were the Pearlman family. We lived at No. 107, my father, mother, and sister until her marriage in the early thirties, and myself. But next door at No. 109, in these small terraced houses with no bathroom, and toilets in the garden, there seemed to live an avalanche of people. It was a wonderful family. I loved them all. The father was a jeweller. He had a great big safe and on occasions he let me stand in it. His wife used to call the family to meals by standing on the front door steps, clapping her hands like an Army call to the cookhouse. I cannot recall how many children there were, but this family raised and reared me as much as my own parents. I was daily in their house. Fay, an older daughter, used to give me a wash or bath at the same time as she washed her sister Leila, my special friend, who was the same age as me. I remember us as two naked kids under the kitchen table, freshly scrubbed, examining each other's bodies and noting the differences. Leila was a tomboy. She would climb with me, play games with me, even box with me.

I adored her brother, Chaim or Hermy, a couple of years older than me. He was a kind of hero. He could make things. One day a builder had left a pile of bricks in their garden, and the three of us decided to build a house with them. We built from the inside and when the construction just needed a roof we were all inside and could not get out without knocking the whole erection down. Not very bright, but planning authorities in later years have done worse.

Margie was also an older daughter. As if five days a week at Hebrew classes were not enough, my parents used to pay Margie to teach me Hebrew privately. I used to rebel when the kids outside were waiting for me to play football or go on some expedition. However, Margie was a good teacher and my Hebrew knowledge and pronunciation made such progress that she displayed me at Jews College, an orthodox rabbinical seminary, where I had to read passages to the students. My love of the Hebrew language was born in those early years, but my studies never progressed in tandem with my devotion to the tongue. Yet throughout my life, dipping into the Psalms or Isaiah or Ecclesiastics has been as natural for me as picking up and reading the daily paper.

Then there was Moshe, the eldest son of the family. I used to lean over the garden wall and ask him questions and disturb him when he was studying. I was a Jewish Just William. I am sure he wanted to throw something at me. But he never did. He was brilliant, became a noted author, broadcaster, archaeologist, British Army officer, Israeli Ambassador, personal assistant to Ben-Gurion. An outstanding man. We were in touch at intervals throughout his life.

Then there was Judith who died tragically aged sixteen; Asher, a doctor, killed in 1943 on the Anzio beachhead in the Allied invasion of Italy; Hindel, just older than Leila; and Pearl, a doctor. David was born when his mother was at some advanced age, and after the East End was a memory.

The Pearlman household was a joy to me. I ate there, washed there, played there. Sometimes at night we lit a torch, put red paper on it and twigs over it, and imagined it was a fire around which we sat, ate and sang. They were a very orthodox family. Despite the size of the house, the downstairs kitchen was used for the preparation and cooking of meat dishes only, whilst on the first floor was a tiny room in which all milk dishes were permitted. There I ate glorious blintzes, filled with cream cheese, and encouraged my mother to make them.

But for food there was no one like my grandmother, Booba. She lived three doors away, on the corner of Smith and Dempsey Street. She had come from a family of cooks and bakers. Her main purpose in life, it seemed to me, was to keep around her masses of family and to preserve them from hunger. It was a poor family. I vaguely remember (was I about two years old?) a little old man, bright eyes, small grey beard, propped up in bed, an enormous pile of white pillows behind, as he prepared to meet his maker. Jacob Kurtz had married twice. His first wife had died early, but my mother and her two sisters Sarah and Celie, (her much-beloved sister) and brother Nathan were from the first wife. I never knew at the time, and not for many years, that all my other uncles and aunts were from the second wife. I adored them all, Sam, Alf, Mark, Harry, Lew, Dora. They were full of fun, jokes, nicknames. They got up to endless practical jokes. They also never grew up. To be with my uncles was my seventh heaven.

Every Sunday was family day. Into that small, open house, came about forty people, sons, daughters, daughters-in-law, children, cousins, visitors. No one knew who was there at any one time. There were no invitations, no formality, no special dress, no presents, just a big, happy, noisy family. The men played endless card games, pinochle (five hundred or clabayash) sixty six, a thousand, poker, solo. Bridge had not yet penetrated our Jewish world.

The women sat and talked or prepared meals, great dishes of boiled potatoes and herrings and tea, and my grandmother's magnificent cakes, strudels, plavas, honey cakes, fritters. I used to watch her roll out the dough with her rolling pin, acres of thin pastry onto which she poured jam and raisins and nuts and fruit and rolled them into long thin shafts of strudel. She used an old coal or coke-fired oven. Sometimes she let slices of orange peel heat up in the oven, giving off a marvellous smell. She was forever preparing and cooking. More meals were served there than in a normal cafe. I had the privilege of eating in three homes; my own, the Pearlmans, and my grandmother's. I am sure my grandmother believed my parents were starving me. 'Eat, eat,' she used to say. How often did I eat two lunches, two dinners?

Those Sundays remain in my mind. They gave us children a sense of belonging, a sense of security, a sense of fun. It is all gone and we have lost something wonderful that cannot be re-created. We have lost a sense of natural unaffected community. Years later Leila went to work on kibbutzim (agricultural settlements) in the State of Israel, where people lived close communal lives, but she confessed it was never like the old East End. We enjoyed our little blinkered, narrow world, where there were few doubts. We shared the same poverty, the same human warmth. We knew no better, no other world.

Our gardens were tiny, although my father had a grapevine and raised chickens. Parks were few, so we played in the streets. Often we joined together in groups or gangs, not to hurt anyone but as a kind of club. We even had gang cries so that we could keep in touch with each other when out of sight. Many of our expeditions were communal in character. We would explore Rotherhithe Tunnel, yelling at the tops of our voices and listening to the strange, recoiling echoes. Frequently we went to our local 'seaside', a patch of sand at the foot of Tower Bridge, close to the Tower of London. How the sand got there I have no idea, but we played around on this beach, especially with the flotsam floating in the river, usually planks of wood. We wandered through the Tower Gardens before returning homewards.

On a few occasions, a couple of us decided not to return straight home, but stood outside nearby Mark Lane Underground

Station offering to carry bags and cases for people. Once I earned a whole sixpence, enough for a ride to Whitechapel on the tube, an enormous ice-cream which lasted all the way home, with money over for sweets for a week.

Everyone who lived in that ghetto has his own memory, his own East End, the East End of the 1880s when the mass of Jewish migration began; the pre-1914 decades as institutions developed; and my own East End of the late 1920s and the 1930s, when the full Yiddish richness and the poverty of the ghetto had begun to decline, to be finally destroyed by the Second World War. There is a Jewish professor who emphasises the political East End - the Socialists, the Bundists, even the Anarchists led by the non-Jew Rocker, who unbelievably became editor of the Yiddish newspaper, Die Zeit, the Times. Years later I met Rocker's son, Firmin, a gifted painter and illustrator, who told me many stories of his remarkable father.

My own father used to mention the Bolsheviks and communists who held gatherings in the East End. He even thought Stalin had participated. Who knows? Yet to me Ghetto Jewry was not a political Jewry, but primarily a religious Jewry. There were hundreds of synagogues in the East End: Rectory Road, Philpot Street, Stepney Green, Fieldgate Street, the famous Machzike Hadass in Brick Lane, the Congregation of the Elders of Jacob in Commercial Road (associated also I gather with my grandparents), little stiebels or prayer rooms, centres for famous rabbis surrounded by their disciples. A deeply religious society.

On Friday nights a walk along the street revealed lighted candles in so many front rooms, gleams of Sabbath light and rest. After a big mid-day Sabbath dinner, we strolled up and down Mile End Waste, meeting, talking, gesticulating, gossiping, walking down the chulant, (potatoes, meat and beans) that weighed heavily on our stomachs. My father knew so many people that a walk with him rarely got beyond a hundred yards. So much talk, so many people. Mile End became a street employment office where master tailors looked for workers, and workers for jobs. I loved the way everyone examined the quality and cut and make of everyone else's clothes, feeling the material and turning jackets inside out.

Sometimes the Sabbath midday meal was so powerful that everyone fell asleep. How often did I look into my grandmother's (underground) sitting-room on Shabbat and find everyone stretched out, fast asleep. I even recall Uncle Harry fast asleep standing up, leaning on an old upright piano!

On the holiest days in the religious calendar, Yom Kippur (Day of Atonement) and New Year, people dressed up to go to synagogue. Some men even put on evening dress and black top hats. We imps played games with them. We tied cotton between wall and lamppost. Unsuspecting solemn well-dressed elders paraded along in dignity, only to find suddenly that their top hats were sent flying into the kerb. Did they ever know what caused their descent from sublimity? Did they ever find the evil, chuckling children, the cause of their discontent?

We expanded this ruse into the never-stopping knocker. We tied the same cotton, almost invisible in colour, to a door knocker, let out the cotton from its reel around a corner, then gave a tug. The housewife opened the door, saw no one, closed the door, and repeated the operation every time we tugged at the cotton. Sadists, we should have all been locked up, but we never ever engaged in any kind of violence, which was totally alien to us.

Worse was our torment of the local shoe repairer, the schuster. He was a stout, grizzled man, sitting in his shop window next to Jubilee Street synagogue. He had thick grizzled grey-black hair, large dark eyes (I see him now), with always tightly compressed lips. Like some robot, he removed tacks from his mouth at an incredible speed, hammering them into the soles and heels of shoes clasped between his knees or resting on a last. We, hell-bent offspring of Satan, stood outside the window making faces, shouting, teasing, trying our wicked best to make him swallow all his tacks. No wonder, possibly as a form of penance, I later took up the profession of law, having spent years trying to destroy it and create total disorder.

We extended our Machiavellian efforts. Between the back-to-back gardens ran a boundary wall. We wandered along this wall daily, looking into everyone's house and garden. Occasionally we came across some small factory built at the rear of a few gardens. We climbed up on to the roof, opened the skylight and peered down at the furniture maker, upholsterer or small craftsman. In those days Jews were craftsmen, hand-workers, they made things. We waited in silence as the workers banged away, puzzled at the draughts and the rain that poured down on them. Eventually they saw us and chased us out of their buildings, but by then we were far away, tearing along the tops of walls and trees. Villains, outrageous villains!

Our most dreadful act involved pears. We denuded a pear tree of all its pears, hundreds. The house-owner, who had been asleep, rushed out pulling on his trousers, threatening to hose us and worse. I was the pear-plucker up the tree, handing the fruit to a chain gang behind me. Somehow I escaped. Later we tried to eat the pears, but they were like rocks. We poured my father's sewing-machine oil over them to soften them – even more ghastly to the taste. We ended the day throwing them through open windows in nearby houses. How anyone survived in the East End, Lord knows. We were beyond redemption, or so it seemed.

In those small houses, all rented from the Mercers Company I believe, small businesses erupted. My father was a tailor; a neighbour made dresses; another neighbour was a furrier. In Smith Street my friend Gerald's father had a small factory at the end of his garden. He was a furrier. Thrown into one corner was a massive pile of fur off-cuts, six or seven feet deep, all kinds of fur, silver fox, mink, Persian lamb, even bits of sable. They felt beautiful. Gerald and I had an idea. Pretend the pile of fur was a swimming pool. We set up a few tea chests on end, climbed onto the top and dived head first into the pile of soft fur. We spent hours diving into piles of soft fur. I hope he grew up free from allergies.

We had few toys. There was a small wooden rocking horse, which I practically destroyed by hammering in nails. An old doll's pram was useful, but otherwise toys were few and far between. We made our own. All the rage was the homemade wooden scooter using noisy ball-bearing metal wheels. We clattered with these all over the East End pavements, splitting eardrums. A journey to my Uncle Phil in Old Ford where he ran a pub, The Old Three Colts, resulted in a massive gift from him of a half-a-crown, an absolute fortune. He remained a favourite of mine until his ninety-third year, his last.

There was too an unstated sense of geographical ghetto. We rarely walked further westwards than Aldgate or further east than Bow. We might wander into Petticoat Lane, with its pickled cucumbers, pickled herrings, salt beef, brown fried latkes (potato cakes), or else buy a penny's worth of chips from John Isaacs in Mile End. Who knew then of cholesterol? In later life, when a lot of men had heart trouble, they knew. Then it was all delicious, and anyway they were doing heavy physical work and needed the energy. Occasionally we visited the Karsberg family in Forest Gate, or the Litmans in Hampstead, or people came to us. We went to my aunt Celie who lived in Wardour Street in London's West End, where another kind of Jewish Ghetto existed. I adored going there, playing with my elder cousin Charlie (another hero), who boxed and played football and sang (he became a dance-band singer) and who introduced me to the early Bing Crosby records, the best he ever did. I drove my wife and children mad in later years with my Crosby version of 'Buddy, can you spare a dime'.

But there was plenty of local East End culture. I knew only bits of it. We went to the Yiddish performances in the Pavillion, Mile End, where Edward G. Robinson is alleged to have made his Yiddish debut, and where I was thrilled with a performer called Jan Kapura. When he asked the audience for their favourite song they yelled 'Eli, Eli', the first words of a Psalm and almost the last words of Jesus, 'My god, my god, why have you forsaken me?' Next door to the Pavillion was the Christian Mission to the Jews. I do wish they would leave the Jews alone and concentrate on the pagan majority. Oy! The arrogance of the missionary with his self-satisfied closed mind.

The Grand Palais, the main Yiddish theatre of the East End, is famous. We used to go there regularly. The plot was always the same, tragi-comedy musicals, always with mistaken identity problems that came right in the end. The audience joined in the plot, advising performers what or what not to do. The audience brought their own three-course dinner to eat noisily, cracklingly, enjoyably, in the theatre. The audience was usually more interesting that the performers. They were all performers.

I recall in the mid-Thirties the visit of the great cantor from Poland named Serota. My uncles became stewards for the disposal of tickets, and I was able to listen to this famous man sing and chant the liturgy. Queues stretched for miles trying to get in. Incidentally he sang in the Assembly Hall, Mile End, where Hertzl first addressed East End Jewry in 1897.

Going to synagogue was as natural as breathing. The service was traditional, all in Hebrew, no English. We did not attend the United Synagogue. It was, I gather, regarded as too anglicised. Of Reform, Liberal, Progressive synagogues we knew absolutely nothing.

Our group of villains loved the festivals of Purim and Simchat Torah when sweets and cakes were distributed to children. We went from synagogue to synagogue, adding to our vast hoard. On those festivals my grandmother made special dishes. I loved the wafer-thin sugary fritters and the little butter beans. On Shavuot we had marvellous cheesecake. On Purim we took presents. On Succot I used the Pearlman's succah and waved the palms and said the prayers.

Pesach was the time for setting out on the pavements shoe boxes with holes in them of various sizes. The object was to roll hazelnuts from the kerb into the smallest holes and win most nuts or coins. Isaac Bashevis Singer in his novel 'Shosha', set in Poland, describes games played with nuts on Pesach. We simply transferred the ghetto from Warsaw to Stepney.

It was a profoundly Jewish life. We had no real insight into the world of our non-Jewish neighbours. In some ways they could be living on another planet. Many of our day-school teachers were Jewish. One locked himself in his room each lunchtime to say his prayers in peace. In the evening Hebrew classes, the teaching method was to limit the use of any English and concentrate on using Hebrew as much as possible, Rev. Goldbloom's Ivrit B'ivrit method. It was competitive. If you answered a question correctly your neighbour had failed and you changed places with him. The top four boys sat next to the blazing fire, an important objective on cold nights.

Day classes were overcrowded, often undisciplined. But good masters like Mr Swaffer made an impression and we really learned. In recent years I have met fellow-pupils of those days and we recalled the influence of these good teachers. I was lucky. My father was usually too busy working to help me, but my mother always had time for me. We used to play learning games together. She mentioned a country and I had to tell her the capital city. In this way, before I was ten, I knew most of the capital cities of the world. She used to give me mental arithmetic sums and if I answered correctly I would give her a sum. In this way I learned to do many sums quickly in my head. Even today I rarely resort to adding machines or computers. I was lucky. It helped me to win a scholarship to Central Foundation School in Cowper Street. It is important to choose the right parents. My mother could speak five languages, even though she left school at fifteen. She improved her English by reading the newspapers. She became a successful businesswoman throughout her life. She hated ostentation, loved modesty and always taught me that 'no one is superior to you and no one inferior.' One part of her family, I gathered, were teachers and lawyers, another part Chassidim.

Having a bath in the old East End was a problem for us. We had no bathroom. Occasionally the zinc bath hanging on the wall was placed on the kitchen floor and I sat in it getting alternatively scalded and frozen as buckets and kettles of hot and cold water were poured in. This was no solution. My parents could lose a son that way. We decided on the public baths. So weekly we walked a mile or so to the baths, where my father scrubbed me black and blue with a hard brush. People used to yell out to the water attendant 'More hot in No. 7!' and 'More cold in No. 9!' I learned something then that I still do to this day. I never leave a bath in my home, in a hotel, anywhere, without thoroughly cleaning it so that it shines perfectly for the next occupant. Habits formed in early years die hard. Occasionally my father took me to the Turkish Baths at Gardners' Corner and I revelled in the hot rooms, the hotter rooms, the steam room and ultimately the breathless splash into ice-cold water.

Once a year the family went on holiday to Westcliff or Cliftonville. When I say the family, I mean the whole family. Twenty or thirty of us went together. We rented a few houses adjacent to each other. We moved a bit of the ghetto to the seaside. We played football and cricket on the sands and we had enough to make two teams from the family. Two uncles had married two sisters and came with their children, and the sisters' family came too. How extended can a family get?

Uncle Harry was a caterer. He catered enormous meals at weddings in La Bohème or the Casino. The latter establishment was opposite my Hebrew classes, and I often slipped in for a snack at some wedding or barmitzvah on my way home.

All this wonderful world - wonderful for me - came to an end in 1939. By this time we had moved to Stamford Hill and then evacuated to High Wycombe to avoid Hitler 's bombs. We had no idea of the unfolding tragedy ahead. My barmitzvah in 1939 was a wartime one. I sang from the Chumash and the Prophets in a little Chassidische stiebel surrounded by swaying sidelocks and gaberdines topped with beards and black flat hats.

I have touched on but a few incidents. Many more remain vividly, pictorially, in my mind. This was my upbringing, my rich Jewish world, not a world of violence but of peaceful, poor but happy characters. I was lucky. The East End others recall was vastly different, consumed by poverty, dissension and illness. We, in our East End, reacted as a community, proud when someone achieved something notable. How we kids exulted and surrounded Max Baer, world heavyweight champion, when he came to Brick Lane. I was often taken to boxing matches, watching the mayhem from the shoulders of champions like Kid Lewis.

My East End world had come to an end. It never recovered from the war. That sense of family, of community, of being part, one of another, had departed. It lives on only in memories, in books, in guided tours, in museums, in a Master's thesis, in talks to Jewish old age homes, informal but sad reminiscences. My children never knew it, my wife never knew it. I knew it, lived through it, and it lives forever in me.

***

In 1947 I began work as an articled legal clerk. Five years later I was able to set up my own practice in Fleet Street, backed by £250 from my mother. In 1954 I married Sheila (who came from a completely different world, brought up as the only Jewish child in the Gloucestershire village of Winchcombe and whose mother was a Rakusen – of matzo fame). I continued as a sole practitioner until 1971 when I joined forces, as senior partner, with another firm. In 1991 I became a consultant. I have worked with a wide range of clients from all walks of life – from shoplifters to entrepreneurs, from kidnappers to prime ministers.

My key aim throughout my career has been the promotion of good race and community relations. I have been particularly involved in assisting immigrants from South Africa, the Caribbean and elsewhere, with their problems settling into the UK. Throughout the Nineties I was involved (as a Commissioner and later Deputy Chairman) with the Commission for Racial Equality and was heavily involved in promoting human rights and democracy in the Commonwealth countries. I have also worked to build bridges with other faiths and have been a member of various cross-denominational bodies such as the Council of Christians and Jews and the Indian Jewish Association UK, as well as being a long time member of the Board of Deputies of British Jews.

A growing passion is ecology. In 1991 I set up and chaired the Jewish Working Group on the Environment, which included leaders from the various strands of Anglo-Jewry as well as professional environment experts. I was very pleased to edit *Judaism and Ecology,* the first ever book setting out the Jewish attitude(s) to and involvement in environmental matters, which was backed by the World Wide Fund for Nature.

A book I wish I had not had to write was *Journey into Immortality,* both a tribute to my elder son David who died of cancer, aged 21, and a personal reflection on family bereavement.

I am still involved in various legal issues, including employment, extradition and setting up educational and medical charities, and you will be thrilled to know that thanks to my involvement as legal adviser to the Lottery Promotion Company, 'It could be you!' every Saturday via the National Lottery. (They tell me my CBE was awarded for services to the community, rather than this latter work.)

I am very keen on gardening, travelling and doing such sports as I can now do. I used to be a football coach for youngsters, and now very much enjoy teaching the finer tackles to my six-year-old grandson.

50   DR. HAROLD ROSE

I was born in Bethnal Green in February 1913, the youngest of a family of five – three sisters and one brother. My parents were Russian and emigrated to England in 1903 to escape the pogroms. My father was a cabinet-maker, and was strictly orthodox. Yiddish was the family language. I met my wife Jenny (Finkelman) at Mile End Central School when I was ten years old. We became friends, ultimately engaged and married in 1937 at the Stepney Orthodox Synagogue (where I was barmitzvah). We lived on a joint annual income of £300 a year.

I won a scholarship to the East London College (now Queen Mary College) where I studied chemistry. In my third year I studied chemical engineering at University College London.

The 1930s were not a good time to find a job. We were at the end of the depression and unemployment was high. Anyone with a Jewish name could not even get an interview. I changed my name from Harry Rosenberg to Harold Rose by deed poll. After a year's unemployment I got my first job as a chemist in Chadwell Heath, earning £2.15s a week.

My second job was as chemical engineer to a firm making building boards from sugar cane fibre. This was a reserved occupation. So I was not called up and joined the Home Guard. From 1943-48 I was technical manager of a pioneering company, Uni-Seco, building prefabricated schools, farm buildings and aircraft hangars. The company received a Government contract to build 70,000 prefabricated bungalows in the next few years. Many of these survived for fifty years, and some have been listed for a further fifty years.

During the early years of the war we rented a flat in Hampstead. When the first incendiary bomb attack on Hampstead took place, we sheltered one night in a neighbour's house and were entertained by Herzl Goldbloom, the son of the headmaster of the local

Talmud Torah. His fund of Jewish jokes kept us roaring with laughter while the bombs rained down.

My work took me to Uganda and Kenya to make building boards from papyrus, and to South Africa to help the Africans build their own Kraals from indigenous materials.

In 1946 I came back to England. I was invited by the War Office to join an Anglo-American intelligence team of five people engaged in the building industry to visit Germany to interrogate German industrialists. This was quite a change from living in East London during the Mosley riots, the Cable Street revolt, and the humiliated Mosley being escorted out of the East End. Whilst in Munich I visited the Dachau Concentration Camp soon after it was liberated. I was able to report on the gas chambers and the ovens and the German guards sunbathing under the eyes of the former inmates.

I then set up in private practice as a technical consultant. The first half of my career in building science ended in 1951 and I then became involved in the textile industry for the next twenty-five years.

We joined Alyth about forty years ago. I have served on the Council, on the Executive and as membership treasurer. In 1986 I was elected Chatan Torah. My connections with Israel have been primarily through the Hebrew University. I was Chairman of Alyth's Friends of the University for ten years during which time we raised substantial funds to establish scholarships in Reform studies. At one time I was invited to become Professor of Building Science at Technion, which I had to decline. We were not ready to go on Aliyah.

In the course of my private practice I invented a process which was to change the clothing industry throughout the world – the replacement of sewing stitches by welded micro fusible dots. I called the product Staflex and in 1951 was co-founder of Staflex International. For this work I was awarded two Queen's Awards for Technological Innovation. As I was approaching retirement I was invited by Leeds University to write the history of the company. It took me five years to write this thesis and I was awarded a Ph.D at the age of sixty-five when I finally retired. We had 250 editions published privately and they sold in twenty-one countries.

I resumed my interest in photography and put on several slide shows at Alyth and other synagogues. During the course of the next ten years I set up four touring exhibitions, which provided 46 one man shows. One of these was at the Festival Hall and the other at The Museum of London.

At the age of eighty my sight deteriorated rapidly as a result of glaucoma. My wife said I should find something else to replace photography and I found I could paint. With a little residual sight I mounted a touring exhibition under the title 'Challenging Blindness' with the idea of encouraging the visually impaired to paint. This exhibition has its own website.

At eighty-nine I am mobile and reasonably fit. Loss of sight is not the end of the world. One has to adjust. I cannot read books but with the aid of magnifiers I read letters and do crosswords. I do not watch TV but listen to documentaries, the radio and to audio books. I walk daily. I have had a happy, busy and active life.

I am thrice blessed in having a caring wife, son and daughter five grandchildren and an extended family of eighty. I have no grounds to complain and remain an optimist.

51   SHEILA ROSE

I spent the first five years of my life in Temple Fortune, only a very short distance from the North-Western Reform Synagogue.

My mother was a businesswoman, long before it was fashionable. Although her father had prevented her from fulfilling her ambition to become a lawyer he nevertheless, when travelling to China on one of his journeys to purchase eggs, left Power of Attorney not with his wife, nor with my mother's two elder sisters, but with my mother then aged eighteen, tacitly acknowledging her prime ability to manage the family's affairs. My grandfather Samuel Rakusen, who must have been an interesting character, actually started not in eggs but as Rakusen's matzos before passing the business over to his brother Lloyd. Thereafter, he made his living travelling to and from China on his egg importing business. At one time he even journeyed back from China through Russia at the time of the Revolution in 1917.

My father Bernard Glassman was born and brought up in Grimsby. Like many others, his parents had set out from Europe to emigrate to the United States, in their case somehow or other landing up in this fishing town on the Lincolnshire coast. My grandfather died when my father was just fourteen, and from then on he had to earn his own living.

At the age of eighteen my mother taught typing and commerce at a secretarial school. Later she started up a business with a younger brother, but then, after she married my father, remained together in business with him for most of their married life. Being a businesswoman at that time was in some ways less difficult than it is today. Help was cheap and easy to get. When I was young my mother employed a nanny to look after me, and later we had a maid who stayed with us for twenty or so years.

When the war started in 1939 we moved to Winchcombe, a village in the Cotswolds about seven miles from Cheltenham, to a house that my parents had purchased the year before as a holiday home and also as a retreat in case of war.

As a young schoolgirl I attended North London Collegiate School, an institution that was closely associated with Cheltenham Ladies College, in view of which my father applied for my transfer there. At the interview he was told that they had a 1% Jewish quota, but that in my case they would make an exception. 'Thank you,' replied my father 'but we won't bother'. So I never went to the College and instead received my education elsewhere in Cheltenham.

The war years were fairly peaceful in the countryside. My parents started a business manufacturing wooden houses for chickens, later branching out into other types of wooden buildings, including some for human use.

With the ending of the war they took a flat in Kensington, where I went to live with an unmarried aunt. For a time I worked in a local dress shop at £2 per week selling hats, which I found very boring, but at least I could buy some of my clothes at a discount. Later my aunt and I started a small dressmaking shop and asked Aubrey Rose, a young lawyer we had met at a Youth Club, to deal with the legal aspects of taking it over. It was only after this lawyer and I had married that I discovered that he had only just started working on his own and that we were his very first case. I thought that most appropriate in the circumstances.

When we were first married, Aubrey and I lived in the same Kensington flat, my aunt having left in order to get married a month after me. It was here that we had our first child, David. I used to take him for walks in Kensington Gardens, almost the only mum among all the uniformed nannies.

When David was two we bought a six bed-roomed house in Highgate for £8,500. If only you could do that today! Here we had our second child, Jonathan.

In 1964, when David was six, we joined the North Western Reform Synagogue, largely so that David could start at Religion School. Aubrey became Chairman of the Education Committee; the two of us were active in the Parents Group, whilst Aubrey also taught the children in the study group for many years.

We organised what I believe were the first holiday activities at the Synagogue, for about two hundred children enjoying themselves over three days in the holidays. This was repeated the second year, a few weeks before our daughter, Esther, was born eight years after her brother Jonathan.

I had always wanted to teach, so when Esther was old enough to start Religion School I attended the Teacher Training Course at the Leo Baeck College for two years. I found this very enjoyable and learnt a great deal. I then started to teach in the classes, mostly the 6-7 year olds, and continued to do this for about thirteen years. I was very pleased that before I gave up Esther joined me, teaching the first reception class, something that she went on doing almost until she had children of her own. But this was not my only involvement with the children of the synagogue. When Esther was seven she joined the Brownies. I asked Elizabeth Spencer, at that time Brownie Guider, if she wanted any help. Fatal words! It resulted in over twenty-two years of great delight and some hard work, though I enjoyed every moment of it, or almost every moment.

A year after I started to help Elizabeth resigned and I was asked if I would become Brownie Guider in her stead. For many years I was almost the only adult involved, although later I had help from Gwen Singer, and eventually from Esther. We had yearly pack holidays at Well End Scout Centre, Boreham Wood, not very far away perhaps, but once we got to the camp we were in a world of our own, a million miles from our usual lives. I think the children thoroughly enjoyed themselves. I know that I did, even though it did involve quite a lot of hard work. Those holidays (and despite everything they were holidays) remain among my happiest memories.

In 1978, while I was helping with the Brownies but before we had started embarking on Pack Holidays, our son David, then twenty, came home from his Law Course at Leeds University for the winter holidays with a lump on his hip. To our horror this was diagnosed as bone cancer. A course of radiation followed and every day I took him to the University College Hospital. David bore this with great courage and cheerfulness and by the summer a period of remission allowed him to enjoy life again, playing the guitar in a small band he had started, writing music and lyrics.

In the autumn he was not well enough to return to Leeds, so we arranged for him to continue his law studies at a college in London. Almost at once, however, the cancer recurred. Further medical treatment was impossible and the doctors held out very little hope.

My husband began to study alternative methods of dealing with cancers and went with David to Frinton, where a naturopath thought that he could be helped with a rigid diet regime. Although I worried about the hardship involved since David had always enjoyed food, it did help him mentally. He started drawing brightly coloured patterns, reflecting a more cheerful frame of mind.

Back at home he had to remain in bed, but somehow, despite continual pain, he remained steadfast and cheerful and we were greatly helped by David's attitude. He lived for a further six months, dying in July, eighteen months after his cancer was first diagnosed and remaining at home the whole of this time. It was, inevitably, a very unhappy time. But there were some better moments, leaving me with many happy as well as sad memories. We played cards with David, he watched TV with enjoyment, especially snooker and sports, and drew his wonderful patterns. He never complained and was always able to look on the bright side of things.

I had always enjoyed needlework and knitting, and gained great pleasure and learnt a lot through helping to make the hangings for the synagogue. What I learnt enabled me to make my own pictures and to turn David's colourful drawings into needlework.

About a year after David's death we moved from our Highgate house to a larger house and an even larger garden in Hadley Green, outside Barnet, where we are still living after about twenty years. We moved partly to provide a home for my mother, my father having died a few years before. My mother had been living in a flat by herself since his death, but as time went by she became increasingly crippled with arthritis and we felt she needed more care. She stayed with us until a few months before her death in June 1999, just prior to her ninety-eighth birthday.

In 1989 Esther was married in the garden of our Hadley Green house. She now has two children, Joshua aged seven and Jessica aged four, both our great joy. Like her grandmother, Esther is a career woman and combines caring for her children with work as a Town Planner.

Aubrey has been very busy over these years, in his legal work and in the communal field, at one time Vice President of the Board of Deputies, also Deputy Chairman of the Commission for Racial Equality, as well as writing and giving talks. Now, although still very active, he takes things easier and we are able to spend more time together.

Jonathan got married in 1998 and lives in a cottage in the garden. With Esther and her family living round the comer at present we are very lucky to have our children so near. I still retain my love of working with children and now help at Joshua's primary school, listening to children read and helping with the stamp club. I have had a very happy life and have been exceptionally lucky.

52   HELMUT ROTHENBERG
A BALANCE SHEET OF LIFE

I am the last surviving member of my generation of our family, born into an era which spanned the years from the First World War, the hyper-inflation period in post-Versailles Germany, the advent of Hitler and the Holocaust, the Second World War and the events thereafter.

My ancestors came from Mackensen near Hanover. In 1742 when the family decided to take a surname they chose the name of the local mountain range, Rothenberg. Previously men were known by their first name and then as the son of their father. My parents married on 24th March 1914 in Frankfurt. My father, Isaak, worked for a metal trading company in the Hartz Mountains. My mother, Dora Moses, came from a religious family that originated from Mainz. The guest of honour at their wedding was Ludwig Lion, Germany's special negotiator in Switzerland during the war. He was a close friend of Prince Max von Baden, the last German Imperial Chancellor. I attended his one hundredth birthday celebration in London in 1998.

In 1914 my father was called up into the Army as a Sergeant Major and was appointed a military administrator at the local hospital in Halberstadt. I was born on Friday, 22nd January 1915 at 29 Lindenweg, Halberstadt. I was underweight as a baby and the doctor thought I would not be over-healthy in years to come. I can still remember being pumped full of tonics. Two years later my brother, Karl Heinz, was born on 1st January 1917 and was known as Heini and then Henry. Food was difficult to obtain during the war and my mother kept two goats in the back garden so that we could have milk.

In 1920 we moved to Frankfurt where my father started work running a factory manufacturing twist drills. Frankfurt had two famous sons who influenced the city greatly: Goethe, Germany's foremost poet, and Mayer Rothschild who founded the banking dynasty. French troops occupied the Rhineland and half of the factory where my father worked was in the French zone and the other half was not. This began the period of hyper-inflation. The cost of a holiday in the north sea coast was 100,00 Marks and 10,000,000 Marks for the return journey. Workers were paid twice a day and their wives would wait at the factory gates at lunch-time to use the money to buy food.

I attended the Musterschule in 1927 aged twelve. I was fortunate that the school also specialised in English and French as well as German and Mathematics. This stood me in good stead for the future. Most of the teachers were former German officers and were very bitter about the outcome of the First World War. They became easy converts to Naziism. In 1930 I was sent on a school party to Cheshunt in England to stay in the house of a chartered accountant, Frederic Porritt. Family holidays were spent in Germany and Switzerland. I was a keen visitor to the cinema, and my class spent many hours performing plays and operas. At the Museum Society in Frankfurt I heard Yehudi Menuhin make his debut aged thirteen.

With the growth of Nazism, boys in my class used to dress alike and were known as 'Boys in Grey', forerunners of the SS. Police officers attended the school to teach the upper classes shooting, which is how I still manage to win prizes at the fair at Hampstead Heath! On 6thMarch 1932 I went to the Festival Hall in Frankfurt and among an audience of thirty-five thousand heard Adolf Hitler speak. When Hitler came to power on 30th January 1933 everything changed. My headmaster, Dr Peter Mueller, advised me to leave Germany by the end of March as after that date Jews would be prohibited from leaving Germany. When I attended a birthday party at a popular café in the centre of town I was forced to spend the night in the café as the streets were full of Nazis looking for Jews to attack. I realised I had to emigrate and left on 31st March 1933 via Brussels to stay with Frank Porritt in England. My father was determined to remain in Germany as he could not comprehend how German people would allow an Austrian vagabond to steal the fatherland from the people. I left with the awareness of the tragic cycle in Jewish history, where in normal times generations built and built and these achievements were then destroyed by forces of incredible adversity.

After a short period at a crammer in Chancery Lane I stayed with Frank Porritt and his family and was articled to his firm of chartered accountants. The firm's principal activities were purchasing shares in rundown companies and then trying to build them up. In 1934 circumstances in Germany became too difficult for my brother and he joined me in England. On 10th November 1938, after Kristallnacht, my father was arrested and sent to Buchenwald. I managed to meet the British Consul General in Frankfurt when he was visiting England and persuaded him to issue entry documents for my parents to come to England. My parents eventually reached England five weeks before the outbreak of the Second World War. Unfortunately the money Frederic Porritt was holding in trust for my father had been lost in commodity trading and we had little money. My brother joined the Pioneer Corps in the Army and I joined another firm of chartered accountants, Bright Grahame & Company. I reorganised the annual accounts for Bell Toys and Games Limited and I was then given a permanent position in Bright Grahame & Co as a manager in their office in Finsbury Square.

At this time I had additional night duties as fire warden in the City of London. I managed to rent a house for my family in Hampstead Garden Suburb at £90 per annum and remember how I had to sell my typewriter to pay the first quarter's rent. At this time all foreigners were known as enemy aliens and were classified according to their risk to the nation. Fortunately we received a low C classification which meant we could remain in London. Our next-door neighbour was Herbert Marcuse who became one of the heroes of the New Left in the 1960s and was one of the triumvirate of Marx, Mao and Marcuse. This is where I met my wife to be, Annema. Annema's husband had died during the war and when peace was declared we decided to get married. Annema and I were married on 23rd August 1945. She went almost immediately to Amsterdam to bring back her aunt and cousin, Henny and Billy Schalscher, who had just been liberated from Auschwitz.

I was determined to start my own firm. I met Bernard Blick who was in charge of insurance at Bright Grahame & Co and we commenced practice together. We called our firm Blick Rothenberg & Company. The firm is still known under this name. We obtained offices in Copthall Avenue. My firm expanded and we took an interest in a manufacturing firm, North & Sons. Eventually this company was floated on the stock exchange and became the biggest producer of industrial safety clothing in Britain. More partners were taken into the firm and it continued to expand. We moved to 3-5 Oxford Street and then eventually to York Terrace, our present address.

By the early 1950s we had four children (Eve, David, John and Bobby) and finally decided to have another and Judy was born. Two of my sons became chartered accountants and joined the firm as partners. Unfortunately I lost my dear wife Annema on 10th April 1991.

I got to know Dr Wiener, founder of the Holocaust Library and persuaded Leonard Montefiore to sponsor the library. I helped in the efforts to bring one thousand children from the concentration camps to England, although only 732 children were found alive. I also greatly assisted the Association of Jewish Refugees in Great Britain.

I have always wanted to live in Regent's Park and therefore it gives me great pleasure to work in an office overlooking the park. My great joy lies in my family, and assisting the various charities and organisations which interest me. I often wonder how my life would have been if there had been no political upheaval in Germany.

53   IGNACZ RUB
A SILENT HERO

I was born in the small mining town of Aknaszlatina in Transylvania in 1922. My parents were wealthy land and mill owners. At the age of eight I was sent to be educated in Frankfurt, over a thousand miles away from home. My time at the school owned by Mr Klibansky was the happiest time of my life.

It was during the school holidays that my lifelong fascination with all things electrical was fuelled and I spent hour after hour in my father's factories. After my barmitzvah I completed my secondary education in Oradia.

In 1940, at the age of eighteen, I was conscripted into the Jewish 7th Division of the Hungarian Army as slave labour. When Hitler declared war on Russia I was sent with 18,000 other Jews to the Russian front to support the Germans who were Hungary's allies. My unit was forced to work for the Todt engineering conglomerate in Dornica near Kiev. We spent our days chopping trees for firewood. In the winter of 1943, after many bloody battles in the Ukraine, the Germans retreated. The Hungarians were demobilised after three long years of hard labour.

A few weeks after I returned home, the Germans invaded Hungary. Along with the town's entire Jewish population my family were sent to Auschwitz. Joseph Mengele was present when the transport arrived. He looked at me, tall, robust and sun-tanned, and asked me my trade. When I replied that I had helped the Reich in the war effort and that I was an electrician, the infamous doctor pointed to the right.

Immediately after selection I was sent to the coalmines at Janina. On one occasion I was wrongly accused of stealing a piece of rag and severely beaten. Some months later I was transferred to the IG Farben plant at Buna, a few kilometres away from Auschwitz. Tens of thousands of slave labourers provided by the SS assisted in the production of methanol, oil extracted from coal. As one of the three largest synthetic oil plants Buna was producing about 33,000 tonnes annually, keeping the German Army rolling on the road and in the air. Here the Germans, recognising my considerable electrical expertise, put me to work on the transformers, which provided power to the factory's anti-aircraft defences.

I remember how well-prepared the Germans were when they heard the Russians advancing. An SS officer informed me that as the camp was to be mined the inmates would all be blown up in the event of a Russian invasion. I decided that if I were to die I would do everything in my power to take revenge for the suffering that the Germans had caused me. Without telling anyone I managed to tamper with the calibration of the fuses in the power supply to the anti-aircraft guns. Despite regular testing the Germans were completely unaware of what had taken place. When American bombers raided the plant in August 1944 the Germans went to operate all of the guns simultaneously. All of the fuses blew and the guns failed, leaving most of the factory destroyed. Within twenty minutes the Germans were seeking my opinion about why the guns had failed. I managed to convince them that the simultaneous starting of the motors must have overloaded the circuit. A quick look at the fuse covers, which showed the misleading calibration, satisfied them.

It was only after the war that I discovered just how catastrophic my sabotage had been. During the Battle of the Bulge, when the Germans had attempted to break through the steadily advancing Allied forces in the Ardennes, they had ground to a halt because they ran out of fuel.

In January 1945 the Germans, who were terrified by the imminent arrival of the Russian Army, fled the camps. On 18th January I and 1800 emaciated inmates were marched out of the camp by fifty armed SS men. No one knew where we were heading and along the way those who could no longer walk were shot by the roadside where they fell. When the column reached Landeshut in Lower Silesia several weeks later only half of us were still alive. Exhausted and starving we were literally stuffed into a stone quarry,

3 metres wide and a quarter of a mile deep – an economy as it only required two SS men to stand guard outside the two enormous wooden doors slammed shut at night. There was lighting inside the cave but within hours the oxygen was depleted. By morning hundreds were dead. Others like myself were semi-conscious. I had seen my life flash past my eyes, convinced it was the end. Miraculously I survived, only to escape and be recaptured. I was sent to the Landshut concentration camp where I remained until liberation on 8th May 1945.

After the war I studied physics in Vienna. During this period the Allies employed German personnel in Austria and Germany to help with administration. Other survivors who had sabotaged German plants divulged their activities to the Allies. I heard stories of Germans passing on this information to SS contacts who tracked down and killed these survivors. This terrified me into remaining silent until 1988 when I met another survivor, Gabriel Ramet, who persuaded me to tell my story. Despite talking at length about my experiences I still feel frightened.

Following university I worked in Australia for three years. I was taken to Melbourne by Yehudi Menuhin's sister, where I worked in a wiring factory where everything was done by hand. I noticed a lot of wooden crates and was told that these contained machinery from Germany, but as no-one could read the German instructions they could not be used. I unpacked the crates and as a result of translating the instruction I was able to get a production line up and running.

I met Thelma from London when she was on holiday in Australia and we married in 1952. Although my boss had offered to pay for all of her family to re-settle in Australia she insisted on returning to England.

In England I set up a successful factory in Dalston where among others I supplied Rolls Royce with the spring which was the basic ingredient of their car seats, and also Leeds jail with some of its wiring. I also supplied many countries abroad including several Arab countries, one of which wrote to me asking if I supplied Israel or had any Jewish people on my staff. I replied to them that mine was a any Jewish people on my staff. I replied to them that mine was a private company and I would not disclose details of either my customers or employees. This country continued to buy from me.

I am now retired and we have two sons, two daughters and six grandchildren. Only one of my sisters survived the war and today she lives in Israel.

NB Most of this information has come from an article by Joe Carver in the Holocaust Survivors' News September 1996.

54   DONALD PEBA SALINGER

I was born on 25th August 1915, the third child and elder son of Alfred and Hilda. My father was born in November 1868 and my mother, Hilda Rebecca née Nathan, was born in New Zealand in 1882. My father was the ninth of eleven children. His father was Maurice Salinger who came to England in 1830 with his mother as a boy of about fifteen. He claims in an affidavit sworn in 1856 when he took British citizenship that he had come from Gnessen in the Kingdom of Prussia. This may have been Gnei or the present city of Gneisenau but there are no longer records. He married into a long-established Anglo-Jewish Sephardi family called Peba, who were one of the original Jewish families to have settled in this county in 1657 at the behest of Oliver Cromwell. My grandfather married twice. His first wife died giving birth and he married his deceased wife's sister and had five children by her, of whom my father was the third.

I was born in West Hampstead where I lived with my father, mother, two sisters and younger brother from 1915 to 1932. My father, who in his youth had travelled widely in South America and South Africa as a salesman for Lever Brothers (now Unilever), eventually settled in London. In partnership with his elder brother he started the firm of H Salinger & Co., which still exists.

My father was forty when he married my mother, just twenty. Six of us, plus two living-in maid-servants and probably a living-in nursemaid when we were babies, lived in a horrible little house in Kingdom Road, West Hampstead. Suddenly in 1932 my father bought a much larger house the other side of West End Lane in Fawley Road. Only my elder sister Joan and I were still living with the family. My other sister Nancy had gone to Oxford University and my brother John followed in 1939 to Reading University. Because of our rather cramped living conditions in Kingdom Road, and in tune with the ethos of the time, I was sent aged ten to Bickley Hall boarding school, a preparatory school near Bromley, Kent, where my first cousins, the sons of my father's younger brother Maurice, joined me. I was there from 1925 to 1928 and then transferred to Mill Hill School in north-west London as a boarder. We were a typical Anglo-Jewish family; my parents were married at the West London Synagogue in Upper Berkeley Street. My father had never had very much to do with the synagogue, but my mother did a certain amount of voluntary and charitable work under the aegis of the Henriques family who founded the Oxford and St George's Settlement in the East End. I received correspondence courses from the synagogue and was barmitzvah there in 1928 but have no recollection of it some seventy-two years later. At sixteen I was confirmed there by Rabbi Harold Reinhart. In due course I became a member of the Junior Membership (JM) as it was then called, because Reinhart, who was from the USA, had brought with him the idea of making the synagogue a communal centre in addition to a Prayer Hall. He did much to encourage the youngsters. At these membership meetings I came to know a number of people, a few of whom are still alive, and we have remained in contact. I suppose the most notable amongst these was my wife, Rena, whom I met there in December 1935.

In March 1936 I was offered a job in Canton, China, by Deacon & Company who are still trading after their 1840 beginning in China. My father's firm was their London agent and I was offered the usual contract for a period of five years at a salary of £20 a month, which included accommodation and free medical attention. There was no allowance for holidays, or leave as we called it, but at the end of five years I was given a passage to anywhere I wanted in the world and a year's salary paid by the firm. In those days there were no air services to the Far East and travelling time to places like Hong Kong was over thirty days from southern Europe and about thirty-six days from London or Liverpool. Although I was only twenty my father allowed me to take this position, so in March 1936 I sailed from Tilbury to Hong Kong in HMS SS Rajputana. This was a P&O vessel, mixed passenger and cargo, and my passage created a precedent. Up till then expatriates to Deacon & Company and indeed most European trading firms in the Far East always travelled first class, but because of my youth and the fact that the firm was cash-struck at the time, they booked me second class. I only learned when I got out there that this created a terrible furore. It was considered to be a loss of face for anybody to travel second class. However when I got to Tilbury, much to my and my father's amazement, I had been upgraded to first class because we were taking a military draft to Bombay and all the second class accommodation was required by the NCOs. Officers and their families all went first class.

In December 1935, I had first met the young lady (she was seventeen) who later became my wife. We had been friends for a short time. We first met at a party in the house of a mutual friend. Afterwards she came rambling with our Junior Membership over the weekend in the Chiltern Hills and I was attracted to her. I liked 'the cut of her jib' as they say in sailing circles. However, when the call to China came I could not resist that and so presumably kissed her goodbye and off I went. Perhaps it is just as well that we don't know what life holds in store, because I thought I was going out to the East for a maximum of five years but in fact it stretched to a period of ten years, and of course World War II intervened.

I joined a special unit of the British Army in the Far East in October 1941, just before Pearl Harbour, and was given a Commission. Our task was to help train Chiang Kai Shek's army to fight the Japanese for China. However, this long spell out East is a story of its own, which I am not going to tell here. I learned the language and became part of the China scene.

I first made contact with Alyth Gardens Synagogue after World War II. During my life in the Far East I had no contact with other Jews because there weren't any around. My Army service was all in China where most of my companions were former Christian Missionaries. Neither of my parents nor my siblings were particularly observant. First time round my eldest sister married a Jewish man from New Zealand and went out to Australia where she spent the war. My younger sister went to Oxford and then shocked our Victorian/Edwardian family by marrying a young man who had been training for the Unitarian Ministry. She started her sixty years of married life as the wife of a Unitarian parson in Rotherham, Yorkshire. So we had a pretty mixed religious background.

In 1946, when I was back in the UK, my father was considered to be an old man at nearly eighty and our family was scattered. My parents had to spend the war without their children – my brother had been on Army service in England and Europe and of my two sisters, one lived in Ipswich and the other was in Australia. When I came home after ten years abroad I had only managed one visit home. That was just before VE-day when the powers in the Far East gave us all compassionate leave and after the usual administrative failures we were given a flight home. So I did come home in 1945 for a few weeks to say 'hello' to my parents. However I had no friends. All my cousins who might have been friends were up to twenty years older, and they were not around either. When I came home in 1946 I had intended to go back and live and work in the Far East, but I thought that I owed it to my parents to live with them and help my father during his declining years because of the nature of our family business (it had ceased trading in 1941 having been bombed out of its City offices). I tried to revive the business when trade with Hong Kong and the Far East became possible.

I returned to find out if I had any pre-war friends left in the West London Synagogue, where Reinhart was still the Senior Minister with Curtis Cassel as his deputy. Most were still in the Forces and had not come home or been demobbed. But I became interested in the running of the synagogue itself. At that time the executive consisted mainly of the older generation including some of the old founding families like the Mocattas and Montefiores. It urgently needed a transfusion of new blood. Reinhart saw this and got hold of me, Monty Moss and the then Honourable Roger Nathan, now Lord Nathan, and had us elected as wardens. Probably for the only time in its history the West London Synagogue had three wardens under the age of thirty-five. There was a lot of work to do and, as wardens do to this day, we had to spend a lot of time in committee. We did not have the secretarial and office backup that the organisation now has. There I started a club for young adults, because we found we had nothing in common with the then Junior Membership who had not been in the Forces. With people like Theo Marx and a few others we started a group called the Berkeley Reunion Group for ex-service people to get together and renew their pre-war acquaintances, and for social company. That was how I got involved in synagogue affairs after the war.

In 1950 by one of those strange twists of fate, fourteen years after I had left Rena, I happened to go into a room in the Stern building, Seymour Place, after one of the innumerable committee meetings in order to get a cup of coffee. When I went into this committee room there was a group of young women sitting around the table in animated discussion. Rena was one and I recognised her immediately, although I could not think of her name. I wondered what she was doing there. I knew by means of letters from my mother that she had been married so I had made no effort when I came home to contact her. I went over to the group to be sociable. They were discussing how much a single woman needed to earn to live in London. It was the first part of the post-war social revolution whereby young people became independent at a much earlier age than when we were young. Anyway, one of the young women whom I knew said, 'Donald, what do you think should be a figure?' Pompously I replied, 'I don't know but I pay my secretary so much.' At this moment Rena turned to look at me. She said the first thing she had said to me in fourteen years. 'What the hell do you know about it?' To which I replied, 'Well, wasn't your name Rena Lawton?' I could not remember what her single name had been. That was the beginning of a long story, which has lasted for another fifty years. I remember that we went up onto the roof at Seymour Place. We talked for two hours before I went home to my mother and said 'Mother, I have seen a ghost!' Rena had been married and her husband had left her. She had three young children. The upshot was that about a year later we got married and I adopted her children.

When I married Rena I was engaged mostly in exporting, acting as a confirming agent for exporters. Not a very successful business. Hong Kong had started up again and I was still doing business with my principals in the Far East. My previous employers were now well established in Hong Kong. By that time China had closed up.

One day Rena came to me and said 'I want to buy a flat.' It has been my very great good fortune that when we married she had recently moved into the house where we still live in Ringwood Avenue, (where she is by quite a long way the oldest inhabitant). 'Who do we want the flat for?' I asked. It was for a young woman who was seven months pregnant, the daughter of a builder who had done some work for us and who was desperate to get accommodation for her. His daughter and her husband were living with them in a council flat and were under notice of eviction due to overcrowding. There was a house at the end of a road not far away, which had been up for sale for some time, and we could not think why because at that time there was very little property for sale. We made enquiries and found that the family who owned the house was selling but they had what were known as statutory tenants who occupied the middle floor. The vendors insisted that the buyer should also give a home to the old family retainer who lived on the top floor in two rooms and shared the bathroom and toilet with tenants on the first floor with a 14-year assignable lease at £1 a week including rates. Thus all the buyer of the property got was the vacant ground floor. However the price was very cheap and so we enquired of the agents who were selling and it turned out that somebody was trying to buy it with a council mortgage.

At that time nobody was giving mortgages on part- possession properties. So Rena said 'All right. If the mortgage does not go through we'll buy it for cash.' The price was so low we thought there must be something wrong because even with a little portion of the house that we got, it seemed that we could make a 10% return on our money. So we did a little turn around the neighbourhood and saw one or two other 'For Sale' signs and found the same sort of properties, i.e. with statutory tenants, who paid anything from 12s 6d to £1 a week rent and usually had a major part of a house and probably a room in the rest of it. Anyway, we found a couple of these. I had a little money left on the stock exchange, which an uncle had bequeathed me, and so we bought two houses in the immediate vicinity. Then the first one we had seen came up, so suddenly we had three. And bingo, we were in business! Shortly after that Rena's father retired from business and we found other people who had capital to spare who were nearing retiring age. We said, 'Look, why don't we do the same thing for you?' We could pretty well guarantee them a 10% return on their money. This we did and within a few years we found ourselves overall managers of a considerable number of residential properties in the area. This is still the family business.

During my time as Cub Master (now called Cub Scout Leaders) I always made it my business to encourage the boys to support and attend synagogue services. We had regular youth services in which the cubs, scouts, guides and brownies took part. Today I have the pleasure of seeing boys who were formerly my cubs bring their children to the services. Such a long time has passed that many of their children have had barmitzvahs there.

It is well over ten years since I joined the Alyth choir. Viv Bellos had recently taken over direction of the music and she allowed me to join them. It has been one of the pleasures of my old age to take part in the services and sing with the choir under her direction. My first introduction to synagogue choral music was in 1935, the first year in which the West London Synagogue had an overflow service. The WLS had, and still has, a totally professional non-Jewish choir and organist under the direction of a Jewish musician. The musical director was Maurice Jacobson who later became a well-known musicologist, teacher and composer. When he was told there was to be an overflow service for the High Holidays at the Wigmore Hall, he asked some of us youngsters from the Junior Membership if we would be interested in forming an amateur choir. I had spent seven years at boarding school and was thoroughly familiar with choral singing in the Anglican tradition, so I volunteered and learned the whole repertoire

265

for the High Holydays, which has come down to the present without many changes. Under such progressive leaders as Viv Bellos there have been many notable additions to the repertoire.

RENA SALINGER
MEMORIES AS TOLD BY DONALD SALINGER

55

S he was the second child of Alfred and Ada Lesley, early members
of the North Western Reform Synagogue, before it had even
moved to Alyth Gardens and when it was still meeting in the
Hawthorn Hall in Bridge Lane. Her parents ran a grocery business in
Tottenham. Her father had served during the 1914-18 war. He had a
science degree (BSc) and had come through with scholarships all
through his career and planned to be a teacher. After the war he found
that with a wife and two children he could not make a living on a
teacher's pay of about £3 a week. His family was in the dress business
but, since his wife's family was in the grocery business and he lived
almost next door to them in Hoxton, he went into the grocery business
with his wife in Tottenham and made a great success of it.

His second child, Rena, went to Tottenham High School
which was one of the leading grammar schools of the area and then for
a short while to Minerva House, a Jewish boarding school for
gentlewomen run by some spinster sisters in Leicester. Because of her
turbulent nature, she must have been quite a handful. She left at fifteen
and came to the sixth form at Henrietta Barnett School where she
initiated Jewish prayers in the face of opposition from the then head
teacher. She could not get the scientific training that she needed to go
to university and so her parents asked the first Rabbi of the North
Western Reform Synagogue, Dr Starrells, if he could take her in hand,
and use her as his secretary. Her predecessor was a Mrs Joseph. Her
princely salary was 12s 6d per week (62½p in modern money).
Initially the synagogue did not have funds to pay her, so they made her
a life member of the synagogue in compensation. This enabled her to
attend the Association of Synagogue meetings as a member of the
synagogue. She ran the office single-handed, and was already very
involved with the Girl Guide movement. She remained a secretary
until two weeks after I said goodbye to her in 1936. Dr Starrells had

returned to America. Dr Perlsweig was the incumbent for a short time and then he went to America.

In 1939 she married Merton Lawton. By that time the minister was Vivian Simmons, seconded from Upper Berkeley Street Synagogue. Merton joined the army immediately afterwards as a fluent speaker of French and German. He had attended UCS in Hampstead and then the Sorbonne and Heidelberg University. He was enlisted into the Intelligence Corps and sent to France, Christmas 1939. He was due to come back to the UK with two stripes as a corporal, to the Officer Training Unit, to take his own Intelligence Squad to France with a commission. Because of the deteriorating military situation in France he never came back to this country and was taken prisoner with the 31st Irish Division at San Valéry in Normandy in May 1940. He spent the next five years as a prisoner of war at a large camp in Poland where he was the hospital administrator.

The Germans emptied the prison camp when they saw that the war was coming to an end. They did not liberate the prisoners but marched them away, attempting to take them back to the Fatherland. They were force-marched but he managed to escape and was liberated by the Russians via Odessa. He arrived home in April 1945. Rena had become very close to her parents-in-law, particularly her father-in-law whom she nursed through his last illness, but unfortunately he died just before his son came home.

The families rallied round and helped them get a home and a business together. Rena, who by then was thirty, decided she wanted to start a family and in her usual enthusiastic way she produced three children in twenty-seven months, which then was as fast as you could do it. After that it is a different story. She and Merton parted company in 1950. In the end he remarried and went to live in Australia. Shortly after that Donald came into the picture. Rena had maintained her contact with the Girl Guides Association, was an active guide and had revived the Guide Company and Brownie Pack at the North Western Reform Synagogue, which by that time was established in Alyth Gardens. Rena was present at the laying of the foundation stone in 1933. She attended the First Conference of Synagogues of Great

Britain, which was a predecessor to the RSGB and at which, at Rabbi Reinhart's request, she took the minutes.

After Donald came on the scene, their children began to grow up. The eldest child, Janice, went to Brownies and Guides and the boys went to the Cubs, which were under Jack Tobin. Donald still maintained his link with Berkeley Street. Somebody then asked if he could give a hand with running the Cub pack, to which he agreed and continued to do for about fifteen years. Rena continued running the Guide Company and Brownies with help from all sorts of people: Joyce King, Rita Slow, Joyce's sister, and others. It was a very successful company. Many of the later leaders came up through the Guide Company and still look on Rena as Captain or Brown Owl. Donald and Rena continued with these activities for many years until the early 1980s. Then they decided that since they were both over sixty it was time to get out. There was a change of emphasis in the organisations. The ethos of youth training and culture was quite different. So they handed over to others and it is a great sadness that both these activities, which gave such a lot of pleasure and useful education to the youngsters, have since ceased at the synagogue.

Then Rena developed a mastoid problem in both ears and was admitted to the Finchley Memorial Hospital where she spent the next six months. She had mastoidectomies on both ears, which left her with impaired hearing in one ear and practically no hearing in the other. To cap it all she developed septicaemia, which in those days was usually a killer because this was before the era of sulpha drugs, let alone antibiotics. She was on the critical list for weeks. Her parents visited her daily and her mother used to take her special food. Her doctor attended every day, several times daily at a certain period – possibly to sign a death certificate. However, she survived and had a long period of convalescence. After this she did not return to the synagogue as a secretary. It has left her energy quite undimmed although now, well over eighty, her hearing has almost disappeared.

56   MONAZZAM SAMYAH

My name is Monazzam Samyah. I was born in Iran on 1st January 1927 into a middle-class Jewish family. I was brought to the south of Iran when I was a year old. My father's name was Shalom and my mother's name was Hallom. I am the first child of the family. I had a brother who died four years ago. Two other brothers died when they were a couple of months old and I have another brother who is alive called Jonathan. My father's financial situation was not very good. He was a shopkeeper and then went into antiques. My mother worked in the shop and was a very brave woman. We lived in a house where three families lived and each family had a couple of rooms.

We had one synagogue in the south to which the family belonged. Life in Iran eighty years ago was not very good for the Jews and they lived in ghettos. I studied in the south of Iran at an elementary school and then went to a Muslim High School for girls during the war, where I learned English. All religions went to the school and there was freedom for women. One day when I was eight years old we were taken to the railway station to meet the Shah. He was very tall and wore a blue cape on his shoulders.

When I was eighteen my parents arranged a marriage for me to my mother's cousin. I was not happy. His family all treated me badly. After a year I went back to my hometown and wanted a divorce. My parents made me go back and two years later I became pregnant. All the time the family was cruel to me - I was treated like a slave - all day I was sewing, knitting and cleaning. When my daughter was born they all blamed me for having a girl.

Due to the cruelty I became paralysed. I went into hospital where after forty days I then began to move again. During this time my husband never visited me. Soon after this my husband put my daughter and me in a taxi and sent us home to my parents. When I got married I had a dowry, which included money, silver and gold, but I left everything behind. After returning to my parents' house for about a year I just lay in bed. I then started sewing, knitting and teaching

English again. I wanted a job, although hardly any Jewish women worked. My parents had a friend working in the government who found me a job working in American educational agriculture projects as a receptionist. I got on very well with the Iranians. Jews lived like kings and queens. The Shah said we were no different - we were all Iranian.

When my husband heard I was working he tried to stop me. In the evenings I supervised an orphanage where the director was a Governor General. One day I went to his office with eyes full of tears telling him my husband had complained about me. He then wrote a letter saying what a good job I was doing. After a year I learned to type and became a secretary. After two years I became the chief secretary. During the time I worked in the orphanage I also did prison work. I had no social life in Iran. I started work at 6am and didn't get home until 10pm. It was often very hot - 54 degrees centigrade. In 1960 I was offered another job with more money and then became a manager for more companies. In 1974 I worked as an office manager for an electrical company and then came over to England as a refugee.

My daughter went to school in Iran. She came to England with me and continued her studies. My daughter is now a lecturer in Hebrew at London University - Leo Baeck - and a translator. She married and divorced, and has a daughter who has graduated from Edinburgh University in genetics. When we first came to England it was very hard for me to leave my work and my friends. I was lucky to escape as they executed some of the Jews in Iran. However the last thirty years life has been better for the Jews and they have been able to integrate. Iran is a very rich country with copper, aluminium, iron and oil.

The saddest thing for me is that I lost my mother eleven years ago. She came over to England with me and lived her whole life with me. My father died in Iran. My brother in Los Angeles died four years ago. My other brother lives in England. Life has not been easy for me but I have always been a strong person ever since I was a little girl.

57 MARCUS SEFTON-GREEN
A LEAP OF FAITH

M y maternal grandfather was born in Poland and blew the cornet in the army of the Tsar of All the Russias. He always retained a ramrod spine and a moustache with heavily waxed points. My paternal grandfather, a tailor, emigrated from Riga to Sheffield and I believe his acting as a minyan man for the synagogue helped him scrape a paltry living.

I was born in Birmingham. My father, a doctor, died when I was fifteen months old. When the war started my mother moved to London and worked as a nurse. I stayed with my grandparents in Sheffield and can recall, after a night of the Blitz, finding an unexploded incendiary bomb on the cellar stairs. Later, my mother brought me to London and I attended Christ's College, Finchley, spending many lesson-less hours in the basement shelters during air raids.

After my mother's remarriage in 1941 I was encouraged to be actively orthodox, attending cheder three times a week until I was fifteen, and competing with Rabbi Lee Wax's father for the best chazan in the children's Shabbat services!

Two aspects of my life have remained very constant: in 1957 I married Dorothy, who I met at Oxford, and we set up home in the house in which we still live; and I joined the law firm to which I am still a consultant. In a third area, however, I made quite a momentous move. I became increasingly disillusioned with, and unable to believe in, Jewish fundamentalism. Rabbi Louis Jacobs' book, *We Have Reason to Believe*, came in every sense as a revelation. I needed to find a Judaism I believed I could pass on to my children.

A chance attendance at a Shabbat service at Alyth helped Dorothy and I decide what to do. We were warmly greeted there by the door warden, Jerome Karet (I had been involved in an amateur dramatic society with his brother and Nikki Van der Zyl). After some heart searching, we took the plunge and, to the consternation of my mother, left the United Synagogue and joined Alyth. Incidentally, the said consternation disappeared when I became a 'macher' in the community!

We started off attending the Forum Adult Education lectures, where Raymond Goldman invited me to prepare the next weekly précis. I had found my community and my friends. I also started to enlarge my Jewish knowledge and experience. After a few years I became a lay reader and have been able to 'inflict' my pleasure in Torah on the congregation for many years since. I was elected Junior Warden and two years later was thrilled to act as Senior Warden at the induction of Rabbi Dow Marmur. To my mind the job of warden is the best and most fulfilling in the congregation – even when it de-camped on High Holydays to the Hendon Odeon – as you get to know so many members. I was a member of Council for sixteen years in all, becoming Chairman in 1980. I was also active on the RSGB Council and later chaired its Congregational Development Committee. In 1976 I was nominated a Governor of the Jewish Joint Burial Society, later serving as Chairman.

In 1971 I merged my firm with those of Aubrey Rose and Jerome Karet – a wonderful professional association, which could never have occurred without our mutual Alyth membership.

My Jewish studies continued and I have particularly fond memories of the Monday evening sessions at the Marmur home. As my children grew up I was able to fulfil my duty by teaching all three of them their Bar and Bnot Mitzvah portions.

When I semi-retired in 1996 I was able to fulfil a long-cherished desire to study at the Leo Baeck College. I went back to basic aleph-bet and re-learned all the grammar I had never really known, and have been able to cope with a range of wonderful and stimulating courses from Tanach to Chasidism, history, philosophy and more. Alyth has been a substantial part of my life and that of my family. And in whatever I have been able to do for the congregation or the Reform movement I have always had the unfailing support and encouragement of my wife.

58   BEN SEGAL

I was born in Newcastle-upon-Tyne in 1912, the youngest of five
children. My father, who had come as a young man to Britain from
Lithuania, was Minister of the Leazes Park synagogue, and from a
very early age I was familiar with the synagogue and Jewish ritual. My
parents were dedicated Zionists. They spoke Hebrew - indeed, my
older brother learnt Hebrew before he learnt English. My mother had
spent her girlhood in Palestine, her parents having been among the
founders of Petach Tikvah. Indeed, my father met my mother after
reading a poem she had written in a Hebrew newspaper.

When I was six my father was appointed member of the
International Zionist Commission in Palestine under Chaim Weizman,
which was intended to prepare the ground for the Jewish National
Home. The rest of our family moved to Oxford. There, from the age of
ten, I attended a grammar school, the only Jewish pupil in the school.
Inevitably I was teased. It was on the whole in good-natured fashion,
though on occasion it ended in a fight. But in any case I was made
aware of the difficulties that beset a Jewish child in a Christian
environment.

In 1927 my family went on Aliya; my father had become
Professor of Bible at the Hebrew University of Jerusalem. I remained
at school at Oxford, living on my own in lodgings. But I went home
for the summer holidays in 1928, visiting Palestine for the first time. I
explored the length and breadth of the country, by bus and on foot, and
I learnt Hebrew. On my second visit in the following summer we
experienced something of the problems of the Middle East. Armed
Arab rioters besieged Talpiot, where we lived, for twenty-four hours.
The Haganah evacuated us just in the nick of time before houses in the
neighbourhood were sacked by the mob.

I went up to Cambridge in 1932 and studied Oriental
languages. I was wholly observant. I was President of the Jewish
Society and the Zionist Society, and I chanted the weekly parasha

in shul almost every Shabbat. I also boxed for the university over two seasons. After Cambridge I spent three years at Oxford, where I wrote a thesis on Passover for my D. Phil.

In May 1939, after a visit to Egypt, I travelled to the Anglo-Egyptian Sudan. In those days that vast country was administered by the British, a few hundred officials in charge of a population estimated at four million. I was - and remain - a wholehearted admirer of the British Sudan Government. True, the system suffered from the defects of colonialism but it had a kindly face, and it was efficient and incorruptible. After a stay in Khartoum I toured the province of Kordofan, and I went to Dilling in the Nuba mountains. At the end of May, on my last day in the Sudan, I was invited to join the Sudan Administration as the Government expert in Arabic.

I signed my contract in London when war was obviously imminent. With other Sudan Government officials on leave in Britain, I heard the declaration of war afloat off Glasgow in what became the first Allied convoy to sail through the Mediterranean. During the next two years I served as Deputy Assistant Director of Public Security at Khartoum, responsible for immigration and passports. I also acted as liaison with non-Sudanese communities, including the small Jewish community.

Life in the Sudan was interesting - it is here that the Arab world meets Africa. But inevitably, as the war progressed, it became a backwater. In January 1942, at the end of my probationary period, I was able to leave Khartoum for Cairo, and there I joined the army as Intelligence Officer at GHQ Middle East. Carried across the Sand Sea by units of the Long Range Desert Group, I had two stints several hundred kilometers behind enemy lines. During the first I spent a complete month with a Belgian officer and two Libyan soldiers in caves near Benina airfield, collecting and radioing information on enemy troops in the Benghazi area. Our informants were everywhere, observing German identity flashes, armour, planes, shipping and petrol dumps. We received information even from an Italian officers' mess, where an indiscreet conversation gave us the date of an approaching enemy advance.

I returned for a second trip behind enemy lines later in the year, with a British officer and two other Libyan soldiers. This time we were pursued for over a fortnight by the Italian carabinieri. We changed our hiding place each night, and finally succeeded in making our way northwards to Derna. When the Germans retreated to the west after their defeat at Alamein, we entered Derna and took control of the city at midday on 16th November 1942. I had prepared a Union Jack from a handkerchief and hoisted it over the Town Hall. The 'flag' is now on display at the Imperial War Museum in London. I was awarded an immediate Military Cross.

The war moved to Italy, but I remained at Derna. I supervised the dropping by parachute of informants in Greece. At the same time I was Officer for Tribal Affairs in Cyrenaica, visiting Bedouins in their encampments. But in early 1945 I moved to Tripoli to organise Arab education there. In the whole province of Tripolitania there had been only one Arab school. Amid great enthusiasm I travelled from town to town setting up schools and enlisting teachers and students. However, in November 1945 there took place in Tripolitania the pogrom in which over a hundred innocent Jews were killed. I helped in the task of evacuating the terrified survivors.

The atmosphere had been poisoned and shortly afterwards, in 1946, I arranged my transfer to headquarters in Cairo. There I was within easy reach of my family in Talpiot. There, too, I was able to visit Leah, who was a sergeant in the Palestine ATS in charge of a unit at the Victoria Augusta on Mount Scopus. We married in April 1946 at my parents' home, and after a brief stay in Egypt travelled to Britain by troopship.

With my return to civilian life I decided on an academic career. I taught Hebrew at the School of Oriental and African Studies, in the course of time being appointed Professor of Semitic languages in the University of London. I have specialised in Syriac, a form of Aramaic. On visits to the birthplace of Syriac, Edessa - now Urfa in Turkey - I discovered and recorded five ornate mosaics of the second century. Local bigots later destroyed them. I also found early Syriac inscriptions in the mysterious Tektek Mountains near Harran, where Abraham once lived. I have written a history of Edessa, and the townsfolk of Urfa elected me Freeman of their city. I have written a book on Passover, and another on the history of the Jews of Cochin in Southern India, which I visited four times. I have given public lectures at an Arab university at Cairo and at the Hebrew University of Jerusalem. In May 1968 I was elected Fellow of the British Academy.

I retired from London University in 1979. From 1981 to 1985 I was Principal of Leo Baeck College and supervised its academic activities after its transfer to the Manor House. I have been Vice-President of RSGB. Until recently I was a Director of the Jewish Chronicle.

Leah and I are long-standing members of Alyth. Our daughters Miriam and Naomi were Bnot Mitzvah there. We value deeply our association with the shul.

59   MANNY SILVERMAN

I was born in the East End of London in Stepney on 2nd January 1932, and like so many of my contemporaries was the son of first generation immigrants. If you listened hard you could hear the sound of Bow Bells, which I suppose makes me a true cockney. My parents had come over from Lithuania, but I am not aware that any of our family who stayed on survived the war. However some of our relatives did manage to leave and get to South Africa.

My father was a tailor and worked in many of the small workshops that were to be found all over the East End of London at that time. Because the opportunity of working was highly seasonal, life was particularly difficult in those days. As far as I can recall it started to get busy the day after the Lord Mayor's show in November, and it would stay busy until about February/March. Then there would be a very quiet period for the next few months. This meant that those working in the trade had to work virtually day and night to earn enough to ensure the families' existence throughout the year.

Looking back at life in those days I can clearly remember from a very early age that it was never an easy life for my parents, my younger sister Lillian and myself, but we survived. None of us can foresee which way life is going to take you and at that time who would have thought that many years later I would find myself participating in the Lord Mayor's Show as the reigning Master of a City Livery Company?

I have to confess that my education was fairly limited. I started school at Wood Close in Bethnal Green at the age of four. As my parents only spoke Yiddish it was not until then that I began to learn English. In between progressing from infant to junior and elementary schools, my education was further disrupted by the need to be evacuated during the war years.

I was evacuated three times during the course of the war. The first time was with my mother and sister to Cambridge at the outbreak of hostilities, (though I don't remember very much about that as I was only some seven years old). We came back shortly afterwards, but I was evacuated again during the blitz in 1941, this time on my own, to Hemingford in Huntingdonshire. During that period I lived with a number of families, some of them very good, others too awful to be believed. Interestingly, nobody I know had ever heard of Hemingford until John Major became Prime Minister.

I came back again to London towards the end of 1943 sadly bereft of any Jewish education. Consequently my Jewish education as such was very intermittent. It had stopped at the outbreak of war, started again towards the end of 1943 when I returned to London and stopped yet again when the doodlebugs started falling in 1944, when I was sent away for a third time. In the end I came back just in time to learn my Barmitzvah portion and be Barmitzvah.

During the whole of this early period we lived just off the now highly fashionable Brick Lane in Bacon Street. But it wasn't always so! The house has gone now, but I doubt that is any great loss. On the other hand the building on the corner is still there. I remember it because during the war years it became a sanctuary for us, as we would take shelter in the cellars of this building as soon as the sirens began to wail.

Compared to life today, living in the East End was primitive to say the least, but it was not all bad. As I think back on those summer evenings, people would sit and talk on the doorsteps in Bacon Street whilst the kids were playing in the road. To say that life was good and we all had it easy would be a bit of a pipe dream. The reality was quite different. Life was still hard after the war, goods were short, there was still rationing and money was very tight, but there was camaraderie, warmth of feeling and a good deal of trust.

If, for instance, you wanted to get into an 'A' film your parents would simply give you the sixpence and an adult would then be inveigled into taking you inside. In those days you could stand outside the Mayfair cinema in Brick Lane, the Museum in Cambridge Heath Road or the Rex in Bethnal Green Road and not think twice about approaching a total stranger and asking them to take you into the cinema. How tragically different things are today.

According to my late Mother (rest her soul) Silverman was not our original name, although I have nothing to prove otherwise. It is quite possible that someday we might find some relevant documentation, but regrettably we have never been ones for keeping family papers. My view has always been that whilst roots are important, they are only so to you as an individual. But as our family grows I am becoming increasingly conscious that we should do rather more to save family documents for posterity, something unfortunately I have not done.

My father (rest his soul) died when I was thirteen. At the age of fourteen I started work as an apprentice tailor with Moss Bros. This was a direct result of joining the Cambridge and Bethnal Green Boys Club when I was twelve. One of the club managers was Harry Moss, then chairman of Moss Bros, and it was through him that I joined the company.

I married Patricia in 1969 and we have one son, Jeremy. During the whole of this period I was still with Moss Bros, gradually taking on more responsibilities and climbing up the ladder, until in 1967 I was appointed a Director. I became Deputy Managing Director in 1975 and ultimately Chief Executive in 1980 during which time the company flourished year on year and produced levels of profit that it had never reached in its 180-year existence.

Life seemed secure but then in 1987, after forty years with the company and in my mid-fifties, I became the victim of a Moss family coup, out of a job and forced to start anew elsewhere. Fortunately things worked out well for me. Norman Hartnell, the prestigious Fashion House, which had made HM the Queen's Wedding Dress and Coronation Robes and had Royal Warrants of Appointment to both HM the Queen and the Queen Mother, had come on to the market. With the help of a number of friends we acquired the business. I became executive chairman of the company, adding lustre to the firm by also hiring Dior's world-famous designer, Marc Bohan, whose unfortunate experience of the politics and jealousies of business had been very similar to mine.

For the last few years I have been involved in consultancy and advisory work in the fashion and retail sector with a number of companies and public bodies including Scottish Enterprise, the Welsh Development Agency, UN Miller Freeman plc, the V&A and many others. I have also become an accredited Law Society expert witness.

Among my other interests is rowing. This began many years ago when some of my friends took to the River Lea down at Clapton and needed someone of suitable size to cox for them. Subsequently, a customer at Moss Bros gave me his address at the London Rowing Club; I happened to mention my interest in the sport and I was invited for a trial with them and became a member of one of the leading rowing clubs in the country. In time this led to my becoming a member of the Steward's Enclosure at Henley Royal Regatta, an associate member of the Leander Club, and a Director of the British International Rowing Fund.

I suppose the one thing that gives me particular pleasure and a degree of pride is that having started life in the East End, I became Master of the Worshipful Company of Glovers of London in 1997. While perhaps it may not be one of the oldest of the City Livery companies - we were not granted our Charter until 1638 during the reign of Charles I - our records nevertheless go all the way back to 1349.

Looking back on my life I feel that I have been very fortunate. I have become increasingly aware that whatever your beginnings, you never know where and how you are going to finish up.

60　　　　　　LIESL SILVERSTONE

M y parents names were Willi and Friedl Fischmann. My mother's maiden name was Dub. I was born on the 15th June 1927 in Puplitz-Schonau, Czechoslovakia, where my parents had always lived. I had a brother who was six years older than me and his name was Heini. My grandmother was born in Central Bohemia.

My father and his brother had glass factories. They were the biggest glass factories in Czechoslovakia for commercial glass, windowpanes and beer bottles. In the First World War my father was an officer in the Austrian-Hungarian army.

When I grew up, German was my first language but we went to Czech schools in my hometown, because after the 1914-1918 war Czechoslovakia was founded out of the Austrian-Hungarian Empire: one year German school, four years elementary Czech school and then I went to high school when I was eleven, by which time the Germans had invaded us. We moved inland in 1934 to Pocebrady near Prague.

My family belonged to the orthodox synagogue. During that time in Europe, whether or not you belonged to a synagogue, you belonged to the Jewish community called the Kahillah through which you paid your contributions to old people's homes, schooling, etc. As far as Hebrew education was concerned a rabbi used to come to teach us at home and I hated it.

When I was growing up my parents were very liberal and I did not hear any Yiddish until I came to England. However, they had lots of Jewish friends and most of my friends were Jewish.

When we moved to Prague I went to another school. The Germans occupied my father's factory.

I came out on the last Kindertransport when I was twelve. At that time I was just told that I was going. I recently met Nicky Winton, the man who initiated bringing out my generation. The government had initiated Kindertransport for Germany and Austria but nothing for Czechlosovakia.

When I first came to England I could not speak any English. I went to a boarding school in Worthing called The Warren. I was then meant to go to Toronto to my mother's cousin but the convoy of evacuee children that left before mine was torpedoed so they stopped anyone going abroad. At first I wrote to my parents, and the Red Cross managed to get the letters out via Spain. During the war I didn't know what was happening and I was just marking time until I could go home.

My favourite maiden aunt was in England. Unfortunately she had just got married in her forties to a refugee from Prague and they did not want me. In fact I found a letter where she had arranged to have me fostered for four pounds a week. I stayed with them in the Midlands and went to school in Dudley and then in Leeds. I must have been to eleven different schools and been taught in three different languages. In 1945 when the war ended I was actually studying for my finals at Leeds University. I used to be glued to the radio every day when the Red Cross read out lists of people who had come back. I didn't know what had happened to my parents. However, one of the Czech soldier boys who returned to Czechoslovakia phoned my mother and she was the only one who had survived.

During the war she went to Terezine where all the Czech Jews were sent. My father was then deported to Auschwitz erev Rosh Hashana – the Germans knew how to pick their days. They invited the women to join their men. My mother did not know where they were going but joined my father. We think my brother had been shot. My mother got out of the train at Auschwitz and there was Mengele. My mother lied and said she was under forty – everyone over forty was gassed. From Auschwitz she went to Freiburg where they were making V2 rockets, and then to Mathausen where she was placed in the mortuary as she had typhoid. Here the Americans liberated the camp and she was taken back to Prague. Eventually my mother and I met again when she came to England. I was about eighteen and it was a strange meeting and the first thing she said to me was 'You're the only one I have left to make life worthwhile'.

I went back to Czechoslovakia with my mother. I had by then graduated from university and was a member of the Institute of Personnel Management. I got a job with the World Jewish Congress in Prague where I was living and used to visit my mother at weekends. We were not allowed to keep our family home as it was too large and she was allocated a flat. However, the Russians came and again we tried to get out. I got out before my mother as I had lived in England. I then tried to get my mother out. The intention was that my mother would come to England and we would both emigrate to Israel. However, when my mother came to England we stayed here.

I worked for the Jewish Congress in London where I met my husband, and we got engaged. His name was Jack Silverstone, and his family were in the wholesale grocery business. I knew his sister from work and she introduced us. I had lost nearly all my family, and at that stage of my life it felt so right to marry him. He had such a sense of humour, which I had been completely cut off from.

We were married in 1949. We had two boys, Daniel and Robert. Daniel is now chief director of the Fiaria Commission for Racial Equality. Robert lives in Rouen and has a restaurant. The boys went to private prep school. Then Daniel went to Orange Hill Grammar and Robert to Hendon County. Daniel went on to Sussex University, then Manchester for a second degree. Robert did voluntary service in his gap year. He dropped out of university and joined a political action group. In due course he went back to university and did a degree in food management and then lectured in various places. Eventually he had his own restaurant in Brighton, and then Rouen, but he now wants to come back to Brighton.

We joined Alyth quite early on. Alfred Goodman rang the bell. He got us involved and I remained very involved with Alyth for many years. I was on various committees, on the Council, the Board of Deputies etc.

One year, I took my son, Daniel, back to Czechoslovakia. My other son, Robert, went on his own. In May I am going back as Daniel wants to see my hometown. Before the war we were very wealthy and

I had a nanny. As times grew more difficult, my parents gave members of staff things to look after for us. After the war, some of the staff did not remember, but others did and returned the items. It was a very difficult time when I went back. There were Jews who were Communists betraying other Jews – you did not know who to trust and it was a dreadful time. It was also difficult for the children. They were questioned at school about politics. Prague was not touched during the war, but an entire democratic regime was destroyed.

My husband left me for a young secretary at work. It was difficult at the time as the boys were in their teens, but we are good friends now. At that time I had already started working as a school counsellor in Brixton. After my husband left I took two more qualifications – I qualified as a counsellor and an art therapist. After this I became a tutor on counselling courses, and gradually evolved and pioneered a form of art therapy. In the Jewish section in Prague (in the Jewish Museum) there is an exhibition of children's art, and each painting gives the date of birth of the child and the date that child was deported. When I went to Prague with Daniel I saw this exhibition. It became a trigger for me to do art therapy and turn what was a horror into healing. There is an approach called the person-centred approach, originated by Carl Rogers – a wonderful American therapist – and his belief is that people can be autonomous if you are directing, controlling and guiding them, at the same time allowing them to reach their own potential. My other inspiration was my father, who was very accepting and very much like Carl Rogers. I have written a book on this new approach called 'Art Therapy in a Person-Centred Way'. I have taught this approach, and there are now six colleges teaching this approach. I am a Fellow of the British Association of Counselling and Psychotherapy, partly because I was very actively involved with them on their executive and various committees, and also because of this work I have initiated.

Going back to Alyth, I found I was getting more and more disenchanted. However, I was eventually introduced to a group concerned with Jewish Spiritual Renewal. This movement originated in America. There are about thirty or forty of us. I find this wonderful.

I am still a member of Alyth and have been since 1949. The boys have dropped away from religion. Daniel is married to a non-Jewish girl and Robert is gay. Although Judaism means a great deal to them because of the Holocaust, they are not in any way religious. I have one surviving cousin in Israel. However, I have not been there very often and he has not been here.

61   ALFRED SILVERTOWN

My parents names were Jack and Ginny. My mother was born in England and my father was born on the border of Germany and Poland. My father came to England in about 1880 with his parents because of the persecution in the border towns and villages.

My father was five when he arrived in England and went to the Jewish Free School. His family lived in Stepney. He was a master tailor and eventually had his own business. Between the two wars he became the biggest retail bespoke tailor in the City of London. The name of the firm was Jerry Silvertown.

I was born in Belgrade Road in Stoke Newington on 23rd May 1914. I had an older brother and sister and a younger brother and sister (I was in the middle). Their names from the eldest were Nathaniel, Esther, Gertrude and Cyril. I started my primary school in 1919, in Princess May Road in Stoke Newington.

What I first remember about the First World War was the bombing of London. In 1917 - I was about three and a half - there were a number of air raids from Germany and one or two on north London. The local community used to pile into the Alexandra Theatre in Stoke Newington for protection against the bombs. I remember one Friday night when the air raid warnings went off, all my family trooped with everybody else into the theatre and sat on the stone steps. Being Friday night my mother had cooked fish in the usual way and when we got back home the cat had eaten all the fish.

We moved from Stoke Newington to Stamford Hill and I went to the Norwold Road Primary School. My parents were members of Shacklewell Road Synagogue, Stoke Newington and we used to go regularly. I used to attend Hebrew classes there and also at a private home in Cazenove Road, North London. I had my barmitzvah at Shacklewell Road Synagogue, where I was also in the choir.

My next school was Upton House Secondary School, boys only, in Homerton. The teachers were all men, all ex-servicemen from the First World War, an excellent school.

My father was not called up in the First World War, but he was ordered to do military work in the clothing trade. In between the wars my school days on the whole were very happy. We were five children and we had a nice house and garden. Sport played a big part in my life. We had a chauffeur at that time and he always called me 'sporty boy'.

I left school at sixteen having matriculated and went into a solicitor's office in Bishopsgate. I was on a few weeks trial but didn't like it and left and went into my father's business. My father was keen for his sons to come into his thriving business at Ludgate Circus, City of London. I was sent to the Tailor and Cutter Academy. At that time we were still living in Stamford Hill.

I left the Academy in 1934 when I was twenty. I was very aware of Nazism and Fascism in England. I used to attend all kinds of political movements for the Labour Party and I also helped to collect money for Spanish refugees coming to Europe at the time of the Spanish Civil War. I met many Labour politicians and became a member of the Fabian society. I used to go to summer schools in Devon. I met Hugh Jenkins, who later became Lord Jenkins of Putney, and he was also Minister of Arts. I also met James Callaghan.

In 1938 I left my father's business as I realised it was not the kind of work I wanted to do. I found a position as an articled clerk in a solicitor's office of Sam Bard. Sam Bard was later in the army in North Africa and awarded the MBE. I stayed at this firm for four years until the outbreak of the Second World War. I wanted to go into the Air Force, but they weren't ready for me. They deferred me for about a year and by that time I had passed my final examinations and begun working as a solicitor.

In 1936 we moved to 36 Beechwood Avenue, near Henley's Corner. As I was deferred from the RAF I joined the Finchley Fire Service in 1940 with my older brother. We had to go to the fire station on the North Circular Road. During this time I was given permission by the Government to take my final exams as a solicitor.

We lived in London during the Second World War - there was no bombing until the beginning of 1941. The Battle of Britain began in the summer of 1940. The bombing was extremely heavy. I was at a loose end for a few months - the RAF had still not called me - so I went back to the solicitors firm, Crone & Son, stayed there a few months and then went into Intelligence in the RAF in 1941. After a year or two they placed me in coding cipher.

At the end of 1943 they wanted men to man the invasion. So the RAF had to play its part, even men on the ground. I was involved in an organisation called Combined Services, in which a combined force of the Army, Navy and Air Force were prepared for invasion. I was still in Intelligence, but they put me on board a ship. The purpose of this ship was to get information on the movement of aircraft, mainly by use of radar, at the time of the invasion. This information had to be coded and decoded. This was done by teleprinter and not by radio.

I was based mainly in the RAF at Stanmore although I moved around England a little. At the beginning of 1944 I was placed on board ship. This was an iron ship made in America, and it had a capacity of 5,000 tons. We were all in training on this ship. In June 1944 we came into the Channel and were at Weymouth where there were thousands of troops, including Americans. On 5th June 1944 we were told to get ready. However the weather was so bad in the Channel that it was postponed. There were 4,000 ships going over from the South Coast. Eventually we anchored seven miles off a French port. We carried out our work of teleprinting back information about German aircraft, but on the night of 22nd June 1944 our ship went down. It was torpedoed and I was on it. Everybody escaped except five men. We managed to swim to a destroyer, and were brought back to Portsmouth wrapped in blankets and given hot tea and rum.

A few days before the ship was sunk we managed to pick up a body from the sea. It was the body of a German airman who had been shot down. I remember helping with a Neil Robertson jacket to pull him on board. A Neil Robertson jacket is a stretcher, like a corset, one for the lower part and one for the upper part of the body, and at each end is a rope. The German was taken down to a makeshift surgeon's table and the surgeon helped to save his life. A week later we realised that this was the Nazi airman who had destroyed our ship and five lives.

About four months later, on 10th December 1944, I was posted to India. I went out on the BOAC sea boat (flying boat). We landed on the Nile and stayed in a hotel. We had to be up at 5am to go on to the next stage from Cairo. We went on to the north-west of India. For the first year I did field work, coding. At that time the war in Europe was over, but not in Japan. They asked me to volunteer for teaching jobs, which they called educational vocational training. I got the job and was a sergeant. It was very interesting going around the different camps in India. At first no-one would talk very much, but once I started talking about football - Tottenham and Arsenal - they wouldn't stop talking. By the end of the war I found India fascinating. Gandhi was still alive, the Governor General was still alive, Mountbatten was still around - it was a tremendous melting pot, and fortunately with the Army, Navy and Air Force behind you felt secure.

After the defeat of Japan I remained in India for another nine months and managed to see many places, all at the King's expense. I came home in April 1946 and went back to my family in Beechwood Avenue and stayed there until I got married in February 1949. I met my wife after the war in London in 1948 at the Overseas Club in Piccadilly.

We were married at the North Western Reform Synagogue and Rabbi Landerdowne married us. In 1938 I became dissatisfied with the noisy services at Finchley United Synagogue and I went to the nearest reform synagogue, which was Alyth. I liked it so much that I stayed on. Our wedding reception was at home in Beechwood Avenue.

When we were first married we lived in a flat in St. John's Wood. I left my original job in a legal firm in 1948 and my father was very keen for me to have my own practice, which was called Alfred Silvertown. Later I joined up with one or two other partners. The practice was in Holborn and two or three years later we opened a branch in Wembley.

We moved to Highgate Village in 1951 and were there for eleven years. We came to Lanchester Road in 1962. We had two children - Jonathan and Adrian. They both had their barmitzvahs at Alyth, under Dow Marmur. Jonathan went to Sussex University and is a professor in ecology. Adrian got a first at Lancaster in physics and has a very good job. Jonathan has two sons.

I sold both my practices in 1985 and had permission to practice from home. This was until 1996 and I then sold that practice. I have been chairman of the university group at Alyth and later on I was elected a member of the Board of Deputies and was on the board for nine years. When I retired I did some academic work. I was introduced to Butterworths and they published a work of mine.

I was very happy about the founding of the State of Israel. My wife and I have been several times to Jerusalem to the meeting of the governors at the Hebrew University.

62   CECILY SOLOMONS

I was born on 27th October 1919 in London and was an only child. Both my parents were born in England. Mother's ancestors were Dutch and father's parents were from the Heim, but he was not sure from where exactly. They must have come to England when my grandfather was quite a young man. He came to take up a job as a shochet in Newcastle.

My father, Samuel, took a teacher training course and was a teacher in elementary school. My mother, Elizabeth, took an English degree at the Royal Holloway College and at one point was also a teacher and later on a social welfare worker. It was very unusual before the first war for a female to go to university. In the First World War my father was in the Royal Naval Air Service and was an instructor somewhere in Scotland.

We lived in Highbury. I went to the local elementary school and then went on to Owens Grammar School, Islington. I then read chemistry at the Royal Holloway College from 1938-1941. We were quite comfortable in those days before the war. My father bought his own house. It was unusual in those days to have two working parents.

As far as my Jewish education was concerned, I went to cheder at a very small Echal Midrash literally round the corner that was an offshoot of Shonfeld's Federation Synagogue. My parents belonged to the United Synagogue. However they eventually joined the North London Liberal Synagogue in Stamford Hill. At that time they met at Stoke Newington Library Hall. I didn't go to any youth activities or clubs until I went to Jewish student clubs at university.

During the war I lived at home and also at my residential college. Then I left and worked at Boots in Nottingham for four or five years doing quality control and analytical development. I left in 1945 and worked for BDH in London. I then worked for Glaxo until I retired.

Life in Nottingham during the war was reasonably good. I shared a small, furnished place with a friend. When I worked in London I lived with my parents. (I lived in Finchley for twenty years in a flat, but I got so fed up with it I eventually moved to Asmuns Place when I retired.) During this time I used to go to concerts. In fact, at one time I used to go to a concert every week, sometimes at Sadlers Wells. I went to the first production of 'Heat of the Night'. One night I saw an Italian lady from Abyssinia who was of the old school and I have never heard anybody quite like her again.

When I worked in Nottingham during the war there were army and airforce men and then the Americans came. I never went out with an American. When it was known there was an American contingent going to Nottingham they sent emissaries round to all the big factories to tell us that if you have a daughter going out with an American soldier it was okay, but not to go out with a coloured soldier. I used to mix in Jewish and non-Jewish circles in Nottingham. I had quite a strong social circle at work and a social circle at a United Synagogue.

During the war the only thing I missed, as far as food was concerned, was not having imported fruit. For most of the war I was in Nottingham and came back to London in 1945 and lived with my parents for quite a while. After the war I went to the Festival of Britain.

I don't feel my life was different because I went to university and got a degree, as people at that time got other types of training such as apprenticeships. Girls did secretarial courses and even if they got married they carried on working. I did not notice much anti-Semitism before the war. One of the things I can remember was that you could go on a trolley bus after six o'clock north or south of the Thames for sixpence. During my working life I was never short of money although I was paid at the women's rate, not the men's. I used to keep up-to-date with my chemistry by reading all sorts of journals.

I joined Alyth in the late fifties as I preferred it to the Liberal shul. I worked on the guild and the library committee. I worked on various embroideries and in the Mizrachi Library for a while. When I joined Alyth, Philip Cohen was there and then Dow Marmur who was very involved in adult education. Now I go to the Sternberg Centre and listen to lectures.

I used to go on holidays abroad and I liked cruising. I went on Mediterannean cruises on the P & O in the fifties and sixties. I have been to Israel. The first time was 1959/60. The refugees were pouring in at that time.

I have done various social activities with the synagogue. I enjoy music and used to play the piano. I had a wide circle of friends who had similar interests to mine. Now I mainly stay at home and listen to Radio 2, as it has a wide selection of music.

63   JOAN STERN

I was born in the East End at Mother Levy's Maternity Home on 2nd July 1932. My parents were Mark and Rose Tressner. My father's family came from Lithuania and my mother's family from Poland. I have one brother called Harold and a sister called Delia - I am in the middle. Delia is very involved with RSGB. The Tressners were a well-known East End family. My father worked in a tailoring business. He was too old to be called up in the war but worked in the garment industry making uniforms.

During the war my mum decided that we were not to be evacuated, which was very unusual. I went from the East End to Dagenham (near where my sister lives), then we came back to Edgware via Golders Green. I went to primary school in Edgware and Orange Hill Secondary School in Burnt Oak.

I didn't have any Jewish education. Although we lived in Edgware we were not as well off as most of the people in Edgware, so we were not very much involved with Jewish life. I was a very introverted child.

I left school at sixteen and went to work as a junior clerk in an office with Middlesex County Council. After that I had a succession of jobs. I worked at M & S for a while as a shorthand typist. I got that job because one of my uncles was a manager of the Kilburn branch. I became bored as a shorthand typist and went to train as a staff manageress. After this they started cutting down on staff, but I think because of my uncle I was not fired. I ended up secretary to the company secretary of British Aluminium and stayed there until I married Ralph.

I lived at home with my parents until Ralph and I met and married in 1968. Before I met Ralph I used to go to dances and theatre. I went to Israel on holiday and came home when the Six-Day War started. After I married I went to work in a family business. I never became involved in Ralph's committee meetings - they did not interest me. My hobbies are music, reading, gardening and knitting.

64   RALPH STERN

I was born in Berlin on 13th February 1931. My parents were Alfred and Lisa Stern. My father came from a small village near Frankfurt and my mother, whose maiden name was Leeser, came from Essen. My mother's family had reform connections since her grandfather was president of the Liberal synagogue in Essen at the beginning of the 20th century - so we have a long connection with the reform movement.

My father was born in 1887 in Germany and came to London in 1906 working as a button merchant with his brother Julius Stern. In 1914 my father was interned and he spent the First World War on The Isle of Man. His main job was producing the Jewish menus for the Jewish prisoners.

In 1918 my father went back to Germany and moved to Berlin where he started his business as a button merchant. My parents were married in the Liberal synagogue in Essen in 1930. Because my father had connections in this country (his brother's family was still living in England), he came here in 1935. My mother followed with me in January 1936. In Germany I can remember my mother's sister who had a kindergarten in Essen where I spent a few months when my father came to England.

In England we bought a house in Eastholme where my parents let out one of the rooms. This is where I grew up. I first went to school at Lees Lodge, which is a type of kindergarten for children aged five to seven. Then I attended Lees House, which was a preparatory school up to eleven. In 1939 I was evacuated with Lees Lodge to Lascombe Castle in Dawlish, Devon. While I was there I managed to get a stomach ulcer so my parents took me back to London just in time for the Blitz. I was in London right through the war. When I was eleven Miss Mulliner, who ran Lees Lodge, gave me private tuition and in 1942 I went to Highgate Junior School, then to the senior school until I was seventeen.

My Jewish education started with my parents joining Norrice Lea when they came from Germany and I attended Hebrew Classes. However, as Highgate School held lessons on Saturday mornings, Norrice Lea was not happy about this. Our dentist Mr Starlish, who at that time was one of the wardens at Alyth, recommended Alyth Gardens. I have been there since 1943 and also had my barmitzvah in 1944 when Vivian Simmons and Rabbi Werner Van der Zyl were there. I was in the same class as Raymond Goldman. We had my barmitzvah lunch at 33 Abbey Road, a very nice restaurant.

Most of my parent's family got out of Germany. My father's mother, his twin sister and another sister all came here in 1939. My grandmother on my mother's side together with my aunt also came. My grandmother lived with us and my aunt took on domestic jobs, although she was qualified as a chiropodist and did this after the war for many years. The only members of my family who did not get out were two great uncles who ended up being hidden in France and survived the war.

When my father came here he started a button factory with Mr Thompson in Long Lane in the City which was bombed in early 1940. They then moved to premises in Australian Avenue but on 29th December 1940 there was a big fire and the building was completely gutted. However at that time there was a button manufacturer retiring in Bedford Road, Tottenham and my father took over the factory. We stayed there until the sixties. In 1969 my father was talking about retiring from the button business and I was blackmailed into going into the business. In fact my father did not leave the business until he died in 1988. At the end my father got Alzheimer's so I ran the business.

We moved from Tottenham to Hackney, Alcoley Street, manufacturing buttons; originally we were manufacturing casing buttons and later casing became too expensive and we went into moulded nylon buttons, which worked very well until the early to mid-nineties. The business originally was known as the Ideal Button and Moulding Company. We bought the Stamford Manufacturing Company and kept the name and used it for the majority of our work. We supplied the button merchants. We supplied mainly white buttons and they dyed them to match the cloth for the manufacturer. Today there is very little manufacturing in this country. In the end we closed the business when I was of retirement age, as the two managers did not want to take over the business.

My interest in the synagogue started when I was barmitzvah. When I was seventeen I became very involved in the Alyth Junior Membership which was run by Ruth Markman. When I was eighteen we started the Alyth Jewish Fellowship. Before I went into the army I went to University, Northern Poly in Holloway Road, to read Chemistry. 1951-1953 I did my two years National Service in the Royal Artillery where I got a commission and spent a year and a half in South Wales at Newport Mon barracks. Whilst I was there I got to know the Cardiff Reform Synagogue and was befriended by the Bogod family. The last job in my army regiment that I did was to organise the troops who were to line the route for the Coronation in 1953. We were housed in Olympia and we watched the Coronation on television and waited for the troops to come back in the evening.

At that stage I was qualified as an analytical chemist. The first job I had was in Maidstone working for Kent County Council Public Analyst Department, analysing food and drugs for contamination. I was there for about a year, living in digs, but I came up to London most weekends for my Jewish life as I was very involved with the Alyth Fellowship and the YSGB (Youth Association of Synagogues in Great Britain). I then got a job with Walls Ice Cream in Acton, analysing ice cream and sausages. This was 1954-1955 and I moved back to my parents' home.

In 1955 I met my first wife, Angela Cowen, whose family was very involved with West London Synagogue. When I met Angela she was just finishing a BA in English. We were married in 1956 at the West London Synagogue and the reception was at the Rubens Hotel, South Kensington. The wedding was performed by Lionel Blue, who was a student rabbi at the time. We had three children - David was born in 1958, Richard and Martin, twins, in 1961. We bought the house I am now living in just before we married. Angela had very serious post-natal depression after David was born and even more so after the twins.

In 1964, when Richard and Martin were three, Angela committed suicide. Members of Alyth were very supportive when I lost my first wife. I just kept going because at that time I was very involved in synagogue work. When I got married in 1956 I was elected to the synagogue council and from 1960-1963 I was a warden of the synagogue. After that I was Honorary Secretary for five years with Alfred Soester.

My children went to Conway House prep school and then all three got into Haberdashers. They all had their Jewish education at Alyth. In 1967 I was vice-chairman of Alyth. In 1968 I married Joan Tressen who was PA to a company secretary and had a very high-powered job. We met through a Jewish introduction agency. We were married at Alyth and also had the reception there. I was then chairman of the synagogue. During my term of office Rev Phillip Cohen retired. I chaired the selection committee that appointed Rabbi Dow Marmur.

In 1967, during the Six-day War and when I was vice-chairman, we became very involved with the JIA, which is now the JPA. Geoffrey Rose was the chairman and asked me to run the JIA campaign during the Six-day War. That was when my interest in Israel began and I have been involved ever since. It was during this time that I started the idea of the daily kaddish service. At that time we started Pro-Zion and I have been on the committee ever since. The primary reason is to support the Israel movement in Israel and achieve equal rights for progressive Jews in Israel. The first time I went to Israel was with my wife in 1969. From then on there is hardly a year that I have not been; firstly on JIA missions and through Pro-Zion I became involved with the Zionist Federation. The first person to get on to the executive was Bernard Davies who was treasurer in 1986. We were also involved in the World Zionist Congress. A big change came a few years ago when we got seventy American delegates and this changed the whole aspect.

My children are not Zionists and all three have married out. David got a degree at Oxford in PPE, then went to America and is now a professor at Iowa University. Richard went to Oxford and got a degree in English. He now lives in East Sussex, is married with one son and an adopted daughter. He was a health service expert on the homeless and is now Executive Director of a National Health Trust for a series of GP practices in Sussex. Martin went to Warwick University and got a degree in history. He had glandular fever for a year after which he decided he would do a PGSE, which he did in Bristol. He became very involved with learning-disabled children. He spent a year at a school in Weston-Super-Mare. He came back and trained as a counsellor and he is now training to be a child psychoanalyst.

As regards the creation of the state of Israel in 1948 - we were all very happy but not that involved. My involvement with Israel started in 1967. When I was involved with RSGB I helped set up new synagogues, one of them being Finchley Reform. I have spent twelve years on the executive of the Zionist Federation, the first four years as treasurer and then four years as Vice-Chairman. I am Chairman of the Zionist Federation at the moment until July of this year. I am the first non-orthodox chairman of the Zionist Federation. I have met many people over the years, am involved with the Embassy and a new organisation called Bi-con. We have three hundred active members of Israel Response Group. These people answer letters in the press and take part in phone-in programmes if Israel is mentioned. I have been involved quite frequently with the solidarity missions to Israel. I am also a member of the ruling body of the World Zionist Organisation, a special status for Chairman, and we meet together two or three times a year. I was Chairman of Pro-Zion at one stage.

I was also involved in the Button Trade JIA committee. I was twice Chairman of the British Button Manufacturers Association. I was also President of the European Button Industries Federation. As far as the business was concerned I did quite a lot of selling abroad - Scandinavia, particularly Copenhagen, Berg and Helsinki, Stockholm, a little in Germany, Austria and we did quite a lot in the States - we had an agent in New York.

Joan and I very much enjoy going to concerts.

KATHE TRENTER
65
BEGINNINGS

My father was born into a very large, very poor family of ten children in Poland. The family migrated to the small towns around Breslau in Germany, and it was there that I was born in 1919. My sister was born in 1917. By that time my father was comfortably off, with his own clothing factory. We had a nanny and servants too.

My mother came from Upper Silesia, not far from Breslau. She was brought up in a much better way than my father. Her parents had a material store and there was already money there. My mother had a governess, and went to finishing school in Neuchatel. So already she could speak French and English a little, and played tennis and swam.

My father was always very good to me. I remember him with a smile and I always say, 'I know what I know from my father.' He taught me everything. I remember one day we were going to work and there was a shop that had a sale - every garment was 25% off. I said to my father, 'Tell me, how much is this one then?' My father said, 'Well, tonight you'll come into my study at 7.30, and when you leave that study you will know what a percentage is!' Unlike my sister I was never brilliant at school. I was the practical one.

In 1933, when I was fourteen and a half, a law was passed that Jewish children should only go to Jewish schools. The teachers in my mixed faith school had always been all right, but not the pupils - they had become very anti-Semitic. Probably this was the influence of the two youth organisations Hitler had created, the Hitlerjugend for boys and the BDM for girls. From now on all the Jewish children would have to go to Jewish schools - and this would have been a horror for my parents, who felt much more German than Jewish. So I was able to persuade my father that I should leave school at fourteen and go to work in his factory. The other workers did not know that I was the boss's daughter. I started at the beginning, learning how to cut out garments. I was very happy, and did well and was really getting on much better than anybody would have thought. Soon I began designing children's clothes too. My mother was disgusted to have 'cutter and designer' in my passport as a profession. I remember it so well – how shocked she was, and how I laughed about it. She was still higher up in this world, playing bridge, going to fashion shows, and so on. She could not come down. But, believe you me, she had to come down!

My father insisted I worked in his office as well, and learnt how to handle everything for the factory. He always said I would be the one to inherit the factory. That was in 1936. By 1937 all Jewish social and cultural life in Germany took place in synagogues. We couldn't go to restaurants, hotels, or theatres anymore - everywhere Jews were not allowed. So it was at the synagogue that I met my future husband, Herbert Licht. I was sixteen-and-a-half, and my husband was nearly thirty. I got engaged very quickly. My parents would never have allowed this in other times because I was far too young, but it was a chance to get married and, maybe, to leave Germany. So I got married in 1937.

We had a small flat in Breslau but Herbert very soon tried emigration. Of course, everyone was keen to emigrate to England, but you had to earn a minimum of around £13 per month. I was lucky. Because of his business contacts Herbert was already working in England. He obtained a permit and I was able to come, too. My sister would have loved to come to London, and was always annoyed with me that she couldn't get a British permit. Instead, she and her husband left Germany for Montevideo, South America. My father, who was sixty, and my mother, forty-seven, also started a new life there. They had to leave their house, flat, factory, everything. On their way to Montevideo they came to see me here in London. I miss my father very much. After he left on the ship for South America, I never saw him again. That is so sad because he did such a lot for me. My mother did come to see me one more time in London.

At that time, I had almost normal sight and very normal hearing. I was born night-blind but, of course, nobody was supposed to know about it. I was always told that I should not talk about it. Many years later the likely reason came to me: you know, Hitler would not have any disabled people. I remember a disabled child living next door, a very sweet little girl who had had polio. One night she was taken and put away. That is what the Nazis did.

In England, Herbert and I were practically penniless. My husband had had his own factory in Breslau and had come from a very wealthy family. I remember in Germany Herbert had given me a little Opel car for my seventeenth birthday. I went on my own to visit my in-laws on the motorway (typical Hitler - you didn't have motorways in England then!). When I got there I said, 'Come on, I'll take you out.' They both said, 'No! No!' They wouldn't go in the car when I was driving! At that time there were not so many women drivers.

We started here in a furnished room in Goldhurst Terrace. No basin, no bathroom, and the loo two floors below. My husband was whistling and singing, ever so happy, but I must confess I was not all that happy. I wrote home to my parents, 'In London, the streets are always wet. They never have the chance to dry. It's really true. Wet - and so cold, everywhere.' My husband took it much better than I did but, of course, I tried my very best to get on well.

It was around 1938 when Herbert became very interested in Alyth Synagogue. I was not at all because I was not brought up to it. I got married in a synagogue because that was the done thing but I didn't know any Hebrew, or anything Jewish. But Herbert insisted, so we went round to Alyth very often. My cousin was Professor Ernst Cohen, and he was already a big shot at Alyth, and he told us we must become members. So we did, around 1940. Alyth was very poor at that time. There were very few members, and they were all English Jews. Then we got together a little circle of five former Germans, called 'The Group'. This included Dr Werner Vander Zyl (later Rabbi at Alyth). It was very difficult because times were tough financially but Herbert went round in the evenings and tried to get people to become members. The Group had a very good idea. If we got children to come to religious classes without payment, then the children would bring their parents, and then we would get new members. It worked very well. So Alyth was very successful in the end.

As a refugee who was a married woman I did not get a work permit. But I met a little Russian girl outside the baker's and, while I was talking to her, her mother came out. We discovered we lived close by and the mother began giving me six shillings an hour to look after her child. Later, I had my own lovely little girl, Anne - the happiest day of my life. We were living then in Highcroft Gardens with Herbert's brother, Bernhard, and his wife, Hilde. Then, unfortunately, Bernhard was interned - many of the male refugees were sent to the Isle of Man. So my husband went to Temple Fortune Police Station - he was the type of person to do that - and he told them, 'Look, there is no point in interning me because I'm much more useful to England organising my export business.' And they said, 'Yes, we need businesses like yours.' So I was very, very lucky that Herbert stayed at home with me.

Of course, we could not keep the house up without Bernhard, so we got a flat in Temple Fortune. This was a wonderful flat, with central heating and hot water! It was at that time that I started to work with my husband. We made little skirts from cloth remnants thrown away by some of the big firms. And that is how we started our very nice business. Slowly but surely we expanded from one room to a workroom in Berner Street. Herbert and I were working very hard and from nothing we built up to seventy machinists. I was in the factory doing the cutting and designing and Herbert was in the administration. But increasingly, I had to go home early because of being night-blind. In 1943, my son, Steven, was born. I took it easier with the business. I still went in every day but I was not really working.

We were very happy and everything went very well until I started not to be able to travel any more as my sight was really getting much worse. And then came the terrible time when I was stuck at home and I really could not cope with that situation. We lived in The Leas and everybody always said, 'You have a beautiful house,' and I said, 'Yes, but it's a cage. I am here and I can't get out.' One day, Herbert came home and said, 'You know, I've got a marvellous idea. You should get a guide dog!' I went to the Guide Dog Centre and had to walk for miles every day with the dog and I liked it very much. I was very happy because I could meet friends again and walk to Kenwood.

Then, unfortunately, Herbert died of cancer when I was only forty-three. It was very upsetting for me. My daughter had just got married and I was at home with my son. The business was finished, of course.

As time passed, I got into the custom of taking my dog for a walk with my good friend, George Trenter. Later we married and were very happy together for a long time. But twelve years ago, while we were abroad on holiday, he died very suddenly. It was a terrible shock.

But I am not complaining about my life. I have some very nice friends who are very good to me and I have carers who make my food, and I can still do a bit of housework - because I don't like to sit and do nothing - and my carers take me out walking every day. My children are wonderful to me. So I am very lucky with my children, my grandchildren and my great-grandchildren. And I have Friday night dinner with either Anne or Steven every week. They are always on the phone or taking me out. I must say I am satisfied with my disabled life. Now I am eighty – though I don't wish to be a hundred – I am managing all right!

66   NIKKI VAN DER ZYL
ICH BIN EINE BOMBSHELL!

I was born in 1935 in Berlin. My father, Rabbi Doctor Werner Van der Zyl, was one of a number of rabbis in Berlin. He set up a college at the West London Synagogue named after his teacher, Leo Baeck.. My mother, Annalesa Lecht, came from a distinguished family. Her cousin, Haman Schluck, was a very well-known artist, and her uncle was the last acting manager of the theatre in Breslau as well as the Mayor. He later became an important member of the Jewish community in Uruguay.

My parents met in Berlin when my father came to see my mother's parents on a religious matter. My mother was then training to become a concert pianist and when they first met they discussed the merits of music and religion.

As a rabbi my father was in much danger, but he had a number of miraculous escapes. Once, when some Nazis came into his synagogue, he stood up to them saying his father had fought in the German Army and that people should not be persecuted just because they were born into the Jewish religion. On another occasion he was held in a house where they collected Jews. If you were moved to the top floor it meant certain transportation to a concentration camp. The man in charge of this particular house took a liking to my father and didn't want him to die, so he kept moving him from one floor to the next to avoid the count for the top floor.

Another time my father didn't come home one day. He had been picked up in the street by the SS. My mother and I went out looking for him at the local police stations – I did not look Jewish as I had blonde hair and blue eyes like my father – but they did not tell us where he was. Luckily, my mother contacted the Hon Lily Montague, who with her sister founded the Liberal Jewish Movement. She knew my father through his work with the Council of Christians and Jews in

England and through her connections with powerful people she was able to secure his release.

My mother and I came to England on 27th March 1939. First we stayed in Hampstead and then moved to Kilburn. My father came over later. By day he worked for the Jewish Board of Guardians in Euston and by night he was a fire warden. On one of these evenings, when my mother and I were on our own, our house was bombed.

When I was six, my parents were placed in an adults-only aliens' camp, so I had to board at the Stockney Russ school for refugees in Haslemere, Surrey. Although my parents were able to visit me - my father held services there - I found it very difficult as I still did not speak any English. I was very naughty and in fact got expelled when I was nine. I then went to a school for young ladies in Farnham, but I was not any happier. I missed my parents and London. I used to go on long walks on my own.

Eventually, when the war ended, we got back together and rented a flat in Swiss Cottage. My father held Shabbat services for the German refugees who belonged to the Belsize Park Synagogue. In 1947 he was asked to come to Alyth. He was rabbi there until 1958 when he moved to West London Synagogue, to be joined by Rabbi Hugo Gryn a few years later.

I failed my eleven plus exam, but I got into Paddington and Maida Vale High School having passed their entrance test with flying colours. At this time I was quite rebellious. Because I spoke German (and maybe to help me settle in) I was asked to re-write a German children's film, as the original soundtrack was missing. I enjoyed this so much that I decided – despite my dreadful German accent – that I wanted to be an actress.

Then fate stepped in. I had suffered for a couple of years with a very bad squint. I used to see double. Eventually, even though we were told there was a fifty-fifty chance I would either be cured or end up blind, my parents booked me in for an operation at Moorfield's Eye Hospital. It was a terrible experience. I woke up in the middle of the operation as they had not given me enough anaesthetic. They bandaged one eye for two weeks and then operated on the other one.

However, during this time of enforced blindness, my hearing became very acute and I worked on my accent. By the time I left hospital I had a proper English voice!

In my early teens I made a new friend – the conductor Malcolm Sergeant. I used to queue up for the Proms and one day he came by and gave me two tickets. I told him my mother was a fellow musician! I got to know him quite well as he used to do recordings at a studio in Maida Vale, near my school. I would sit in on these recordings during my school lunch break, and he introduced me to people like Sir Thomas Beecham, which was very exciting. My mother and I met Brian Pedlar, the head of BBC Light Entertainment. She would play the piano and I would sing German songs.

Forging ahead with my acting ambitions I spent a year at RADA and loved it. My first job in the West End was as an understudy in a play called *The Pet Shop*. I then met Brian Rix and toured in his company for about two years, doing stage management as well as acting.

When I was twenty-one I got married and soon had two children. I could fit in my work with looking after the children, and it was then that my unusual career as the voice of famous foreign bombshells began. Although Ursula Andress and Raquel Welch and a host of other Bond girls had the looks, they could not always speak clear English. So I was employed to re-voice their parts, complete with a sexy – but intelligible – foreign accent. I got on very well with Gerd 'Goldfinger' Frobe. I coached him with his lines for that famous scene when Sean Connery is tied to a table and about to be cut in two with a laser. (Gerd also told me that his family helped hide Jews during the war).

I worked with at least two English actresses (who shall remain nameless) whose natural Cockney twangs did not fit their ladylike characters in various films. I also did stunt work on several 'Carry On' films.

In 1968 I got divorced and married George, whom I had met at a guitar club – I write poetry and songs. My father was not overjoyed about me marrying a non-Jew. The divorce proceedings proved to be both highly traumatic and rewarding. They dragged on for ten years ending up in the High Court, but as I couldn't afford a lawyer I conducted my side of the case myself.

As a result George suggested that I study law. So I went back to college and eventually entered the Bar and joined a set of chambers. Then in 1978 I got an EEC scholarship and took up a job in Brussels. My children were doing their O and A Levels at this time, and George stayed with them in London, coming out to see me every other weekend.

My job involved working closely with UK ministers, and I became very interested in politics. When I returned home I worked with the MP David Mellor in the House of Commons. I was then asked to become a journalist for the independent television company TVS, based in Southampton. I think I had the skills and experience they were looking for: I was an actress, I knew how to talk to people, and understood the Westminster and Brussels political scene.

After this, and a one-off (but well paid) job for the Conservatives monitoring the television campaign for the 1992 General Election, I returned to my first love - the stage. I started a Jewish theatre company and we took shows to the Edinburgh festival.

I am proud to have been elected onto the international group of the Board of Deputies. I am still writing poetry and songs, painting (next time you are waiting around at Barnet General Hospital, you may see one of the twenty-four paintings they commissioned from me), giving concerts and talks.

So life is very busy - even though I am no longer 'ze voice' of Raquel or Ursula!

67

MARGARET WEISS
A CHILDHOOD IN NAZI GERMANY

I was born in 1921 and was twelve years old when Hitler came to power. I had a very happy childhood as my mother did her utmost to protect me. She never shared her worries with me, but I soon learned to guard my tongue and this fear of making any kind of controversial statement stayed with me long after I left Germany.

My father died when I was four, leaving my mother with three children – my brother, a severe asthmatic of fourteen, and a sister who was fifteen years older than me. We lived in a large house in a beautiful suburb outside Hamburg. As my brother lived in the mountains due to his asthma there was no man in the house, which in fact made life less stressful than for most families. We lived a very sheltered life. Many men who were employed by the state lost their jobs soon after Hitler came to power in 1933. This affected teachers, lecturers, judges and lawyers, hospital doctors and dentists who were not in private practice, and even members of orchestras and entertainers, as well as journalists. Businesses were boycotted, but as there was an international outcry this was soon discontinued. In hindsight, those who lost their jobs were lucky. Many of them emigrated, which at that time was much easier. They were able to take out far more money at that time than the 10 Marks, which I took in 1939 (equivalent to 80p today).

I was twelve years old in 1933 and like so many assimilated Jews was unaware of my heritage. All that changed in some odd ways. I was a keen Girl Guide and when our troop was taken over by the Hitler Youth I went home and told my mother. She told me that they would have to manage without me, as I would not be welcome. Next came the break from my constant playmates. One of them showed me his father's uniform and told me proudly that he was a personal friend of Goering. I knew we could no longer be friends, although we parted amicably and there was no animosity, just an acceptance that this was now a new stage in our lives. At school we had to produce our family tree. Mine, with its typical Jewish names, was read out by the teacher, but as I was blond and blue-eyed nobody ever suspected I was Jewish. Even the form I had to fill in asking if I was in the Hitler Youth or if not, why not, got lost among the hundreds. I belonged to an athletic club with a similar uniform to that of the Hitler Youth. How strange it was to see boys wearing kappels as they ran and jumped. I later joined the sports club Schild and started to join my friends at services at the synagogue and became proud to be Jewish. At that time I felt uncomfortable in school and went to my teacher and confessed that I was Jewish. There was a teachers' emergency meeting and they consented to keep me.

The teachers behaved as before, but one told his wife who then told a friend. As bad luck would have it her son was in my class. Some pupils had the courage to be on my side, which was a great help when many turned against me. There was no major anti-Jewish legislation in 1934, which helped to create the illusion that all would be well. Then in 1935 came the Nuremburg Laws which took away our citizenship, as well as adding a whole string of restrictions against non-Aryans. In 1936 Hitler put Germany on a war footing. It should have been obvious what real danger there was. We divided our house into flats and a garage was added in the basement, which had to be strengthened, as it was to become a shelter.

It must have been in 1937 that I was caught in a mock air raid where everyone had to seek shelter. In 1938 came the notorious Kristallnacht – the night when windows of Jewish shops were smashed and synagogues burnt. Soon there were signs everywhere – 'Jews forbidden' – outside theatres, cinemas and restaurants. Jewish shops had to display signs saying they were owned or run by Jews. It was as if a noose was being pulled tighter and tighter. The Jews were asked to pay one billion Marks and as we had been asked to declare all our assets, everyone was asked to pay accordingly. Our silver and jewellery had to be handed in, which must have been very sad, but was just one more act to humiliate the Jews and make the government richer. Non-Aryans could not study, train or work in German companies and as one Jewish enterprise after another folded there was little chance of making a living.

Suddenly emigration was an urgent matter, but no country wanted an influx of penniless Jews. We were terrified for my brother, as men were arrested on certain days. He would be warned and disappeared into the mountains, while outside his window groups would chant 'When Jewish blood drips from the knife.' For a man who needed medical care it was nearly impossible to find a country to take him. My brother eventually went to Shanghai and my sister to Argentina. Unfortunately my mother was sent back to Germany when Italy entered the war. She had been on her way to join my brother.

England took in many children, and young women and girls worked as domestics or as probationary nurses. Others found guarantors and were allowed to work in jobs for which no English applicant could be found. The war altered the refugees' position. Many were interned, then later joined the army or did war work. I arrived six months before the outbreak of war, at first being given hospitality in English homes.

After six weeks I started my training as a probationer in Peterborough, then a sleepy cathedral town. The work was hard, the pay very poor and the discipline like a strict school for young offenders. I was eighteen years old and while on night duty for three months I was acting as a runner, which meant that energy was essential.

One of my tasks was laying out bodies. I must have laid out about fifty during that time. Even in my first year I was left in charge completely on my own during the night. There was endless cleaning: I had to rinse sheets in cold water and grumbled, 'I do hate washing these bloody sheets'. I could not understand why I had shocked those that heard me. These sheets were soaked in blood. I had a lot to learn!

We were given tickets for variety shows but the English jokes went right over my head even though I spoke very good English.

The worst effect of being a refugee was that I lost all confidence. It certainly was the end of my childhood.

68   EMANUEL WEISSAND

B oth my parents came from Warsaw in Poland. I find it difficult to remember, but my sister to this day can remember everything about the family. My father's name was Oizer and my mother's name was Sarah. In Poland at this time my father was in the Russian army and my mother was working in Berlin making cigarettes. Then in about 1912 they came to England where my father was a tailor by trade. In 1914 when war broke out my father went into the English army. I was born at the Middlesex Hospital, London on 18th October 1915. At this time my parents lived in a small flat in Broadwick Street. My father was a ladies' tailor and he earned good money, so my mother never had to work. In time my father opened up his own workshop near Bond Street and employed twelve people.

My sister Ida was born in 1917 and I had another sister who was born in 1919. We went to school in the West End in Poulteney Street. As my father was doing well, he moved and bought a house in north Kensington. We all thought this was magnificent as previously we had all lived in one room. I went to school at Oxford Dans School and from there I went to Sloane Secondary School in Chelsea. Another school I went to was in Portobello Road Market. My parents sent me to Pitman's college to learn typing, etc. I left when I was sixteen.

I had some religious education – my father did not believe in religion at all. I used to go to Bayswater synagogue to learn Hebrew. I did not go to any youth clubs. I went to work for a transport firm. From this job I got to know all the West End and the river where all the transport was going.

I married Kay during the war on 6th September. When we first got married we lived in my father-in-law's house and then moved to St John's Wood. I started working for my brother-in-law, Max Sennit. The company was in the clothing business. Max's father said I should learn the trade and the first thing to do was go on the machine – it was piecework and I earned good money. I did not suffer from the slump before the war but the firm eventually went bankrupt. Then Max

Sennit opened an office with his father selling property. I worked for him for quite a few years.

Then the Second World War came and I was in it for five years in the Royal Army Service Corps. I was made a sergeant and ran a petrol depot and went to France, Belgium and Germany – this was because I could speak a little German. As far as Dunkirk was concerned I got papers to go to a town in Belgium, but when I got as far as Dover I was told to go back. Apparently the troops were coming home.

During the war I saw fighting in France. I was with the unit, front line troops, and we were issued rifles. We would always be at the ready. One day we came across a bunch of Germans and we started firing at each other until they gave way. Eventually I was told I would be going to the Far East but I didn't fancy it as I was being demobbed.

After the war I came home. I couldn't go into my father's business as he was working for someone else so I had to look for a job. I went into partnership with my cousin in a fruit shop in Aylmer Parade. I was not there for very long. The shop did not do very well as there was a lot of black market fruit (which we could not get) which was wanted by the Jewish people in that area. So we had to close. My next job was in the watch trade – a Jewish firm and they went bankrupt. I then got a job in another watch firm. I was the office manager and stayed there until I retired.

In 1946 we had a baby called Gina. We lived in a flat in St John's Wood. In 1951 we had a son called David. Eventually we moved to Falloden Court, as the children were growing up, and joined Alyth because my sister was also a member (we previously belonged to Upper Berkeley Street). Both children went to a little school in St John's Wood. Gina then went to a High School in Maida Vale. She learned journalism at the Regent Street Polytechnic and became a reporter in Coventry. She then went to Israel for a year – I have relations there. David went to university and studied environmental sciences. He obtained his degree and became an income tax inspector.

69   FRED WINTER

M y name is Fred Winter, though at one time my surname was Winterberger which is logical since I come from a town called Winterberg, a small place in the western part of Germany in Westphalia where I was born on 26th August 1929. Look at any good map and you will come upon the source of the river Ruhr. There, quite nearby, you will find the town of Winterberg, a market town and ski area well known to sports enthusiasts.

My family had lived in Winterberg for some hundreds of years before I was born, and in my research I have even been able to trace the name all the way back to the very first Jew who ever settled there, a man by the name of Solomon the Jew. One of the treasures in my possession is an illustration of his gravestone. In time there came to be a lot more Winterbergers living in this little place, and at one stage there was both a synagogue and a cemetery. Over the course of time, however, most of the Winterberger Jews, for whatever reason, departed so that in the end only my family remained, without the support of any Jewish facilities.

Without a synagogue in town my father was forced to attend one elsewhere at the nearest commune available to him in another town, and his Jewish education remained on the whole very meagre. During the First World War he served in the German army, as far as I know with the rank of Private. When the fighting was over he went to work in his father's business. My grandfather was a man of property who also had a small shop selling clothes and various household items. In time my father took over from my grandfather Emil who in turn, I believe, had taken it over from his father before him. The handing down from father to son had gone on for many generations.

In Germany we did not start school until the age of six years. There I learnt quickly, so that by the time I was seven, I could already read books and newspapers. That, though, was about as much as I would receive in the way of German education, for by the time I got to be eight years old Jewish children were already barred by the Nazis from attending all non-Jewish schools. I clearly remember being told by my teacher in school one day that he was sorry, but would I mind going home? When I got back my parents told me that they too were upset, but Jews it seemed could not attend state schools anymore. Whilst I had no further formal education in Germany this did not matter too much to me since I could still learn from reading books.

My mother came from Leipzig, in the eastern part of the country, a large town quite different from Winterberg. She was a very lively person and participated a lot in amateur theatricals and was also one of the first women to be admitted to a university in Berlin. She was introduced to my father by friends and, despite their different backgrounds, lived a contented life and I do not recollect anything but love in their relationship.

Living with my brother and parents in Winterberg for the first ten years or so of my life, I only gradually began to appreciate a little of the persecution being unleashed on Jews. However, I still remember much of it including events such as Kristallnacht, even though I was only a young lad. I used to get up early in the morning and three or four times on different dates came down to find that all our windows had been smashed with glass lying everywhere. Once, after one such occasion, a German walked into our house, gave the Nazi salute and said, 'Yes I did it and what are you going to do about it?' What indeed! To be fair, we did have one or two reasonably friendly neighbours at first. But they were soon frightened off by the Nazis, fearing prosecution if they persisted in their friendly behaviour towards a Jewish family, especially as it had already been explained to them that the Jews were unworthy, being dirty as well as exhibiting other anti-social tendencies. I even have a document of that time in which a local citizen had been seen talking to my family. Such a disgrace – but for whom I wonder? Not surprisingly under the circumstances my father was arrested once and sent to prison merely because he was a Jew. Amongst other documents I possess are some in which certain brave people had actually written to the authorities to ask why my father had been arrested since he had done nothing wrong.

It was all terribly unjust, but that was how it was. On the other hand I do know that my parents were very popular residents in the town and most established families were known by a name attributed to the house in which they lived. Our house was known as David's, and I was accordingly known as 'David's Fred'.

The countryside around Winterberg was very picturesque, with mountains, forests and great walks. I recollect with great affection the long walks we had, both in summer and winter (sometimes on skis). One particular walk I had with my father I still have as one of my fondest memories of him. Our journey that day took us to the actual source of the river Ruhr. When we got there we saw an old man who had a few bottles and glasses set up on a trestle table. My father bought a glass of schnapps from him and then, as the old man turned away, emptied the whole glass on the ground. 'Why did you buy schnapps if you were not going to drink it?' I asked, and back came the reply, 'That old man needs money to exist and by selling drink he does not feel like a beggar and retains some dignity as a human being.' Although this event occurred some sixty-five years ago, it still seems as if it had happened yesterday and I am sure it still influences the way I live today. My parents tried very hard to get out of Germany in 1938/39, but found it impossible to obtain the necessary visas. They, I believe, considered me too young at the age of eight or nine to send away on my own. I was later told the final straw that persuaded them otherwise, was when I had to go into hospital in a nearby town for a minor operation. Apparently I told one of the nurses confidentially that I was a Jew. She reported this to her superiors, with the result that none of the medical staff would attend to me, and I was sent home again as fast as possible. It was then that my mother contacted a friend in London (another story in itself), who approached the Jewish community, relating the plight of this sole Jewish boy in Winterberg and the intolerable situation he was facing. My older brother was more fortunate in a way, having been sent earlier to school in Holland while I stayed behind in Winterberg.

Kristallnacht was an experience sobering enough but even more so for me was that of being sent out of the country to England in a Kindertransport in 1939, alone and without my parents who were forced to stay behind, eventually to perish in Auschwitz. Thinking back, I would have died together with my parents had I not been sent away. In my own case salvation came in the form of an organisation in London called the Cricklewood Weekly Appeal Fund run by a Mr Henry Cohen. He operated what was known as a 'tally business', selling clothes from door to door. It was Mr Cohen who collected money for the charity with the aim of bringing over Jewish children from Germany, generously giving his male work force leave every Friday in order to solicit funds for the cause. With the monies they received, Henry Cohen was able to rescue many German Jewish children and bring them over to this country, myself among them.

Only later did I discover that someone had written to Henry's organisation on my behalf, telling them about this one little Jewish boy in a German village and could they please get him out. Someone must have listened, for in June 1939 I found myself together with a lot of other Jewish children, on board a train at Dusseldorf bound for the Hook of Holland, from where we were to proceed by ship to Harwich. Even as we left the station however we discovered that our troubles were not yet over. To ensure that no one took out of the country more than the permitted ten marks per person, suspicious German officials proceeded to give us a hard time on the train. Still, in the end, we did manage to get to the Hook safely and from there sailed to Harwich. At the Essex port we all disembarked and were given a medical before then being shepherded on to a train once more, eventually to arrive in London's Liverpool Street station. I was now in my newly adopted country, though quite unable to speak a word of the language. Still I was not the only one, with many of my travelling companions in the same boat as it were.

In retrospect, the day that my parents delivered me to the assembly point for the train to Holland still remains the saddest and most dramatic day of my life. I know they tried to act their normal kind selves, but it was perfectly clear to all that this could be the last time that we would ever see each other again. The situation was made worse by the fact that outside the station there were many shops with notices saying 'Juden unerwunscht' (Jews not wanted).

My fellow travellers and I were at first placed in a hostel in Shoot-Up Hill in Cricklewood. When war came we were all sent away as evacuees to different schools, in my own case to Bedford. I teamed up with another boy, Emil Steinberg, and together we were taken through the streets looking for billets until we came to a lady who said, 'I'll have these two.' Her home was not exactly palatial. There was no bathroom and no electricity, and the family was very poor, but we were taken in and cared for and were content. I only wish we could have actually talked to our carer, but as yet we could speak no English.

At first I would hear from my parents quite regularly via the Red Cross. They were allowed twenty-five words in every letter, the last one I received from them sometime in 1943 telling me that 'we are going away and you may not hear from us for some time.' Unfortunately 'sometime' lasted forever, as I never heard from them again. They had managed to survive in wartime Germany for nearly four years, but then they too were taken away to the camps. From once being relatively wealthy owners of land and property my parents were, I later learned, reduced virtually to begging. The Germans had taken advantage of the fact that everything they owned was well documented and now used that knowledge to force them to sell out on very unfavourable terms. They had nothing left. The Germans took their home, their property and their business. My father ended up digging roads. How he managed that I do not know, but the documentation mentions this quite clearly. The realisation from the sales of all our properties and belongings were, of course, kept by the Germans, but after the war we managed to obtain a schedule of the amounts involved and obtain formal restitution. These assets were then resold by us at very low prices. Had I known what I know today I would have kept it all and been rich, but I needed the money at the time and therefore sold everything. The fact was I needed cash to live and also to help my brother, who had somehow survived the war and was now in America. He was lucky. When the Germans invaded the Low Countries in 1940 he was trapped in Holland, together with an uncle and some cousins. Told to report for transportation to the East, my uncle smelt a rat and managed to collect enough money to bribe someone to get a lorry and take them out of Holland, to Belgium, France and the Swiss border. Their guide advised them to run for it, adding encouragingly that 'They will try to shoot you, but once you are in Switzerland you will be all right.' In fact everyone made it safely to the border, living out the rest of the war quite happily in Swiss camps, though not without having to pay their way to some extent by doing housework as a way of recompensing their hosts.

They all returned to Holland after the war, but could not settle. My uncle went to Germany where he died many years ago, while my brother emigrated to America. As for myself, I enjoyed a twofold education in Bedford, one secular and the other religious, the latter under the auspices of the same Cricklewood Fund that had brought me to this country just before the war. The Fund had rented a building in Bedford as a Jewish Youth Centre open to all Jews, not just us, and it was here that we had Hebrew classes and held Passover services.

At first Jews were a novelty in Bedford, few of the townsfolk having ever seen one before, but then as the war progressed more appeared, especially from London, which was not too far away. In time we even had a rabbi for our swelling congregation and, as I have said, the youngsters were then obliged to attend Hebrew classes every Sunday morning. At first we kids only spoke in German to each other. Of course the local authorities objected. Here we are at war with Germany, they complained, and these little kids are bellowing away in their language. It just won't do. So we stopped and within a month could all speak passable English!

To earn a little pocket money some of us also delivered papers, including Saturday mornings. This did not always go down well with some of our co-religionists, who no doubt looked upon it as a desecration of the Sabbath. But then we could hardly ask those who had taken us in as lodgers for money. They themselves were only getting ten shillings a week (50p in today's coin) to look after us, and whilst the value of such a sum was undoubtedly more then than it is now, it was still barely enough to feed us. Certainly no one got fat on the relatively poor offerings at mealtimes, though we were otherwise treated well enough.

So far as my education was concerned, I had no trouble with Hebrew. On the other hand the question of entrance examinations to a better school was another matter. I did actually sit for the eleven plus, but with my limited knowledge of English at the time could hardly understand the questions let alone pursue the answers, and so quite understandably failed. However, this meant that unless I did something about it I would remain stuck in a school where the standard was extremely poor. Young I may have been, but I was of a persistent nature. I nagged my headmaster and the local education committee to help me and eventually, in 1941, was given a place at a school known as a Central School, where the standards were higher. The results justified my persistence. In due course I sat and passed my School Certificate, as it was then. I could even have progressed on to University, having been offered sufficient funds to do so, but now felt that it was time for me to go to work, so I decided to become an accountant, a profession for which a university degree was fortunately not then necessary.

I left Bedford in 1946 and returned to London in the bleak days after the war. I lived at first in a hostel in Willesden for the homeless young girls and boys, supported by the Cricklewood Fund, despite the fact that their finances were no longer in such good shape. After about a year however I managed to find some lodgings of my own consisting of just one single room. It was not much but it was a step up. In the meantime I had resolved to become an articled clerk, but that was easier said than done. When I began to look for an opening in 1947 to a firm of chartered accountants it was not possible then, generally speaking, to become articled unless one first paid a premium. Even worse, I accepted that there would be no salary. I could not go along with such an inequitable arrangement. I persisted and managed to find a firm which not only did not require a premium, but also offered a small salary on a sliding scale, starting at £1 a week for the first year, working up to £2 and later to £3 a week and then to

£5 in year five. Again I persisted, suggesting that we split the difference and that they pay me two pounds ten shillings a week from the start! Luckily for me they agreed. To make ends meet I took on additional bookkeeping jobs privately in the evenings and, at least once or twice a week, stayed up all night to catch up with my studies. Nevertheless, in the end I qualified as a chartered accountant, sufficiently well to be awarded a prize in the Institute's final examinations.

A great hurdle had been overcome and now I gradually worked my way up until at length I founded my own practice, F. Winter & Co, where my knowledge of German helped many of my Kindertransport friends and which still exists in London's West End.

Over forty years ago I met my wife Sheila at a party at the Majestic Hotel in Bournemouth. We became engaged and were married at the West London Reform Synagogue in Upper Berkeley Street; not that we were necessarily Reform, simply that the orthodox were not prepared to allow anyone to marry in an orthodox shul unless they could prove where their parents had married. In my own case, and that of many of my contemporaries, this was simply not possible, though apparently this was no excuse as far as they were concerned. Later we joined Alyth, living not far away in a house I had had built and where we have stayed ever since. We had three daughters, one of whom died quite young, and a son Paul. Susan and Paul both married at Alyth, Emma is still single. We travel a lot and I play a great deal of golf and Bridge. We still go on annual skiing holidays and enjoy our small holiday home in Spain.

After all these years I still keep in touch with some of the children from the Kindertransport and have acted professionally for quite a few of them. Emil from Bedford eventually went to America. We were going to have a reunion with him there three years ago, but two months before we were due to meet, his wife rang to say that he had died of a heart attack. Perhaps for this reason I dislike going to reunions almost as much as I hate going to Germany. So many of my Kindertransport contemporaries are no longer with us that I can only console myself with the thought that at least I am still here and leading a happy life with my wife, children, grandchildren and friends.

WOMAN OF VALOUR
(Anonymous)

70

I was born in Berlin, in Germany, in the summer of 1923. When I was only eight months old my father died of an illness that nowadays could be cured with antibiotics. After a year looking after me at home my mother had to go out and earn money, and so my grandmother came to Berlin to live with us. I also had a nanny. I loved them both very much.

My nanny's husband worked for the postal service and after Hitler came to power there were all sorts of restrictions. Her husband was obliged to sign an agreement that neither he nor his wife would have any contact with Jews. So that was that - well almost. I remember how, when children in Germany started school, they were given cone-shaped cardboard bags filled with goodies and you had your photograph taken to commemorate the day. I believe this custom is still prevalent in Germany. My first school was a state primary school. My form teacher was not a Nazi, but a lot of the other teachers were. If the father of a Jewish child had fought in the First World War, the child was allowed to go to a mixed Jewish and non-Jewish state grammar school at secondary level. But I was very pleased that I was sent to a Jewish school by my mother.

As I said, when Hitler came to power there were many restrictions. After my mother lost her job she worked for a Jewish organisation which helped people to leave Germany. On Kristallnacht our synagogue was burnt down, and our flat was surrounded by masses of people shouting Nazi slogans. Among the crowd was the man who had worked as caretaker in our synagogue. People came to our flat and demanded to know if there were any men in our home, but my grandmother went to the door and told them that ours was an all-female household – which it was, except that we happened to be hiding two men at the time! Luckily they did not search our flat.

It was after Kristallnacht, (the night of the broken glass), when many Jewish buildings were attacked, that my mother remarried. After Kristallnacht more and more people were trying to leave Germany. My mother, stepfather and I left for England. Sadly my grandmother did not make it, as war broke out. She was taken to Terezin concentration camp and did not survive.

I was to see my old nanny one more time. One evening when it was dark, just before I left Germany, she came to say a last goodbye to me. To this day, I don't know how she was contacted or who told her we were about to leave.

I came to England with the help of the movement for the care of children and was taken to a hostel financed by members of West London Synagogue. In the hostel were people from Austria and Germany, and as far as I can remember we all got along together very well. In fact I am still in contact with some of them. Rabbi Harold Reinhart, the rabbi at West London Synagogue, used to come to the hostel and give us lessons. On Friday evenings we went to the service at his synagogue.

Our English was not very good. Amongst ourselves we spoke German, although Matron always told us to speak English. We were sent to school, and had to wear uniforms, which made us feel self-conscious. Most of the girls still had parents alive in Austria or Germany. Some had older siblings in England. We were given pocket money and stamps so that we could write to those we had left behind.

In September 1939, the day before the outbreak of the Second World War, we were evacuated with Matron to a small village in Hertfordshire. We were all assembled so that the local villagers could pick out the girls they were prepared to board. I must say it is very much to their credit that they were prepared to take in German speaking girls when they were at war with Germany. What's more, they had probably never seen a Jew before. I was very lucky. I was given a lovely big guest room for my bedroom and I was always given enough to eat. Some of the girls were not so lucky. For example they were not given enough food.

Not surprisingly there were quite a few misunderstandings between our respective hosts and us. I remember one in particular. Very early on the first morning in my new household, the man of the house knocked on my bedroom door. I was rather worried about his intentions, but all he did was to leave an early morning cup of tea outside my door. I had never heard of that custom!

We were all sent to school. This meant walking about forty-five minutes through country lanes and in all weathers. I feel sure this did us some good. All the evacuees would often assemble for a regular get-together, which would take place at Matron's billet. There we read Alice in Wonderland.

By the beginning of December 1939 all we really wanted to do was to get back to London, which we did, just in time for the Blitz! Only the youngest children were then sent back to school. My school days were over. I found a job with a dentist, which I enjoyed and stayed for seven years. It was before the days of masks and gloves – all we could catch from a patient was a cold.

When I was eighteen years old I moved into the home of my mother and stepfather. I met my husband during the war years and we were married at Alyth while he was still in the army. I have two sons, and both were barmitzvah at Alyth, but two of my four grandchildren were bar and bat mitzvah at West London Synagogue. So you could say that life has come full circle, because my first connections were with West London.

I am very grateful that some sixty-one years ago I found a home in this country.

71

HAZEL WOOLFSON
FIGHTING SPIRIT

I was born in 1918 and in my eighty-third year have been asked to write something of my life. I am the eldest of a family of four. My grandparents left Russia in the 19th century to escape the pogroms. My father served in the British army in the First World War. I recall my father telling me, 'If your religion is not good enough for you, no other religion will be any good.' He also said 'Anytime you are ill, say 'I am strong. I am strong'.' Gardening and Russian literature were my mother's pleasures. (Later I spent happy hours in Kew Gardens where my mother was often given rare cuttings.)

I came from an exceptionally musical family through the line of my paternal grandmother. She was an indomitable woman. I admired her greatly. My father's youngest brother was a genius on the pianoforte. I remember Sundays listening to him playing. This musical genius came out once again in my brother's son. When he was young I loved taking him to concerts. I loved the great singer Conchita Supervia. I remember her dying in childbirth. When my nephew was thirteen he was given the 'Martin Award' by the New Philharmonia Orchestra - a gift of a glorious Steinway piano. He was taught by Maria Curcio Diamond.

I enjoyed my young life in swimming, dancing, wide reading and intellectual curiosity. I had red hair curling down my back and a penchant for very high heels. I recall the German organised pogroms before the war – Kristallnacht, when the Great Synagogue was burned. The Germans destroyed everything belonging to the Jewish citizens of Dresden. It was then that my outlook on life changed. Like any young girl my thoughts were of myself - studying, college and so on, up until Kristallnacht, That made me grow up and it changed my attitude to focus on my family first.

I remember when Prime Minister Chamberlain went to meet Hitler. My father asked me to go to the country and find a house - a matter of a 'pin in a map'. I found a suitable house in Hertfordshire.

Chamberlain returned saying, 'Peace in our time'. I returned to work and was immediately sacked.

I was in Piccadilly in 1940 when the Germans destroyed the City of London - a great red sky. That same year a landmine destroyed our London house - a huge crater.

I married my dear Sidney Solomon Woolfson before he joined the Royal Air Force, 617 Squadron Bomber Command. He sent me a postcard from Blackpool saying, 'Will write later'. I did not know where Blackpool was and I had no address! But I got on a train to Blackpool station, which was filled with thousands of airmen. I found the house that was my husband's billet. For food on the table there was one lettuce leaf, one sardine on each plate, bread and marge (the flies having a field day). I waited at the gate until Sidney came running towards me. Did he say 'Darling what a surprise!' or 'I love you'? No, he said, 'You can't stay here!' (I still smile at this memory - apparently this billet had a reputation as a house of ill repute.)

The next day I decided to speak to the Commander. Try to speak to a commander in wartime, or even peacetime! Eventually I found a small house (brown lino, brown table). I faced a powerful man, physically and intellectually. I was wearing a cream straw boater, bought at my favourite, miracle-fingered milliner opposite the London Hospital in the East End. I told the Commander that his men would not be able to fight on such shocking food. He made a note and I understand that there was an improvement after that. I asked him if Sidney could 'live out'. Horror of horrors, men do not live out when training! I told him my parents' home had been destroyed. He said he would think about it. Shortly afterwards Sidney was given a living-out pass and I quickly found a flat for us in this most ugly of towns.

When it was time to leave, I went to see the Commander to thank him. He asked, 'What do you want now?' I told him my husband's brother was fighting in Burma, another brother in the army in Scotland. Why, I asked, should Sidney be posted miles away? This man and I understood one-another and we shook hands. Three weeks later I received a hand-written letter saying, 'You will be pleased to learn your husband has been posted to Hendon Aerodrome,' signed Arthur Harris. (Later he was better known as Bomber Harris). What a sweetie! I was later heartened to learn that he planned and executed the bombing of Dresden, 617 Bomber Command together with the United States 8th Air Force - it shortened the war. In my opinion Dresden citizens got what they deserved. This was justice for the future, with no sentimentality. Air Force Marshal Sir Arthur Harris was a great national leader - the free world was in need of him. His statue is at St Clement Danes, Aldwych, City of London.

Sidney and I had an idyllic year at Hendon but I knew it could not last. Sidney was then posted to Bomber Command Hemswall. Lancaster planes all over the ground. I moved into 'Dog Kennel Farm', adjoining the aerodrome. No gas, electricity or water, only a well. The WAAFs came to the farm to cry on my shoulder when their beautiful airmen boyfriends did not return from the raids. Thousands of them died.

Although it was dangerous, I was allowed to walk freely on the 'drome'. I bought my food rations there. A weekly bus from Lincoln brought fish. Thanks to Shrek (the kosher food manufacturer) occasionally a parcel of kosher food arrived. I bought a bicycle for a pound and had eggs galore.

In 1946, Sidney was asked to stay permanently in the RAF. He turned the offer down and was demobbed. After the war we lived in Hendon. In 1967 we became members of RSGB Alyth Gardens. It is 'a home' to me. My work was interesting - producing films for TV advertising.

In 1970 the Leningrad Trials took place in Russia. It was illegal in Russia for children to become Bar/Bat Mitzvah. A group of Russians, mostly Jews, but with a wonderful non-Jewish pilot, attempted to leave Russia (where emigration was strictly controlled and refused to Jews, the 'refuseniks') by hiring an aeroplane to airlift the whole group out. However someone gave them away and they were brought to trial at the Leningrad Trials. The pilot was given the death sentence and all the others got seven to ten years. There was such enormous worldwide reaction that the pilot's sentence was changed to fourteen years and eventually the Russians relaxed their rules. Some of the original Jews did get out and I met them.

The Trials propelled a whole movement to put pressure on Russia to free the Jews to allow them to emigrate to Israel and the National Council for Soviet Jewry was founded - Alyth played a part, with all the Reform shuls working together at the Sternberg Centre. I came up with the name 'Exodus'. We marched and demonstrated.

I was also a member of 'Conscience' under the chairmanship of the brilliant Alan Howard. Our aim was to get scientists out. That wonderful chap Bernard Levin, of the Times newspaper, gave us a very high profile. We even had a spy in our midst - Erwin van Harlem, a Russian posing as an Amsterdam Jew and using his membership of 'Exodus' as a cover to spy on Britain. The Secret Service got in touch with me asking about him. As he was an artist he had offered to create posters for the group - the only poster he created had a rather obvious give-away - his slogan read 'Let Your People Go'. Eventually, he was imprisoned at Her Majesty's pleasure for ten years.

During this time Robert Maxwell, the newspaper tycoon, helped me personally at a public meeting he attended with the Russian ambassador and other high-powered dignitaries. At question time I jumped up first with a letter from a refusenik, who had been refused permission to attend his son's funeral in Israel and proclaimed Russia a prison. Maxwell said, 'Give me all your case papers and I'll do what I can.' I quickly got a letter from him with an introduction to someone who managed to obtain permission to leave for some very difficult refuseniks.

I am the last active member of 'Exodus' as it was disbanded when the Russians finally allowed Jews to emigrate. My last case is of one young Russian, tortured and imprisoned, who now lives in Israel but still needs support because of his experiences. I arranged for the Medical Foundation to support him.

My daughter Diana and I have been members of the 'Women's Campaign for Soviet Jewry' since its conception. I hope my granddaughter, Claire, will join us when she has completed her studies.

I was sixty when I enrolled in Camden College of Art - advanced portrait painting -1 couldn't draw a line! It is a struggle, but my work has been accepted by the Royal Academy Summer Exhibition. I do hope for a peaceful world - in my opinion the most important thing is to have 'good jokes'.

LONDON 1948 by Hazel Woolfson

I lift the floorboards of my mind,
See a hole where a house stood,
Mahogany and green room, Orange peel under the
Bedroom, examine my face for a blemish, room.

See a sunny dining room
Family replete,
Sweet toothed Mother, Sharps creamy toffee
Raisin coated,
Dip pecans and walnuts in wine,
Table strewn with shells.

See make music room
Tetrazzini, Supervia, The Street Singer
Father jumping like a goat, wished he
Would jump in a dried up moat.
Music teacher, a cover up of perfumed powder, sleep.

See midnight summers in the garden.
Green white stars of stock, heavy perfumed,
Mystery, talk, politics, talk,
Friends lingering quietly,
Neurosis years of war coming.
See black rags moving in the breeze,

Once curtains which the light diffused,
Mother mine, you never saw the mine.
Rhode Islands sedately pick their way thro' rubble,
Indifferent to our madness.

Father and I give them away, give everything away,
Except our feelings.
The staircase stands, leading to nowhere.

72   CECILY ZIMMERMAN

I was born on 25th November 1904. My father was from Latvia and my mother from the border of Poland and Germany in Katowice. My father's father was a scribe in the synagogue. The scribes had to be very careful - one mistake and they had to start all over again. I remember that eventually, when my father was about fourteen or fifteen, he was sent to England to escape the army and there he learned garment skills with relatives in Leeds. He was a passionate idealist and socialist and he led the first Jewish garment workers' strike for a 13-hour day instead of a 14-hour day. The strike was successful, but the result was that my father was boycotted and none of the local bosses would give him a job.

So he went to America, where he met my mother who had been sent to Boston by her brother. He had a friend there with a rich suitor who wanted to marry her - she was very beautiful. Unfortunately she fell in love with my father who was a buttonhole maker. Her brother was so incensed that he kicked my father out of the house, but my mother eloped in the night and joined him.

My father had many socialist friends and when he and my mother got married each friend helped - one gave a table, one gave a chair. They were very, very poor. My mother became pregnant and then my father developed a tubercular fistula and had to go into hospital. My mother had a very hard life washing, scrubbing, working and eventually she gave birth to my oldest brother.

When my father came out of hospital he was very frail and weak. A relative in England knew of a doctor, a Dr Dearth, who specialised in tubercular things and they took him to see this doctor. My father, who had a terrible temper but great charm, intelligence and wit, seems to have won his heart because the doctor said to him 'Look, I can cure you. I am going to take you into my private nursing home and cure you.' Which he did.

I was born in Forest Gate. I was the only Jewish child in a Roman Catholic school and I experienced considerable confusion in my attitude to Jesus. My father considered, rightly or wrongly, that being no beauty I should adopt a profession with a pension, so I became a schoolteacher. However, after two years in training college and five years teaching in Limehouse, I married a very charming young man called Zimmy.

I had met Zimmy at the house of a friend. He had just come to England from Poland. He was working with a journalist. My father had seen him, taken a fancy to him and secretly invited him to tea. Zimmy's father had been one of the few modern men in that part of Austria, which afterwards became Poland. When the Russians started to overrun Poland, the father hired a cattle-truck and there were seven children, neighbours and all sorts of things piled into it and they all went off to Vienna. Zimmy had memories of being in the big Platz trying to buy bread. His father was a very capable man and he found a large flat and somehow or other he negotiated, (he was one of those men who could negotiate, do all sorts of things), and he started a sawmill in Yugoslavia. Things would have gone well if it had not been for his brother whom he took into his business. They quarrelled and - it's a long, long story. This was before the First World War.

Zimmy wanted to go to Israel (Palestine), that was always his dream. In those days you had to pay £1000 for a bond to get to Israel (Palestine) and Zimmy's father said 'No, you don't know what a hard life it is there.' As he was a timber merchant he had a shipload of timber, which he had sold to Egypt. The Egyptians decided not to take the shipment so Zimmy and his father went up the coast to Israel (Palestine). Jaffa was just being built and his father showed him Jaffa. The people all came out longing for the wood and the timber, which he gave them. There is a theory that somewhere or other there is a deed saying that we have a large patch of land in Jaffa but nobody has ever discovered it. So we are not millionaires as perhaps we could be. Then Zimmy came to England and that is where we met.

In 1931, after we were married, our business failed due to the fall of the pound. We eventually found ourselves travelling in Scandinavia with a series of British goods in thirteen packages. We stayed in the same small hotel as the West Ham football team and they helped us carry our various samples across the channel.

In 1938, the time of Munich, I gave birth to my only son, Jeremy, and I joined Zimmy, who was based in Sweden where he was an agent for a British sports firm. We lived in Sweden until 1939 when the Swedes decided that we were selling too much and asked us to leave. We decided to return to England and Jeremy and I went first. Zimmy was meant to follow us two weeks later but there was a mistake with the tickets. Unfortunately, Hitler invaded Denmark and Norway and we were cut from each other for three years.

During this period Zimmy joined the British Legation in Stockholm where, because of his languages and his general ability to mix with people, he was very useful. But after he learned of the massacre of his entire family in Theresienstadt he became exceedingly depressed and wished to return to England to join the Pioneer Corps.

Meanwhile, I was approached by one of the top members of the British Legation in Sweden who told me that Zimmy was much more useful to them in Stockholm and they were prepared to fly Jeremy and myself back to join him. We would have to fly at night in a bomber from Aberdeen. After five aborted attempts due to enemy aircraft we finally reached Stockholm.

During this period, Stockholm was known as the 'first-class waiting room'. Refugees who were lucky enough to have visas for English-speaking countries were allowed in, but without money or valuables. I was approached by the Jewish community to open a class giving English lessons. I did so and was moved by the courage, humour and enthusiasm which I met from people who had lost so much. In many ways I think this is when I grew to really understand what life was all about. I learned so much about courage and optimism from my pupils.

When peace finally came Zimmy was offered a post in Germany, which would have led to an ambassadorship. But neither of us could face living in Germany, so we returned to England to start all over again.

After our return from Sweden we went to see Dr Dearth who had been so kind to my father but unfortunately he died on the day we went to see him.

During my stay in Sweden I had written a book of children's stories and was approached to be appointed London correspondent for the Bonniers magazine, which was the Vogue of Scandinavia. In this capacity I sent monthly reports and articles about London life, fashion, art etc. Also, I met another friend who had been writing during this period and we decided to join forces and to try our luck with television. To our amazement we sold our first attempted script to the BBC for a vast sum and it seemed we were made for life. Alas, it was soon dropped because we had no knowledge whatever of television techniques. But for ten very happy years we wrote together for the BBC - plays, series and even two dreadful films. My friend's name was Osiakovska and it was felt that Zimmerman and Osiakovska were not quite suitable names for an English team so we changed to Finn and O'Connor but we were always know as 'the girls'.

During this time I joined ORT (Organisation for Rehabilitation through Training), the world's largest educational, non-political organisation and then I was approached to become their organising secretary. For the next fourteen years I built up British women's ORT. These were very happy and wonderful years, which I shall always remember. I retired in 1973 with a big luncheon at which the guest of honour was Ingrid Bergman.

My dear husband died in 1982 and since then I have done little of interest or importance. I am now a very old lady but my son and his family are a great help by showing continual patience and affection to me.

GLOSSARY

AJEX	Association of Jewish Ex-Servicemen and Women
Alyth/Alyth Gardens	Jewish community and synagogue in north-west London from where this anthology has been drawn
Aliyah	Hebrew for "ascending" - term generally used for emigrating to Israel
Anti-Semitism	Hatred of Jews
Ashkenazi	Jews from eastern Europe
Auschwitz	Largest and most notorious of the Nazi death camps. Liberated by the Russians in 1945
Barmitzvah/Batmitzvah	Synagogue coming of age ceremony for boys/girls at the age of 13
Blackshirts	The League of British Fascists headed by Sir Oswald Mosley
Belsen	Notorious Nazi Concentration Camp. Liberated by the British in 1945
Beth Din	Jewish Court responsible for adjudicating on all religious matters
Black Market	Illegal trading in consumer goods during World War Two
Blintz	Eastern European pancake – can be filled with cream cheese, sour cream, apple
Blitz	German aerial bombardment of London during the latter part of 1940
B'nai B'rith	Jewish organisation uniting Jews in service to the community and the world
Board of Deputies	Jewish organisation that protects, supports and defends the rights, interests and religious needs of the Jewish community in the United Kingdom
Buchenwald	Nazi Concentration Camp, liberated by the Americans in 1945
Buzz bombs	See "Doodlebug"
Challah.	Traditional plaited Sabbath loaf
Chalutz/Chalutzah	Hebrew, literally "pioneer" Jewish boys/girls settling on kibbutzim
Chasidim	Orthodox Jewish religious sect, distinguished by its traditional black coats and fur hats

Chatan Torah	Literally "Bridegroom of The Law" - an honour bestowed on a distinguished member of a synagogue congregation on the festival of Simchat Torah (Rejoicing of the Law)
Chavurah	Social, communal meals
Cheder	Hebrew language/religious study school for children
Clabayash	Card game
Dachau	Nazi death camp
Doodlebugs	German pilotless flying bombs that targeted London and the south-east of England during the latter part of the War
Dunkirk	Seaport in France where the British army evacuated and rescued troops in 1940
Erev	Hebrew for "the eve of"
Evacuees	Children sent out of British cities to escape the bombing during the Second World War
Gedudim	Plural of Hebrew "Gedud" - troop, or platoon
Gefillte fish	Boiled or fried chopped fish balls (literally meaning – filled/stuffed)
Gentile	Non-Jew
Gestapo	Nazi Police
Get	Jewish divorce document
Ghetto	Specific locality where Jews were confined
Goldene Medina	"The Golden Land" – America (literal)
Goy	Yiddish word for non-Jew (derogatory)
Grand Palais	London's premier East End Yiddish Theatre
Habonim	Zionist Youth Organisation
Hagannah	Pre-World War Two Jewish defence force in Palestine
Hatikvah	The Israeli National Anthem – word means Hope
Holocaust	Universally accepted term that describes the slaughter of six million Jews by the Nazis during World War Two
Hora	Communal, linked-arms, round dance
High Holy Days	Jewish New Year and Day of Atonement
Hillel Foundation	Organisation that promotes the education and welfare of Jewish students and graduates

Hitler Jugend	Hitler Youth - Nazi Youth Organisation
Jewish Agency	Jewish staffed organisation in Palestine, pre-1948, which dealt with matters of Jewish interest
JNF	Jewish National Fund – originally formed to purchase land for Jews in Palestine
Kaddish	Traditional prayer for the dead
Kehillah	Congregation
Kashrut	See "Kosher"
Keren Kayemet	See "JNF"
Kibbutz/Kibbutzim (pl)	Communal settlement(s) in Israel
Kiddush	Traditional prayer over wine
Kindertransport	Trains carrying Jewish children from Eastern Europe to refuge in Great Britain
Kosher	Food that is acceptable according to Jewish dietary laws
Kristallnacht	"The Night of Broken Glass", November 1938. Terrible night in Nazi Germany when Jewish lives and property were destroyed by rampaging mobs
Latkes	Fried potato cakes
Liberal Synagogue	Less religious than Orthodox or Reform
Leo Baeck	20th century Rabbi, philosopher and scholar
Leo Baeck College	Seminary named after the above
Maccabi	Jewish youth and sporting movement
Maccabi Hatzair	Educational branch of Maccabi
Maccabiah	International sporting competition and Jewish equivalent of the Olympic Games
Macher	Yiddish expression for important person: sometimes "ganzer macher" or VIP
Matzo	Unleavened bread, similar in appearance and texture to water biscuits
Mazel Tov	Literally "Good Luck" but generally meaning "Congratulations"
	The Fascist German National Socialist Party
	New immigrant to Israel
	Strictly observant (Jews)
	Former geographical costal region of the Middle East. Administered by the British under the Mandate granted to it after the First World War. Became the State of Israel in 1948

Parsha	Portion/chapter of the Torah which is read each week in synagogue
Partisans	Underground fighters against the Nazis in Europe during World War Two
Plava	Sponge cake
Pogrom	Term for orchestrated attacks on Jews, originating in Tzarist Russia
Rabbi	Religious leader of a Jewish community
Reform	20th century synagogue movement with less strict interpretation of traditional observance
Refuseniks	Post World War Two Russian Jews who wanted to emigrate to Israel but who were refused by the Soviet Authorities
Rosh Hashanah	Jewish New Year
RSGB	Reform Synagogues of Great Britain
Sabra	Native born in Israel (named after the Sabra fruit – prickly on the outside, soft on the inside)
Schnapps	Eastern and central European spirit drink
Seder	Symbolic recounting at Passover of exodus from Egypt followed by meal
Sephardi	Jews from Spain and parts of North Africa
Shabbat	Friday evening/Saturday. The Jewish Sabbath
Shiva	Traditional seven days of mourning following a death
Shtetl	Term for Jewish towns and villages in eastern Europe
Siddur	Jewish book of daily prayer
Shoah	Hebrew term for the Holocaust
Shul	Another word for synagogue
Six Day War	The 1967 war between Israel and the surrounding Arab states
Sitzfleisch	Patience, the ability to sit still
SS (Waffen SS)	Nazi elite military unit, notorious for its callous brutality
Sternberg Centre	Jewish study centre and museum in north-west London
Stiebel	Small "one-room" synagogue

Succah	Traditional roofless booth, decorated with fruit and vegetables. Used for prayer and celebration during the Festival of Succot, or Harvest Festival.
Synagogue	Jewish House of Prayer
Talmud Torah	Childrens' Hebrew and study classes
Tanach	Commentaries on the Jewish holy books
Terezin/Thereisenstadt	Showcase Nazi concentration camp in Czechoslovakia
Tiyul	Hebrew word for hike/outing
Torah	The Five Books of Moses, also known as the Pentateuch
Tzedakah	Charity
Ulpan	Study of the Hebrew language taught only in Hebrew
United Synagogue	Traditional orthodox synagogue movement of Great Britain
Volksturm	German Home Guard
Weiner Library	London archive of the Holocaust
Winton, Sir Nicholas	Saved nearly 700 children from Czechoslovakia by sending them on trains to safety in England
WVS	Women's Voluntary Service. Civilian charitable organisation founded during the Second World War
Yeshivah	Jewish religious study seminary
Yiddish	Jewish dialect of German, written in Hebrew characters
Yom Kippur	Day of Atonement. Most solemn day of prayer and fasting of the Jewish High Holy Days
Youth Aliyah	Organisation encouraging young Jews to emigrate to Israel
˙eppelin	German airship bomber of World War One
˙ism	The belief and philosophy in the establishment of the State of Israel as the homeland for the Jewish people. Originally formulated by Theodore Herzl in Basle, Switzerland, at the end of the nineteenth century

˙he transliteration of Hebrew into English, any word which
˙ Scottish pronunciation of *ch* as in Lo*ch*